To Qaisra !
Lots of Love
Lovely & to m
keep in tou
Irena
manila APWT
24/10/2015

Independent
women

The story of women's activism in East Timor

Irena Cristalis and Catherine Scott

with contributions from Ximena Andrade, Isabel Casimiro, Ruth Jacobson,
Caroline Roseveare and Brigitte Sonnois

CiiR

Published 2005 by the
Catholic Institute for
International Relations
Unit 3, Canonbury Yard,
190a New North Road
London N1 7BJ, UK
www.ciir.org

ISBN 1 85287 317 5

A catalogue record for this book
is available from the British
Library

CIIR is registered in the UK as a
charity (number 294329) and a
company (number 2002500)

Design: Twenty-Five Educational

Print: APG (APG holds ISO14001
accreditation for International
Environmental Standards)

Cover picture: Bilesse, a Falintil
fighter, with her son Agildo
(photo Irena Cristalis)

Contents

This book is dedicated to East Timorese
women victims of violence and
East Timorese women peacemakers and activists

Abbreviations

See also appendix 1 for a glossary of terms on gender issues and women's rights.

CAVR	Comissão de Acolhimento, Verdade e Reconciliação – Commission for Reception, Truth and Reconciliation
CEDAW	Convention on the Elimination of All Forms of Discrimination Against Women
CNRM	Conselho Nacional da Resistência Maubere – National Council of Maubere Resistance
CNRT	Conselho Nacional da Resistência Timorense – National Council of Timorese Resistance
DK	Democratic Kampuchea
ET-Wave	East Timorese Movement Against Violence Towards Women and Children
Falintil	Forças Armadas de Libertação Nacional de Timor Leste – Armed Forces for the National Liberation of East Timor
Fokupers	Forum Komunikasi Untuk Perempuan Lorosae – East Timorese Women's Communications Forum
Frelimo	Frente de Libertação de Moçambique – Mozambican Liberation Front
Fretilin	Frente Revolucionária de Timor Leste Independente – Revolutionary Front for an Independent East Timor
Funcinpec	Front Uni National pour un Cambodge Indépendant, Neutre, Pacifique et Coopératif (United National Front for an Independent, Neutral, Peaceful and Cooperative Cambodia)
GFFTL	Grupo Feto Foinsae Timor Lorosae – East Timor Students Women's Group
Impettu	Ikatan Mahasiswa dan Pejalar Timor Timur – East Timor Student Association (based in Indonesia)
InterFET	International Force for East Timor
IRC	International Rescue Committee
KPNLF	Khmer People's National Liberation Front

KWA	Khmer Women's Association
NGO	Non-governmental organisation
NWV	Namibia Women's Voice
OMM	Organização da Mulher Moçambicana – Organisation of Mozambican Women
OMT	Organização da Mulher Timorense – Organisation of Timorese Women
OPE	Office for the Promotion of Equality
OPMT	Organização da Popular da Mulher Timorense – Popular Organisation of East Timorese Women
PLAN	People's Liberation Army of Namibia
PRK	People's Republic of Kampuchea
Rede Feto	Rede Feto Timor Lorosae – the East Timorese Women's Network
Renamo	Resistência Nacional Moçambicana – Mozambican National Resistance
Renetil	Resistência Nacional dos Estudantes de Timor Leste – National Resistance of East Timorese Students
RWAK	Revolutionary Women's Association of Kampuchea
SOC	State of Cambodia
SWAPO	South West African People's Organisation
SWC	SWAPO Women's Council
UDT	União Democrática Timorense – Timorese Democratic Union
UN	United Nations
Unicef	United Nations Children's Fund
Unifem	United Nations Development Fund for Women
UNTAC	United Nations Transitional Authority in Cambodia
UNTAET	United Nations Transitional Administration in East Timor
UNTIM	Universitas Timor Timur – University of East Timor
WAC	Women's Association of Cambodia

Acknowledgements

We would like to thank all those involved in researching, compiling, writing and producing this book:

Milena Pires, Kirsty Sword Gusmão, and CIIR staff who read and commented on the original outline;

Ivete de Oliveira, Emily Roynestad, Deirdre Nagle, Ildefonso Guterres, Maria Antonia Velasco, Januario da Costa and Tomas Fernandes Nunes of the CIIR office in Dili, who supported us over the years that it took to put this book together. Ivete commented on the original outline and, like Emily, on the first draft. Their assistance in the many interviews we conducted was invaluable, while the other members of the team lent us their logistic and moral support;

Judy El Bushra, Kathryn Robertson Marcal, Rolando Modina and Estevao Cabral for their insightful and constructive comments on the first draft;

Elizabeth Traube for ther much appreciated and comprehensive advice on the anthropological section;

Ruth Jacobson for her much valued encouragement and advice;

Mara Stankovitch, our clearheaded editor, for her patience, guidance and recommendations, and Nick Sireau and Alastair Whitson of the CIIR communications department;

Above all, huge thanks to James Collins, CIIR's director of finance and administration, without whose faith in the project this book would not have been realised.

Last but not least, our gratitude goes to all the East Timorese women (and one man) who generously gave us their time and their life stories:

Laura Abrantes
Bertha Oliveira Alves
Sister Esmeralda Rego de Jesus Araujo
Marito Araujo
Laura Menezes Lopez Belo
Mana Bisoi
Olandina Caeiro
Teresa Cardoso
Etelvista da Costa

Maria Lourdes Martins Cruz
Maria Dias
Maria Domingas Fernandes
Bela Galhos
Sister Guilhermina Marcal
Cipriana Pereira
Manuela Pereira
Maia Reis
Maria Madalena dos Santos Fatima
Florentina Smith

Their contributions made this book possible.

No-one can tell the whole story of a social movement, and this account does not pretend to. Everyone involved in it has their own perspective, and the authors acknowledge their role as privileged outsiders, only telling a part of it. We hope that our contribution will encourage others, particularly those involved in this story at first hand, to record their own perspectives and to tell the story of women's activism from their own standpoint.

Irena Cristalis and Catherine Scott
London, August 2005

Foreword

By Olandina Caeiro

INDEPENDENT WOMEN by Irena Cristalis and Catherine Scott is a profound testimony to the unique character of East Timorese women (of which I am very proud) and to their resolve and courage in the long process of struggle for the liberation of their country and now for their own liberation.

The authors' interviews with several East Timorese women are remarkable and show their heartfelt concern to contribute to women's development and promote women's participation in rebuilding East Timor – and especially in rebuilding peace.

The authors describe in detail how the women of East Timor showed the world their maturity when they took part in the struggle for national liberation (on the armed, clandestine and diplomatic fronts), and then promoted peace and stability to help East Timor to evolve and build itself as a nation.

Up to now, many East Timorese women have made their contribution by leading a simple life, making no demands, saying that if they suffered, if they worked, if they did anything at all it was not because they were forced to, but because they wanted to contribute towards an independent East Timor.

Now, they are looking forward to the day when women will not have to face poverty and injustice, and will find equality in education, health, economy, politics and justice.

The authors have made many visits to East Timor from the early 1990s onwards, Catherine as an advocacy officer with CIIR, Irena as a journalist who has invested a lot of time and commitment to well-informed and quality reporting. They have both done a great deal from the outside to support the East Timorese struggle over the years.

CIIR supported East Timor from the beginning of the Indonesian occupation through lobbying and mobilising faith-based organisations, religious institutions, the Bishops' Conference and the UK government on the East Timor issue, and raising awareness through the pages of *Timor Link*, a quarterly newsletter produced by CIIR between 1985 and 2002. CIIR continues that support today through its development worker programme based in East Timor, which was established upon East Timorese independence.

The contents of this book reflect the resolve, courage and character of East Timorese women. I hope readers will find within its pages stories and insights with which to enrich their knowledge of the Timorese woman of yesterday, today and tomorrow.

For all that is said in this book, I would like finally to say two of the most important words of my life: thank you.

Maria Olandina Isabel Caeiro Alves
Dili, August 2005

Introduction

THIS BOOK is about the activism of East Timorese women and their part in the struggle for liberation from Indonesian rule. It explores how participation in this struggle has empowered them and set them on a path towards greater equality with men. It examines the challenges that lie ahead for women as they work together to consolidate the achievements of a newly independent nation.

East Timor, the eastern half of Timor island, is located 300 miles north of Darwin, Australia. The island was settled by Malay, Melanesian and Polynesian peoples until the 1600s, when the Dutch and the Portuguese arrived and fought each other for control of the territory. In 1945 the western part of the island, which had been colonised by the Dutch, became part of Indonesia, while the east remained under Portuguese rule.

As the Portuguese colonial empire broke up in the 1970s and the 1974 'carnation revolution' overthrew the dictatorship in Lisbon, East Timorese political parties sprang up. Their options for the future were federation with Portugal, full independence, or full integration into Indonesia.

The Frente Revolucionária de Timor Leste Independente (Fretilin – Revolutionary Front for an Independent East Timor), a left-wing party with majority popular support, declared independence on 28 November 1975, after a brief but bloody civil war sparked by a coup attempt by the more liberal União Democrática Timorense (UDT – Timorese Democratic Union). On 7 December 1975 Indonesia, which had been covertly destabilising its small neighbour, staged a full-scale land and sea invasion with the tacit approval of western governments. Indonesia's illegal occupation claimed the lives of an estimated 200,000 people and lasted until 1999.[1]

The East Timorese were incapable of defeating Indonesia militarily, but their clear cut and United Nations (UN) sanctioned quest for self-determination captured the imagination and eventually the support of the international community. Fortunately for the East Timorese, this happened at a time – the end of the 1990s – when change had become politically possible. East Timor finally broke free from occupation in August 1999, when the UN supervised a referendum in which four out of five East Timorese voted against autonomy within Indonesia – and so, in effect, for separation from Indonesia. Indonesia retaliated: its retreating army destroyed and looted 70 per cent of the country's infrastructure. In 2002, after a transitional period under UN administration, East Timor finally gained formal independence.

As in other places where long guerrilla wars have raged, women and children were the most vulnerable victims. But women did more than passively suffer abuse and war crimes: they played an active and crucial role in resistance and survival. They developed coping mechanisms to take care of large families on their own. Many also organised with others, either to fight the enemy, often in a non-violent way, or to establish and sustain a support network for the armed resistance.

There is a growing literature that focuses on the way women's movements cope with transitions to peace and try to secure advances made during conflict.[2] Wars and liberation struggles often change the traditional roles that women play in their societies. When the conflict is over, communities must come to terms with changed lives and sometimes, also, changed aspirations. Women often find themselves resisting social pressure to reconstruct life as it was before the conflict began. Some may have become heads of their household through widowhood. Some may have been combatants. Many more are simply unwilling to abandon the process of empowerment they have undergone: the new skills learned and the greater sense of independence, self-worth and self-confidence. Often a women's movement emerges to claim new rights and roles.

This book has two aims. The first is to look at the East Timorese journey from occupation to independence from the women's perspective and to record the achievements of the East Timorese women's movement, in particular during the decade leading up to the 1999 referendum. The second is to examine the challenges which face women after independence. It looks at efforts to consolidate the gains women made in wartime through the state (constitutional reform, legislation, government machinery) and in civil society (through pressure, advocacy and attempts at cultural change). It concludes by posing some key questions that East Timorese women will have to resolve.

The book draws on a variety of sources, both primary and secondary, including interviews with East Timorese women activists who are raising women's issues at both governmental and non-governmental levels.

The East Timorese women's movement came into being in the final years of Portuguese colonial rule, at the same time as East Timorese political parties were emerging in anticipation of imminent independence. Women's organisations previously had been mainly for wives of colonial cadres, or hosted by the church. With the founding of the Organização Popular da Mulher Timorense (OPMT – Popular Organisation of East Timorese Women) as the women's branch of Fretilin in 1975, women were organising politically for the first time, drawing on the learning a tiny group of activists had brought back after studying in Portugal and Mozambique.

No sooner was it founded than the women's movement had to go underground with the rest of the resistance to the Indonesian occupation. For the next 24 years it had to subordinate its agenda to Fretilin's national liberation struggle. Towards the end of that time it began to gain the strength to make its own voice heard – assisted, paradoxically, by activists on women's issues from Indonesia, among others.

The book refers to the 'women's movement' rather than the 'feminist movement' because it is unclear to what extent East Timorese women identify with the term 'feminism'. Some view feminism as a dangerous and degenerate western phenomenon. Clearly some East Timorese women activists are motivated by feminist concepts – equal rights, political emancipation, and liberation from subordinate and oppressive social roles. But the majority would describe their quest as one for greater equality and a modicum of economic independence, and against violence.

East Timor is frequently cited by analysts of UN interventions and peace-keeping missions as one of the success stories of the 1990s.[3] This applies to both the military intervention by the International Force for East Timor (InterFET) and the administration of the United Nations Transitional Administration in East Timor (UNTAET), which saw the country through its transition to independence between 1999 and 2002. UNTAET's efforts to promote equality by mainstreaming gender[4] in the transition period has been described as path breaking.[5] This book will illustrate that although the UN certainly made an extremely helpful contribution, the process was driven by East Timorese women themselves. Without their determination and persistence, progress would have been far more limited.

East Timor's transition unfolded at a time of significant progress for women in international human rights law and development theory. The establishment of the International Criminal Court and the elaboration of theoretical concepts such as 'gender and development' and the rights-based approach to development have shown how the women's movement has been able to introduce into development theory a sharper and more political framework for action.

This progress has shaped the context in which East Timorese women activists, inside East Timor and in the diaspora, fought to expand the frontiers of their own entitlements and terrain for action. In so doing, they have to a large degree pursued a rights-based approach rather than resorting to the efficiency arguments that dominated the 'women and development' interventions of the 1980s. However, a backlash from male politicians has prompted activists on women's issues to reconsider their rhetoric, if not their ultimate goals.

Lessons from elsewhere

The experience examined here leads to the wider question of what happens to women's movements in periods of transition, and particularly in the reconstruction phase. Are there lessons that the East Timorese women's movement can draw upon from elsewhere to help formulate its own strategies? Women need to make advances for themselves collectively, but also to preserve the independence and opportunities gained in wartime as the dust settles and men try to regain ground they perceive they have lost.

There are parallels to be drawn from a variety of liberation struggles and transitions from war to peace in different parts of the world. Women's experiences from Cambodia to Guatemala to Nicaragua, Eritrea, South Africa and Namibia demonstrate that women need to be present and participate in the negotiations throughout transitions, not only in the reconstruction phase. This was acknowledged in Security Council resolution 1325 on women, peace and security in 2000. In some conflicts with many women combatants armed groups practised inclusive policies and equality during the conflict and strong women's movements emerged (for example in Nicaragua and Eritrea). But even in these cases, once the conflict died down social pressures were exerted to return women to their previous subordinate position. As Sondra Hale explains:

> In most societies, men position women within the culture to serve male-dominated institutions. Likewise, in political movements, men position women to serve the movement. Men expect women to preserve the culture or the family, often as symbols of resistance or to maintain 'authentic culture' in the face of chaos and violence.[6]

In East Timor too, men have put forward cultural arguments to convince women that they must return to the hearth and their traditional roles. But even East Timor's poor majority of women, most of whom are illiterate subsistence farmers, have begun to adopt the rights agenda following the UN's civic education campaigns for the 2001 constituent assembly elections.

It is not that East Timor's women activists want to abandon their culture: its diversity and richness provide them with a strong sense of identity both as Timorese and as members of particular tribes. Olandina Caeiro, a prominent East Timorese activist, puts it quite simply: 'I like my culture, but some things have to change.'[7]

East Timorese women activists were networking internationally before the 1999 referendum and were keen to hear how women in other parts of the world had fared in similar circumstances. A conference held by CIIR at the end of 1998 provided some ideas.[8]

East Timorese participants in the CIIR conference were interested to hear about the experiences of women activists from Guatemala, South Africa and Haiti. As in Haiti, East Timorese civil society ownership over the peace negotiations had been very limited. Only one forum was open to East Timorese representatives, and this was heavily controlled. Only four women managed to gain entry out of 38 East Timorese participants. The concern, given this reality, was how to ensure that women's rights would receive both attention and guarantees in any peace agreement. The danger was that abuses such as rape, which had gone unchallenged in the conflict, would continue unchecked, particularly if the culture of impunity was not addressed. Incomplete disarmament and demobilisation of former combatants – militias in particular – as in Haiti, Guatemala and South Africa, was also noted as a potential danger in East Timor.[9]

The experiences in Guatemala and South Africa demonstrated the importance of obtaining peace or decolonisation agreements which promote women's rights and constitutional arrangements which outlaw discrimination based on sex. East Timorese women argued for constitutional guarantees of international standards but also for affirmative action to correct gender imbalances. South Africa had adopted a 30 per cent quota for women candidates in the 1994 elections, which brought many women into parliament. However, there was little participation from grassroots women, with the result that gender issues were low on the rural agenda. In contrast, participation among rural women in Haiti had been much better.

Both South Africa and Haiti set up offices for the status of women or women's ministries, with regional representations to support them. The scope and depth of commitment to women's rights was greatly influenced by the quality of civil society participation in the peace process. For East Timor, there would be much ground to make up, given the intense repression of women and their marginalisation from politics.

The content of peace agreements was sometimes less important than the democratic space that opened up for civil society in their wake. In East Timor, civil society organising intensified after the removal from power in Indonesia of General Suharto in 1998. Women's organising was an increasingly important part of this. Even the massive violence and destruction that the Indonesian army rained down on the East Timorese after the vote for independence had no lasting impact on the groundswell. Twenty-five years of oppression had taught activists, male and female, how to organise in adversity.

For a more detailed comparison, this book offers case studies of women's movements in Cambodia, Namibia and Mozambique. These examples were chosen for what they have in common with East Timor. All have been through transitions in the past 30 years. In all three the UN was involved in the transition, and in the case of Cambodia and East Timor the UN supported women's attempts to consolidate changes that had benefited them. The contributors explore how the conflict changed women's economic, social and political roles, and examine whether, and how, women's status changed as a result of armed conflict. They look at how domestic actors – government, political parties, civil society, religious institutions – helped to consolidate or obstruct gender equity, and consider the role of external actors such as international non-governmental organisations (NGOs) and the UN.

The case studies also hold some warnings about potential threats to women's well-being in East Timor, notably external pressure for neoliberal economic policies and the spread of HIV and AIDS.

Unity in peace

The East Timorese women's movement in the early 21st century is struggling to find common cause in a newly-established democracy. There is a need to build trust between generations of activists, and between 'insiders' and returnees. Those who remained in East Timor during the occupation organised with determination and ingenuity, both to support the independence movement and to address issues that affected women (particularly violence against women). Women in the diaspora worked more through UN structures, and linked with the international solidarity movement and the feminist movement. These were generally women from the younger generation. Given how dispersed they were – throughout Australia, Europe and Asia – they managed to network increasingly effectively, facilitated from the second half of the 1990s by e-mail. Although they kept in touch with colleagues and compatriots inside East Timor, their experience of activism was quite different.

The diverse wings of the movement were reunited in 1999, when many diaspora-based activists returned to East Timor. The immediate need was to work together to promote women's rights to political representation and constitutional guarantees of equality. This provided a strong basis of unity. An umbrella organisation, Rede Feto Timor Lorosae (the East Timorese Women's Network), was formed, and the UN was encouraged to set up a gender affairs unit.

But for civil society in general, as well as for the women's movement, divisions multiplied after the 2001 elections. Political parties quarrelled, and the old debates and enmities of the 1970s resurfaced. Rede Feto was formed out of a diverse collection of organisations and groups, new and old, some with international links and some linked to political parties. The generation gap combined with insider/diaspora tensions and personal, family and party political rivalries to disrupt the relative cohesion that had characterised East Timorese civil society during the occupation.

The advent of a large number of foreign agencies created further complications. The World Bank adopted a strong gender focus through its community empowerment programme. UN agencies such as the United Nations Development Fund for Women (Unifem) and government funders wanted to be seen to be working on gender, and international NGOs were also eager to support women's activities. All had an analysis to offer and grants to hand out. In their desire to be recognised as key supporters of gender projects, they may have inadvertently fed tensions between East Timorese organisations.

Manuela Pereira of the East Timorese NGO Forum Komunikasi Untuk Perempuan Lorosae (Fokupers – East Timorese Women's Communications Forum) says that at the moment when East Timorese women's organisations felt ready to use the resources offered to the maximum effect, the money had already begun to run out. Some East Timorese women's organisations may have become dependent on foreign funding, as was the case in Cambodia.[10]

The first East Timorese election was fought with an eye to the past and who had contributed most to the liberation struggle.

Fretilin's victory was never in doubt, but posed real problems for democracy and pluralism.

Although Rede Feto's campaign to secure a quota for women in the Constituent Assembly failed, more than a quarter of the parliamentarians elected were women, mostly Fretilin members. The assembly itself is under-resourced, under-trained, and dominated by factional agendas. Fretilin women must toe the party line – or else they are effectively silenced. As for women belonging to minority parties, they feel completely powerless and at least one has already relinquished her seat in frustration.

Lack of experience, confidence and trust has so far prevented women parliamentarians from uniting across party lines in the interests of women. In these circumstances the question remains, will women's failure to make an impact on parliamentary proceedings prompt men to mobilise against women candidates at the next election? If the experiment in women's representation is seen as a failure, male politicians – in particular those in charge of government budgets – may see an opportunity to erode the few gains that women have made so far. UN support for efforts to mainstream gender has provided women's NGOs with ready access to external financial and moral support and help with training. This will not always be the case. 'Wait until the UN goes,' some men have threatened. 'Then we'll get our power back.'

But women's struggle for equality in East Timor did not start with the UN, and will not end with its departure. This book concludes with an assessment of women's achievements to date, and raises some key questions for their future.

Notes

1   Statistics on killings in East Timor are subject to fierce debate. However 200,000 is thought to be a reasonably accurate estimate and is the figure given by Amnesty International and Asia Watch. See also Defert, G (1992) *Timor Est: Le génocide oublié. Droits d'un peuple et raisons d'etat*, L'Harmattan, Paris.

2   See for example Meintjes, S, Pillay, A, and Turshen, M (eds) (2001) *The aftermath: Women in post-conflict transformation*, Zed Books, London; Turshen, M, and Twagiramariya, C (eds) (1998) *What women do in war time: Gender and conflict in Africa*, Zed Books, London; Rehn, E, and Sirleaf, E (2002) *Women, war, peace*, Unifem, New York.

3   See for example Fine, L, 'US wants to end UN peace keeping in East Timor', Reuters/Alertnet 28 February 2005; statement by Ambassador James B Cunningham, United States Deputy Permanent Representative to the United Nations, on the situation in East Timor, UN Security Council, 31 October 2001; Galpin, R, 'East Timor, birth of a

nation', BBC News, 19 May 2002; Heinlein, P, 'UN/East Timor', Voice of America, 14 May 2004, No 2-315924.

4   For a definition of gender mainstreaming and other technical terms, see the glossary given in appendix 1.

5   See International Alert (2001) *Gender and peace support operations: Opportunities and challenges to improve practice,* International Alert, London.

6   Hale, S (2001) 'Liberated but not free: Women in post-war Eritrea' in Meintjes, S, Pillay, A, and Turshen, M (eds) *The aftermath: Women in post-conflict transformation*, Zed Books, London, p139.

7   Quoted in Carvalho, M (2001) 'Os dois lados da moeda', Instituto Brasileiro de Análises Sociais e Econômicas (Brazilian Institute of Social and Economic Analysis), 2001 (www.ibase.br), translation by Catherine Scott.

8   See CIIR (1999) *Humanising peace: The impact of peace agreements on human rights*, Catholic Institute for International Relations, London.

9   History has borne this out. UN sources fear that automatic weapons remain at large in East Timor. The newly formed police force is weak, and former combatants who were not recruited into the regular armed forces have formed private militias.

10 See USAID (2000) *Aftermath: Women and women's organisations in post-conflict Cambodia,* USAID evaluation highlights no 67, Center for Development Information and Evaluation, US Agency for International Development, Washington.

Chapter 1
Women's traditional roles

This chapter gives a short overview of the history of East
Timor and the traditional roles of women in its society. It draws
on written sources on the role of women, which are scarce.
A few anthropological studies conducted in the last years of
Portuguese rule give only a limited insight into some customs and
traditions in a few selected areas. A distinct study on the role of
women has not yet been undertaken.

The pre-colonial era

A collection of statues, carefully packed in wooden crates, lies hidden in the cellar of a building in the East Timorese capital, Dili. The skilfully crafted wooden figures are female, with prominent sexual organs. Before the Indonesian invasion, such statues and totems had their own special place on sacred mountain tops and in sacred houses, where they were revered as symbols of fertility and the continuation of the clan.

After the invasion, Indonesian soldiers collected many of the statues and shipped them to Java. Others were removed by zealous Roman Catholic priests, who replaced them with crucifixes and statues of the Virgin Mary. A few of the old statues remain crated up in Dili and the Catholic church is still deliberating on where their future home should be.

The presence of the statues indicates that the power of female fertility was, at least at one time, revered. But how far this reflects the status of women in pre-colonial East Timor remains as obscure as the statues in the crates. Indeed, the entire history of East Timor before the arrival of the Portuguese is obscure and subject to the distorted interpretations of outsiders.

Documents from times before the European arrival can be found in the logbooks of Macassar, Chinese and Arab merchant ships that plied the seas in the eastern part of today's Indonesian archipelago. The merchants travelled in search of spices and, in the case of Timor, of its fragrant sandalwood. In 1225 a Chinese trade official referred to the island in a report as rich in sandalwood.[1] The traders bought sandalwood, bees' wax and slaves from the people living on the coast. They stayed long enough to conduct their business but did not settle in Timor, although they may well have left their mark on the island's rich ethnic patchwork.

Timor, the eastern part in particular, was populated over the centuries by consecutive waves of migration. Some ethnic groups are related to Aborigines in Australia; others have Melanesian or Malay features. Even today, East Timor has at least seven distinct language groups, and more than 30 dialects are spoken in the isolated valleys and high mountain villages.

Portuguese colonial times

Most of the written history of East Timor is colonial. It documents the arrival of the first European merchants and missionaries in the 16th century and the subsequent colonisation of the island. The earliest settlers from Portugal were Dominican friars accompanied by a group known as the Topasses or Black Portuguese – *mestizo* Timorese (Timorese of mixed parentage), Portuguese soldiers, sailors and traders from Macau and Malacca, and their native wives.[2] The community settled at Lifau on the north coast in an area that is now the enclave of Oecussi. In the following century they successfully resisted the authority of the Portuguese and the Dutch, the other powerful colonial power in the region, who established a trading post in Kupang in the far west of the island.

In addition to the lucrative sandalwood trade, both the Dutch and the Portuguese carried on a flourishing slave trade well into the 19th century. Among the people sold were children as young as eight years.[3]

In 1522, the captain of a Spanish ship anchored at Batugade, west of Dili, and noted some evidence that the Portuguese had been there too. One tell-tale sign was the presence of the European disease syphilis, known to the Timorese as the 'Portuguese disease'.[4]

The colonial powers, however, did not venture far outside their coastal trading posts. They used a kind of tribute system, already set up by the Chinese and Arab traders.[5] It was not until 1695 that the Portuguese crown established a foothold in Lifau. A century later this was evacuated and the capital moved to Dili.[6]

In the 19th century, the British explorer and naturalist Alfred Russell Wallace (a colleague of Darwin) reached the shores of East Timor. He took an instant dislike to Dili, which he called a 'most miserable place'. He observed further that 'the Timorese take every opportunity of kidnapping unprotected people of other tribes for slaves' and that, 'except a few half-breeds in the town, there are no native Christians in the island of Timor. The people retain their independence in a great measure, and both dislike and despise their would-be ruler, whether Portuguese or Dutch.'[7]

Wallace was not impressed by the Portuguese colonial government either, concluding that: 'Nobody seems to care the least about the improvement of the country, and at this time, 300 years of occupation, there has not been a mile of road made beyond the town, and there is not a solitary European resident anywhere in the interior.'[8]

As Wallace observed, Portuguese colonial power did not extend much beyond the coastal settlements. However, that changed at the end of the 19th century. With the near extinction of the sandalwood tree and a change in Lisbon's policy towards its colonies, the Portuguese looked for other ways to profit from East Timor. They started to clear land in the mountain forests to plant coffee trees. Women and children worked as labourers picking the coffee berries, while the men processed the beans.

With the expansion of the Portuguese into the interior, their impact on the traditional kingdoms grew. These kingdoms had remained largely intact, although colonialism had some impact on clan politics through the tribute system. Now the foreign rulers used the labour of the population directly. The Portuguese bestowed titles and other privileges on the local chiefs they favoured and who cooperated with them, and exploited local rivalries to fight rebellious chiefs. They established administrative centres (concelhos and postos, replacing the traditional sucos), and created a 'royal' elite whose children were groomed to become useful civil servants.

The colonial power also imposed a new head tax, which led to a major uprising in Manufahe in the south of the island at the beginning of the 20th century. In 1910 the Portuguese fought the rebel chief Dom Boaventura with the help of rival chiefs (and a gunboat) and killed all the males in his family.

In 1916 the Portuguese and Dutch finally settled the colonial boundary between East and West Timor and so sealed the future fate of the people on both sides of the island.

Comfort women

East Timor became one of the lesser-known tragedies of the Second World War, during which Portugal adopted a neutral position. The Allied forces used East Timor as a forward base, which meant that Japanese troops invaded in 1942. Timorese died defending 400 soldiers from Australia and Holland, who eventually fled. It is believed that up to 70,000 Timorese died in reprisals at the hands of the Japanese-assisted militia recruited from West Timor or in the famine and disease that followed.[9]

As elsewhere in occupied Asia, thousands of women were forced to provide sexual services to Japanese soldiers. Of these perhaps a thousand survive today. Some have found the courage to speak out about their experiences and have joined international efforts to obtain a formal apology and compensation from the Japanese state. Two East Timorese women gave evidence at hearings of the Women's International War Crimes Tribunal on Japan's Military Sexual Slavery, held in Tokyo in 2001 (see box).

It came to light during the Tokyo hearings that Portuguese officials colluded in recruiting the women. Australian journalist Jill Jolliffe has revealed that there may have been racist motives:

> A secret report by the governor released in Lisbon some years ago shows that he collaborated with the Japanese in rounding up Timorese women, against the protests of other Portuguese officials. His justification, he said, was to save European women from rape by Japanese soldiers by providing them with indigenous women who were already prostitutes – although there is no evidence the women in question were.[10]

Comfort women speak out

[Taken from paragraphs 51-54 of the transcript of the oral judgment delivered on 4 December 2001 by the judges of the Women's International War Crimes Tribunal on Japan's Military Sexual Slavery]

Esmeralda Boe testified before the Tribunal that she was only a child when the Japanese soldiers kidnapped her from a field near her home in East Timor. She did not know her age at the time of her capture, but recalled that she had not begun her menstruation yet and that her breasts were just beginning to grow. The Japanese soldiers took her to a house where a commander named Shimimura raped and sodomised her. Esmeralda Boe described her first harrowing experience with sexual violence committed by the Japanese military:

> He took off his clothes and took my clothes off. I was so young I had no idea what he was doing. And he pushed me to his bed and then that's when he start[ed] to rape me.... [H]e did the sexual intercourse through my vagina and also my anus.

Although she was allowed to go home, Japanese soldiers returned to her home every evening to take her to Shimimura's residence to sexually service either Shimimura or two other Japanese commanders. This lasted for three years....

Another East Timorese survivor, Marta Abu Bere, also testified before this tribunal that ... at night she was taken to the homes of Japanese soldiers where she was gang raped by up to 10 men at a time.... In addition to her live testimony, Marta Abu Bere also recounted her ordeal in a statement submitted to the Tribunal:

> During the night the Japanese ... entered my room. At that moment I didn't know anything, my clothes were stripped with force and I was pushed to the bed. I was forced to service 10 men; I was treated like an animal. They told me not to yell, [that] if I yell they would kill me. In the morning I couldn't walk because I was in pain.... During the day I had to service four to five men. When they entered the room they wore civilian clothes and their gun[s] were kept away. I had to service them for three months.

Marta Abu Bere got out of the 'comfort station' when her parents succeeded in persuading the Japanese army commander that their daughter was too weak to remain in the station any longer.

[Source: Violence Against Women in War – Network Japan website, www1.jca.apc.org/vaww-net-japan/english/index.html]

A slow road to independence

The Japanese occupation did not spawn an independence movement in East Timor as it did elsewhere in South East Asia. A simple explanation for this might be that while other colonial powers had educated an elite, the Portuguese in East Timor never bothered to invest in education. (It was not until the 1970s that the first university graduates returned from Portugal and trained priests came back from Macau.) Nor was Portugal under external pressure to decolonise. The US saw a strategic interest in supporting Portugal's dictator António Salazar and did not call for decolonisation as it did with the Dutch in Indonesia.[11]

In East Timor the Portuguese secret police suppressed any attempt by the population to organise against their colonial masters. An uprising in 1959, instigated or at least inspired by two exiled Indonesian communists, was quickly and forcefully quelled.[12] Portugal controlled all print media and radio (television did not exist) and the East Timorese were largely kept in the dark about what was happening in the rest of world.

In 1974, however, the Portuguese fascist regime crumbled. After a bloodless revolution the new government started the long over-due process of decolonisation, which paved the way for the estab-lishment of political organisations in East Timor.

Of the five parties, the two largest were the União Democrática Timorense (UDT – Timorese Democratic Union) and a social dem-ocratic party, Associãçao Social Democrática Timorense (ASDT – Timorese Social Democratic Association), which soon shifted to the left and changed its name to Frente Revolucionária de Timor Leste Independente (Fretilin – Revolutionary Front for an Independent East Timor). Both parties drew their leadership from the urban elite and had rather similar platforms. Fretilin's shift to the left was influenced by a group of students who had returned from studies overseas. Together with academic qualifications, they brought ideas and ideologies inspired by Paulo Freire, Marx, Lenin and Mao. They had witnessed the 'carnation revolution' in Portugal and had close ties with liberation movements in Portuguese Africa, in particular Mozambique.

The UDT had a strong following among landowners (often smallholders) and local leaders, known as *liurais*. But Fretilin's pol-icy of agrarian reform was popular in the mountains, where people still lived under a feudal system, and it soon became clear that Fretilin enjoyed more support, even among some *liurais*, than the UDT. The smaller parties included the pro-Indonesia party Associação Popular Democrática Timorense (Apodeti – Timorese Popular Democratic Association), which wanted East Timor to become an autonomous part of Indonesia.[13]

Fretilin and the UDT drifted so far apart that in August 1975 the UDT, urged on by Indonesia, staged a coup. A short but bloody civil war followed, which ended with the defeat of the UDT. As soon as the civil war broke out the Portuguese evacuated the island, leav-ing their arsenals behind. They never returned.

Indonesia closely watched the developments in East Timor. Cold War 'domino theory' and Indonesian president Suharto's hatred of anything that could be interpreted as communism led him to order his special forces to infiltrate the border area. Fighting broke out between Indonesian forces and Fretilin's army, Forças Armadas de Libertação Nacional de Timor Leste (Falintil – Armed Forces for the National Liberation of East Timor). So when US president Gerald Ford and his secretary of state Henry Kissinger, on a state visit to Indonesia, gave Suharto the green light to invade East Timor, Indonesia wasted no time.[14] On the day after the Americans departed, 7 December 1975, Indonesia launched a full-scale invasion.

The war and subsequent occupation lasted for 24 years. Human rights organisations estimate that 200,000 people – about a third of East Timor's population – lost their lives in the first five years of the war.[15] It would take a change of regime in Indonesia to give East Timor an act of self-determination. This came in 1999 when, under a UN-supervised referendum, the East Timorese voted overwhelmingly against autonomy within Indonesia. After a period of transition, the Democratic Republic of Timor Leste was declared in 2002.

Oral history

Historical accounts leave no doubt that the Timorese had a strong warrior tradition, which included the ritual collection of enemy heads. They fought their colonial rulers relentlessly. The Timorese have a term for this 'historic' struggle: *funu*.[16] As one Portuguese administrator put it: 'Rebellion in Timor continues successively, leading us to conclude that revolt is a normal state and that peace is exceptional.'[17]

As to what the Timorese thought of the intruders and the colonial powers, there is no written record. The Timorese never developed a script to write down their rich oral history and until today most of their literature is in the form of narrative recitation, typically involving repetition, rhyme and alliteration to help performers memorise the verses. Poetry remains a favourite way to express personal and political passions.

Much of the oral history that had been passed on from one generation to another was lost in the 20th century as the effects of war, mass displacement and famine wiped out entire clans during the Second World War and the Indonesian occupation. In 1999 a Timorese civil servant, who had worked for 40 years as an administrator in several districts and made it his task to write down numerous local stories and legends, saw his cultural treasure go up in flames in the random destruction that followed the 1999 referendum. He died soon afterwards.

Social structure

Under Indonesian occupation East Timor was closed to western researchers and the most recent anthropological studies date back to the early 1970s. None of these studies focused specifically on the role of women. They covered a limited range of East Timor's diverse cultures, but they concluded that East Timorese social structure showed similarities with those of its neighbours in Melanesia and Indonesia.

As anthropologist James Fox observes, 'Timor is not one place but many.'[18] This chapter will not delve into the complexities of East Timor's traditions, but look briefly at the social structure that most of the different linguistic groups have in common.

The many independent 'kingdoms' had a relatively similar social structure. This was highly stratified. Political authority rested with the local kings or chiefs, known as *liurais*. They stood at the top of the hierarchy, followed by nobles or princes (*datos*) directing the fate of groups of small settlements (*knuas*), and several classes of people, with slaves at the base of the pyramid.

These *liurais* are often compared to feudal lords. They were a land-owning elite who received tribute from the commoners and kept large numbers of slaves captured from other clans.[19] An important difference, however, is that the *liurais* were (and still are) often chosen by the village elders. Although the new *liurai* had to be of royal descent (descended from the clan's sacred house or *uma lulik*, which traditionally holds political power), the elders looked for an intelligent person who had shown leadership qualities.

For example, when Carlos Felipe Ximenes Belo grew up in Quilicai in the 1950s, the village elders favoured him, the youngest child of a *liurai* family, as the ideal candidate for their new leader. But he firmly declined because he had other plans. He went on to become Bishop of Dili.[20]

The social structure was based on an intricate system of kinship relations that secured a community's survival and its territory. Family groups with a common ancestor lived in *knuas* spread over the rugged mountains. Several *knuas* formed a hamlet. Life in these settlements revolved around the clan's *uma lulik*. This was often the oldest dwelling of the hamlet and it was believed to have been built by the common ancestor. In this house the clan elders kept sacred objects. It was opened only on special occasions.

The oldest settlers were considered the 'lords of the land' and had ritual authority while relative newcomers quite often held political powers.

A large clan could have several *uma lulik*, each with a different responsibility. Thus one house might be responsible for rituals while another held political authority, or provided security, or even music and dance.

The *uma lulik* is protected by what is called taboo in Polynesia. It is known by different names in East Timor but it is at the heart of the traditional religious spirituality.

The traditional power structure was uprooted during the Indonesian occupation because of mass displacement. Entire villages were annihilated and people were concentrated into so-called strategic villages – camp-like settlements often far removed from their inhabitants' ancestral hamlets. However, the Indonesians, like the Portuguese before them, also used traditional structures. In some areas members of the *liurai* families collaborated, willingly or under duress, and became *kepala desa* (Bahasa Indonesian for 'village head'). But in many places the *liurais* were also part of the underground resistance.

Some of them paid with their lives for opposing Indonesian rule. For example, Verissimo Quintas, the respected *liurai* of Los Palos, was killed during the 1999 referendum when Indonesian-backed militia terrorised the country.

That the Timorese traditional power structure did not fade into obscurity during the Indonesian occupation became clear soon after the Indonesian army left the country. Many people who had been forced to live in 'strategic villages' went back to their ancestral lands high up in the mountains.

Communities that could afford it rebuilt their *uma lulik* even before they rebuilt their own destroyed houses. Anthropologist Elizabeth Traube observed such projects across the district of Aileu.[21] At the same time the traditional local leadership structure was revived, and in many places where *liurais* had held the respect of the population they were reinstated. In other places the village elders would gather to choose a new leader from the local aristocracy.

These recent developments occurred in parallel to two other processes. The Conselho Nacional da Resistência Timorense (CNRT – National Council of Timorese Resistance) had developed a shadow administration in many places and was demanding some kind of political recognition, and the UN was attempting to establish democracy. The revival of traditional power structures sometimes worked against the democratic principles that the UN tried to introduce: for example, local leaders used their traditional influence to advise people which party to vote for.

Women leaders

Historically women were not by definition excluded from the traditional power structure and could even fulfil a leadership role. Although the *feto ferik,* as queens or female chiefs were known, were more common in the western part of the country (especially among the Bunaq, a matrilineal society), women in other areas sometimes assumed the paramount position, especially in the absence of an adult male heir.

Women could also become warriors fighting alongside the men

in battles against (colonial) invaders or other tribes. For example, when the Indonesians infiltrated the border area two sisters, Leonia Pires and Ravu Letok, took up arms. They rode astride ponies, in full battle-dress, often accompanied by a Portuguese soldier who had stayed behind when his colleagues withdrew from East Timor. The sisters became legendary for their courage and determination to fight. They terrified the Indonesian soldiers who, like the local population, believed that the women were immune to bullets. Their fame reached as far as Jakarta.

However, after the Portuguese soldier died the women surrendered. The military took them to Jakarta to be interrogated by Intel, the Indonesian intelligence. When they were away their husbands remarried; the women were forced to marry Indonesian soldiers.[22]

Marriage traditions and *barlaque*

Marriage played an important role in the complex system of family alliances that maintained (and still today continues to maintain) the social structure and the security of an area. These intricate clan relations were carefully recorded in oral history and recited by the village elders on appropriate occasions such as marriages and deaths.

As in other Asian cultures, marriages in East Timor are often arranged. The match is made with care by a *lia-nain*, or spokesperson of each family, and it is more a contract between families than a love match.

In East Timor the family of the groom has to pay a bride price, or *barlaque*, often in the form of livestock (horses, buffaloes, goats) and jewellery. The family of the bride brings *tais* (traditional handwoven cloth), pigs, rice, baskets and other things considered 'female'.

After the wedding the bride moves to her husband's family, unless the husband could not pay a sufficient bride price, in which case the husband moves in with his wife's family. *Barlaque* can be so expensive that many young men cannot afford it and in the 1990s some opted to marry a 'cheaper' bride from Indonesia.

Nowadays the tradition of *barlaque* remains prevalent and it is singled out by East Timorese women activists as one of the underlying reasons for the problems many married women are facing. The fortunes paid often serve as an excuse for her new family to treat the bride as a commodity and even subject her to violent attacks if she fails to conform to expectations.

The value of fertility

Anthropologist David Hicks, who studied Timorese traditional belief systems, confirms the prominence of the feminine in rituals – a phenomenon which is believed to go back to Paleolithic times and the Venus figures of 27,000-20,000 years ago. He writes that traditional East Timorese myths and rituals abound with masculine/feminine dualism and polarities. The village environment also draws on human bodily analogy to describe everyday human life and experience. In the Viqueque district, where Hicks studied the Tetum Terik-speaking people, traditional beliefs hold that human beings originally climbed out of two holes or vaginas – Mahuma and Lequi Bui – using a sacred creeper. These first people became the ancestors.

Traditional homes, Hicks writes, have doors called vaginas, and the interior is regarded as a 'womb' – a feminine space. Tetum Terik people in Viqueque hold that the universe is divided into an upper-world and an underworld connected by vaginas. The underworld is feminine, material and sacred, while the upperworld is masculine, paternal and secular. These two worlds must come together in Tetum birth, marriage and death rituals, but only within that context – otherwise infertility, sickness and death may result. According to Hicks, women play an influential role in religion, whereas men dominate the secular affairs of the upperworld. Women are mediators between the two worlds. This function is considered crucial for the maintenance of human life and the contentment (and containment) of the spirits human imagination has devised. It defines the status of women in Tetum Terik culture.[23]

Elizabeth Traube also noted the abundance of symbols of the womb, mother earth, union, creation and the importance of the sacred ancestral house. Writing of the Mambai, who inhabit the mountains south of Dili situated around the sacred mountain Ramalau (also known as Tata Mai Lau), Traube says they:

… take pride in preserving their common belief that all living creatures are descended from Father Heaven and Mother Earth, who unite on the peak of Tata Mai Lau, the mountain of origins, at the centre of the world. Father Heaven removes the power of speech from his firstborn, the trees and grasses, so that they may be used to construct the first house, where Mother Earth gives birth to the ancestors of humanity. At first the ancestors cluster together in the Lone House. Human history begins with their dispersal from the mountaintop and their migrations across the land. Each of the male ancestors takes a share of the primordial patrimony, cuts a slip from the house pillar, and sets off for the outside, where after a period of wandering he 'plants' a new house.[24]

Hicks also studied the role of fertility in the marriage tradition of the Tetum Terik people, for whom fertility was a powerful and sought-after asset.

Some families were designated as 'wife givers', whose female offspring were offered as brides to the 'wife takers' (often of the same clan). In East Timorese society marriage is an organisational principle linking groups over time. The repetition of marriages over generations can produce lasting alliances between social groups.

To weave this intricate web of relationships a strict hierarchy was observed. Although often branches of the same clan, the 'wife givers' were always superior in the hierarchy to the 'wife takers'. The 'wife givers' were often associated with the value of fertility. It was not perceived that the woman, as an individual person, passed on to another family, but that the value of fertility was handed to 'wife takers'. The wife givers were almost always also the 'lords of the land', and the ownership of land and the fertility of women given in marriage are seen as closely connected.[25]

The clans were extensive and tightly knit. In an environment where rivalries between clans and villages could be deadly, the family members linked by blood were often the only people to be trusted. Such alliances prevented communities going to war.[26]

Treaties were entered into on the basis of these family links. In this way, even the kings of relatively small kingdoms could wield considerable authority over a large area.

The female line of the clan is as well documented as the male, so that the female line has been preserved down the generations.[27] Both sides of the extended families are invited to major family occasions.

Traditional law

Law was governed by tradition and local custom, known as *adat*, modified over the ages by the adoption of certain Chinese or Muslim ideas.

Adat does not work in favour of women's rights. It does not, for example, allow women to inherit land, and widows would have to hand over their land to a male heir. *Adat* also allowed polygamy, which could leave a woman without any economic means if her husband was too poor to support more than one wife.

Another tradition that often works unfavourably for women is that in many places a council of elders arbitrates in family disputes or problems between husbands and wives. The old men of the village sit together drinking palm wine deep into the night, discussing the matter until they come to a consensus. Often the settlement includes a payment in kind directly to the 'victim' or the victim's family. Depending on the seriousness of the matter, a chicken or a buffalo might be required.

Local Catholic priests can play a similar mediating role. It has been common for their advice in marital disputes to be more concerned with re-uniting the couple come what may than in taking account of any mistreatment of the wife by the husband.

Women's roles

Despite differences among the ethnic and linguistic groups, in general the most important tasks of women were (and still are in most cases) to bear and raise children, look after the house, and cultivate the vegetable gardens. Preparing food and collecting firewood and water are also seen as women's tasks. Pottery, silver work and weaving baskets are women's trades. Men looked after cattle or went hunting, and both women and men worked in the rice and cornfields. Ploughing was typically the task of men.

Outside the house, women assisted other women in childbirth, and looked after the sick and elderly people.

Women also had ceremonial roles. They performed ritual dances and played musical instruments such as the *tupalo* (a hand-held wooden drum) and gongs on special occasions, for example to welcome important guests or when men went out to or returned from war.

In many rural areas the daily chores of women have changed little. The ceremonial role has evolved to include welcoming important visitors by presenting them with a piece of handwoven cloth and performing traditional dances.

Wallace noted in his journals – one of his first observations when he landed on the island of Timor – how the women were unlike those he had met in Java and other parts of Indonesia: 'The way in which the women talk to each other and to the men, their loud voices and laughter, and general character of self-assertion, would enable an experienced observer to decide, even without seeing them, that they were not Malay.'[28] The women had, perhaps, more freedom of movement than many women in the Europe of Wallace's time. This freedom was eroded, especially in urban centres, when Catholic missionaries succeeded in spreading their social values among a larger part of the population.

Educational opportunities

At the time of Wallace's visit there were no schools in East Timor. It would be more than a decade later, around 1878, that the Roman Catholic bishop opened the first primary school in Soibada, followed in 1902 by a boarding school for girls run by the Canossian Sisters of Charity. The nuns taught the girls Portuguese and catechism, but mainly concentrated on preparing them for domestic duties with lessons in cleaning, sewing, embroidery and weaving. Only seven years after it opened, the school was closed again by the new anti-clerical Republic of Portugal, which launched a persecution of Catholic missionaries throughout the empire. The Jesuit priest and Canossian sisters were obliged to abandon their mission and the girls' college was closed, its new zinc roof removed by order of the governor who wished to use it to cover a state building elsewhere.[29] This was a serious setback for the children, who had no other opportunity for formal education than these few church-run schools. It was not until 1923 that the Canossians were able to return and re-open their school.

Whether or not the missionaries intended it, the schools in Soibada were accessible only to children of the ruling classes.[30] This changed when the Bishop of East Timor established a school for cathechists in 1935. It educated both men and women and had a strong influence on missionary work in East Timor. The church put much thought into how to christianise East Timor, recognising the strong resistance to new forms of education. Graduates were encouraged to spread their knowledge and went back to their villages to set up schools. These very simple primary schools were often run by husband and wife teams whose vocation it was to prepare youngsters for the sacrament of baptism. Often the children influenced their parents to become Catholics.

The spread of Roman Catholicism also had an impact on women's lives. It emphasised a woman's role as a mother and homemaker who had to put her own needs behind those of husband and family. This traditional position of women in the family, even in highly educated families, means for example that women, often as part of hospitality rituals, have to serve men and their guests, and only eat (the leftovers) when they have finished their meals. To this day, conservative views on women held under Portuguese times have changed little. Wives are expected to submit to their husbands and divorce is very difficult to obtain.

Olandina Caeiro notes that at the end of the Portuguese colonial era, women were not allowed to work outside the home:

Only a few women enjoyed what you might describe as a 'normal life' like we have now. They were generally very suppressed. They were not allowed to work outside the home and only around five per cent were educated. And this was only in such things as sewing, cooking and the catechism. Only a few people went to school in Portuguese times – and they only received up to middle school courses. There might have been 50 women altogether who had been educated back then, and only one or two had gone for superior studies – such as Ana Pessoa [Minister for Justice in East Timor's first post-independence government]. You had to come from a very privileged background – the parents had to have money, work for the government, have good links with the church, etc. Pretty much no East Timorese had managed to get access to tertiary level education outside the country before the 1970s.[31]

The state-run schools were almost exclusively for the privileged middle classes or so-called *assimilados*.[32] For ordinary Timorese it was virtually impossible to gain access to these institutions. For boys who wanted to study beyond primary school, the seminary was the only possibility. Girls had fewer options still. For them the only chance to learn a little more than reading, writing and home-making was to become a nun. Although education had improved since the first girls' school opened, by 1970 there was only one government high school, one business school and one teacher training college in the whole of East Timor.

In the 1970s the first batch of students returned from studies in Portugal, Mozambique and Macao. They were part of the local elite, the future leaders of East Timor. Not surprisingly, there were few women among them.

Notes

1 Boyce, D (1995) *East Timor: Where the sun rises over the crocodile's tail*, Dili (self-published); and in *Asia Pacific Journal of Anthropology* Vol 2 No 2, September 2001, pp89-113.

2 Jolliffe, J (1978) *East Timor nationalism and colonialism*, University of Queensland Press, St Lucia, Queensland, p23.

3 Jolliffe, J (as above).

4 Boyce, D (see note 1).

5 Gunn, G (2001) 'The 500 year Timorese *funu*' in Tanter, R, Selden, M, and Shalom, S (eds) *Bitter flowers, sweet flowers: East Timor, Indonesia and the world community*, Rowman & Littlefield, Maryland, p5.

6 Gunn, G (as above), p8.

7 Wallace, A (1869) *The Malay archipelago*, Macmillan & Co, London, reissued by Oxford University Press, 1989.

8 Wallace, A (as above).

9   Geoffrey Gunn estimates the total pre-war population at around 450,000. Gunn, G (1999) *Timor Lorosae: 500 years*, Livros do Oriente, Macao.

10 Jolliffe, J (2001) 'Timor's haunted women' in *The Age* (Melbourne), 3 November 2001.

11 Gunn, G (2001: see note 5), p8.

12 Little or no independent research has been done into this uprising and it remains unclear who was behind it.

13 The other two parties, Kota and Trabalhista, never exerted much influence, although Indonesia managed to use them as pawns in its attempts to destabilise East Timor.

14 Burr, W, and Evans, M (eds) (2002) *National Security Archive electronic briefing book no 62*, George Washington University.

15 Based on a calculation of the natural population growth if there had been no war.

16 *Funu* – war – is used not only for war against colonial forces but also to describe fighting between clans and villages.

17 Quoted in Gunn, G (2001: see note 5), p8.

18 Fox, J, and Soares, D (2000) 'Tracing the path, recounting the past' in Fox, J, and Soares, D (eds) *Out of the ashes*, Crawford House Publishing, Adelaide, p1.

19 Slaves, however, could sometimes inherit property and land after their masters had died.

20 See Kohen, A (1999) *From the place of the dead*, St Martin's Press, New York.

21 Traube, E (2001) 'Housing the nation', unpublished paper presented at the Pacific Islands, Atlantic Worlds symposium, Asian/Pacific American Studies Programme, New York University, 26 October 2001.

22 Father Balthasar Kehi in an interview with Irena Cristalis, May 2002.

23 Hicks, D (1984) *A maternal religion: The role of women in Tetum myth and ritual*, Special Report No 22, Monograph Series on Southeast Asia, DeKalb Center for Southeast Asian Studies, Northern Illinois University.

24 Traube, E (see note 21).

25 Hicks, D (1976) *Tetum ghosts and kin: Fieldwork in an Indonesian community*, Mayfield Publications, Palo Alto.

26 Ospina, S, and Hohe, T (2001) *Traditional power structure and the community empowerment and local governance project*, Final Report, World Bank, Dili.

27 Benjamin Corte-Real in an interview with Irena Cristalis, August 2001.

28 Wallace, A (see note 7).

29 See the website of the *Sebastião Aparicio da Silva project for the protection and promotion of East Timorese languages* (http://www.ocs.mq.edu.au/~leccles/easttimor.html). Father Sebastião Maria Aparício da Silva was the author of the first printed book in Tetum, a Catholic catechism (1885), and the first dictionary of the language (1889).

30 Maria Lourdes Martins Cruz in an interview with Catherine Scott, June 2004.

31 Interview with Catherine Scott, June 2004.

32 This literally means families which have become 'assimilated' into Portuguese culture, although not necessarily of Portuguese blood.

Chapter 2
War and resistance

This chapter examines the history of the women's movement in East Timor and the role women played in the struggle for independence. Although an embryonic women's movement preceded the Indonesian invasion, its character was shaped by the invasion and occupation, as were the lives of two generations of women. The period of the Indonesian occupation can be divided into the war years (1975-1979) when a large part of the population lived as refugees in the hills, and the years after 1979 when first a village-based resistance and then an urban resistance developed. Women and children became an invaluable support network for the armed resistance.

Birth of an East Timorese women's movement

When, on 28 November 1975, Rosa Bonaparte unfurled the new red, black and yellow flag with a white star, symbol of the Democratic Republic of East Timor, an invasion by Indonesia seemed imminent. The Frente Revolucionária de Timor Leste Independente (Fretilin – Revolutionary Front for an Independent East Timor) had hastily organised the ceremony, a solemn rather than triumphant affair, to swear in the new government in the hope that an independent East Timor could rally more support and protection from the international community. But less than nine days after Rosa Bonaparte hoisted the flag, Indonesia invaded East Timor.

The war changed women's lives radically, not only because of the death and destruction it brought, but also because it transformed their roles in society. Until then, women had seldom played a public role. Rosa Bonaparte's flag-raising was by no means an indication of women's growing equality within Fretilin, nor in the liberation movement. Of Fretilin's 50-strong central committee, only three were women.[1] A reason for the absence of women might have been the lack of education and preparation (indeed, lack of capacity would be an argument later used by Timorese politicians to reject a quota for women members in the Constituent Assembly).

The female members of the central committee were Rosa Bonaparte, Maria do Ceu and Guilhermina Araujo. They were among the very few Timorese women with a higher education, and rarer still, they had studied abroad. When they returned they brought back political and feminist ideas and applied these to the Timorese situation. The women did not, it appeared, draw on particular texts or thinkers; rather, the ideas came largely at second or third hand from the interpretations of others in the radical political movement that was developing in the early 1970s. Their concern was to open up a space so they could organise themselves.

At this time Fretilin's central committee was devising a strategy to make East Timor independent, and was setting up mass organisations[2] which sent high school students to the countryside to organise villagers for the liberation struggle. An important part of the strategy were the so-called 'revolutionary brigades'. These consisted of 10-60 people, including secondary school students, teachers, health workers and members of Fretilin's central committee. There were two pilot centres, one in Aileu and one in Bucoli. Rosa Bonaparte worked in Aileu. They conducted a cultural campaign, reviving traditional music and dance; held literacy classes and training sessions on basic hygiene; and gave information about agricultural cooperatives and crop-diversification.[3] These activities went on for two and a half months until the coup against Fretilin on 11 August 1975 by the União Democrática Timorense (UDT – Timorese Democratic Union) put an end to budding democracy and civil society in East Timor.

The coup and the subsequent civil war between the UDT and Fretilin left an estimated 2,000 people dead and many children orphaned. The fighting inflamed old rivalries as animosities between tribal groups flared and old scores were settled.

On 28 August 1975, in the aftermath of this civil war, the women's front of Fretilin, the Organização Popular da Mulher Timorense (OPMT – Popular Organisation of East Timorese Women) was formed. Its founders included Rosa Bonaparte, Maria do Ceu, Maia Reis, Aicha Bassarawan, Dulce da Cruz and Isabel Lobato. This was the first indigenous political women's organisation. None of the other parties set up a women's wing at this point.

Initially the OPMT worked alongside other organisations such as the International Committee of the Red Cross and the Australian Council for Overseas Aid to address the humanitarian crisis. Their major projects worked with displaced persons, placing orphans in the care of local families. They also set up crèches in Dili and the districts and ran literacy programmes. But the creation of the OPMT had other objectives too: first, to participate directly in the struggle against colonialism; and second, to fight the violent discrimination that Timorese women suffered in colonial society. The

OPMT aimed to promote the emancipation of women in all aspects of life. The crèches also gave mothers more opportunities to participate in the world outside their homes.

Rosa Bonaparte, who was elected OPMT's secretary, described the new movement as 'a mass organisation of Fretilin – which will work to enable women to participate in the revolution'.[4] Maia Reis, who was involved with the OPMT from the beginning, explained that Fretilin included three political movements. Apart from the OPMT, these were a general youth wing, Organizaçao Popular Juventude Timor Leste, and a labour movement, Organizaçao Popular Trabalhista Timorense. These organisations formed a support base of Fretilin and later the base of the resistance struggle.[5]

As a wing of Fretilin, the OPMT followed its ideology. The factions within Fretilin – a radical left wing and a moderate centrist wing – were reflected in the OPMT. (This divide continues to influence the women's organisation today: see also chapter 3.) But as Olandina Caeiro has pointed out, it was the party that was radical, not the women's movement.

The youth organisations and the OPMT also followed Fretilin's organisational structure which had grown roots in the villages. Each region had committees responsible for education, culture, logistics, health and hygiene, political organisation, nurseries for orphans and agriculture.[6]

The OPMT was open to women of all ages, but recruited mainly among the young women from the 'revolutionary brigades'. The girls who joined their ranks as 'barefoot' teachers, health workers and political educators were often as young as 15. They disseminated the ideology of Fretilin and also raised issues such as human rights, women's rights and the culturally sensitive issues of polygamy and bride price.[7] But it was not until after the Indonesian invasion that the OPMT really penetrated deep into the countryside.

Effects of the invasion on women

On the day of the invasion, Dili saw indiscriminate killing of men, women and even children. Isabel Lobato, one of the founding members of the OPMT and wife of Fretilin leader Nicolau Lobato, was executed by Indonesian soldiers on the wharf and dumped into the sea together with at least 100 other people. The next day Rosa Bonaparte's body was washed up on the shoreline near Dili.[8] Many other members of the OPMT were also killed in these first days. The Indonesian military had a list of the names of radical women, thought to have been provided by East Timorese who opposed the hard-line faction in the OPMT.[9] The Indonesian soldiers killed any

Timorese whom they suspected of being communist.

Soon after the invasion the population of the coastal areas and towns fled into the hills, to seek refuge in the strongholds of Fretilin and its armed forces. The refugees, mainly women, children and the elderly, often travelled in large groups of hundreds of people, resembling entire villages on the move.

The OPMT adjusted its activities to the changing situation. The majority of the population had fled from the coastal areas to the mountains, where women bore arms alongside men, provided logistical support, and carried out a broad range of clandestine political and armed resistance activities. They also took primary responsibility for their communities and families. Florentina Martins Smith, who fled to the forest after the invasion and became an OPMT organiser, says they continued to organise literacy courses for women. They also conducted health awareness training with the Forças Armadas de Libertação Nacional de Timor Leste (Falintil – Armed Forces for the National Liberation of East Timor) and taught them about traditional medicine. Some women did agricultural work, growing food for Falintil. It was dangerous, insecure work, and they had to keep on the move most of the time. 'When there was an attack, we divided up,' she explains. 'Then we would reorganise ourselves again afterwards.'[10]

One of these refugees, Bertha Oliveira Alves, the wife of a Fretilin leader, recalls that on the day of the invasion she fled into the hills above Dili with her small children and many people of her neighbourhood. They could take only what they could carry: a few clothes, a sleeping mat, a jerry can for water. Only a few people stayed behind: the very old who could not make the journey into the hills and a few families who had decided to wait and see what would happen. People who went into the hills often found shelter in existing villages, where they built temporary houses or moved in with family members.

Bertha and her group walked to Remexio, where they built a temporary settlement out of palm leaves around Falintil's barracks. In the group of families she travelled with, more than 20 women were members of the OPMT – 'women of all ages, from teenagers to the elderly. Their main duty was to cook for the military. Sometimes the soldiers helped to collect firewood but it was the women's task to search for food, cook it and bring it to the men in the barracks.' But cooking was not their only task. When the population lived around the barracks women also took it in turns to do guard duty, armed with automatic rifles.[11]

Recalling these early days in Remexio, Constancio Pinto, who grew up there and is now East Timor's ambassador in Washington, describes the activities of the OPMT as follows:

> ... the OPMT would help other women make crafts and baskets, and also cook for the guerrilla fighters and take food to the front lines.... The OPMT had its own political programme. OPMT activists often delivered speeches on women's issues. They also challenged some East Timorese traditions like polygamy and *barlaque*.[12] [*Barlaque* is a form of bride price: see chapter 1.]

Xanana Gusmão, then a junior member of the central committee, recalls:

> The debates that took place in the mountains involved men as well as women. This resulted in mutual respect and an ability to accept opinions of others. The women gained the respect and understanding of the men for their work, political opinion and contribution to the struggle.[13]

But this was just one side of the story. Although women might have been consulted in the decision-making process, it was the men who took the decisions. There were no women in the command structure of the army, and this was mirrored in the political hierarchy. The three women in the central committee of Fretilin had junior positions and none of them was a minister.

Esmeralda Rego de Jesus Araujo: freedom in the forest

Esmeralda was 15 years old at the time of the invasion. As a daughter of the *liurai* (local chief) of Hatolia in Ermera, she was one of the few girls with an education. She had joined a student brigade in 1975. In that year, Fretilin became East Timor's most popular party and many students and young men and women joined teams of barefoot teachers and health workers. Like her colleagues, Esmeralda taught villagers some reading, writing and rudimentary health education, and also political education. When the war broke out she joined the stream of refugees into the mountains of Ermera, where she was chosen as the local vice-secretary of the OPMT in Falintil's Base Quatro (Sector Four). She was 'small and young,' she said, but she felt she 'had to do it.'

Sister Esmeralda often thinks back to the time in the forest with a mixture of horror and nostalgia. Her work meant she had to move from one village to another, staying for a month 'to educate and politicise the people'. As the war proceeded her group could only move at night. In the daytime they hid in bushes and holes in riverbanks. Falintil soldiers would lead and the civilians followed. One night in 1977 they arrived in Maubara. At 4am the aeroplanes came. She found a tree to hide in. The bombs exploded all around them but no-one died. 'God walked with us,' she says. If she had to, she would do it again. 'Although occupied,' she says, 'we were free.'

[Interview with Irena Cristalis, 2001]

The war years

The war continued for much longer than anyone had expected. The Indonesians, who thought they could bring the territory under their control in a matter of days, faced resistance from almost the entire population.

But with their superior weapons, such as the Bronco anti-insurgent aircraft and the Hawk fighter jet supplied by the US and UK respectively, the Indonesian troops gradually gained more terrain. The refugee population and Falintil were pushed higher and higher up the mountains to areas were no food or water was available. Many people either starved or died in bombardments, and Mount Matebian, to which the resistance retreated, soon became a large graveyard.

Entire families hiding in the big boulders that lie strewn over the higher reaches of Mount Matebian were wiped out when the bombs struck. Other families were separated. The men were either killed or fled to avoid capture by the Indonesian army, leaving the women to look after themselves and what was left of their families.

But Fretilin was not only fighting the occupiers. The radical leftist wing gained the upper hand, and purged the party of people they saw as reactionaries. The ideological battle was ferocious and untold numbers of Fretilin members died at the hands of their own comrades.

Maria Madalena dos Santos Fatima: coming to terms with history

Maria Madalena dos Santos Fatima was 13 years old when Indonesia invaded East Timor. Her whole family took part in the struggle against the occupation, and many members of her family were killed as a result.

Maria Madalena remembers that in 1975, when the bombardment started, women formed groups and organised themselves. They would brief each other in the marketplace as to what was happening. The OPMT gave women the opportunity to organise, both for resistance and to fight discrimination against women. Maria, too, joined the OPMT.

Like many others, Maria Madalena's family fled to the mountains after the Indonesian invasion. At the time, she says, women were treated as equals in theory, but the practice lagged behind. 'There was a vision of equality,' she says, but 'the Fretilin commanders did not really practise what they preached.' The gap between theory and reality caused conflict. The vision was that men and women would work together cooperatively. In practice, the men used the women as 'wives'. The cultural attitudes were that women were there as a 'comfort' for the men. The resulting babies (and some unions produced several) unfortunately disrupted many a family and the unions that resulted were not particularly respected. The Catholic church did not recognise the resistance relationships. The families had to decide how to deal with the complications themselves and the injustices that arose were usually borne by the women. The children grew up malnourished and ill-educated and because so many children were born, there was often no time for normal affection.

While they were in the mountains, Maria Madalena's family fell out with a group in Falintil that was trying to promote communist ideas. Many of the men in her family were executed by this group. She believes she was spared because she was very young at the time.

Despite this devastating experience, Maria Madalena clung to her vision of an independent East Timor and continued to fight for it. After three years in the mountains, she returned to her village in 1978. She worked for the clandestine movement throughout the 1980s. Her husband was a soldier in the Indonesian army and stole uniforms, boots and guns which she helped to smuggle through to the resistance fighters. The Falintil trusted her because she had been involved in Fretilin from the beginning. In the 1990s she also became a courier for correspondence between the Falintil and the Bishop of Baucau, Basilio do Nascimento.

In 1997, her car was used in a Falintil attack in which 19 police officers were killed. After that, the military began to distrust Madalena. Her brother was assaulted and her car vandalised. The Indonesian military began investigating her and came to her house. But the International Committee of the Red Cross heard that she was being harassed and took up her case. The harassment stopped.

After the Indonesians left, the Comissão de Acolhimento, Verdade e Reconciliação (CAVR – Commission for Reception, Truth and Reconciliation) invited Maria to tell her story to them. She was reluctant to speak at local hearings organised in her home town of Baucau, fearing repercussions because some of the commission's local staff were Fretilin members. She was afraid she might be killed if she testified. But she decided to speak out in the more neutral atmosphere of Dili, where she felt safer. She sees her experience as part of a much wider national problem which needs to be addressed. Telling her story to the commission, she believes, is part of coming to terms with history.

[Interview with Catherine Scott, June 2004]

By 1979, after three years of fierce fighting, the Indonesian army had decimated the armed resistance and its last stronghold, the Matebian, had fallen. Heeding a call for amnesty, most of the refugees, mainly women and children, came down from the mountains and returned to the towns and villages. As a support network for the remaining guerrilla groups, they became crucial in keeping the spirit of the resistance alive.

Maia Reis: from the jungle to clandestine resistance

Maia Reis has been part of the East Timorese women's movement since the OPMT was inaugurated in August 1975. The organisation was just three months old when Indonesia invaded and the OPMT relocated from Dili to the jungle.

Maia fled to the jungle in the Baucau area with her parents and sisters. She continued to organise for the OPMT, explaining the basic principles of human rights and self-determination to mobilise support for Fretilin.

In 1977 she came out of the jungle. She was interrogated and then subjected to indoctrination by the Indonesian military. She remembers being forced to dance with Indonesian soldiers: 'They would call our names on the microphones and tell us to go and dance with such-and-such.'

In 1979, she joined the clandestine movement, receiving instruction from a Falintil commander based in Suai. She passed information and made contacts, and she and her sister made

Fretilin badges and flags. They also provided the guerrillas with food, medicine and clothing. However, the group of clandestine activists she belonged to was exposed by an informer, and some of the members were arrested. One of them gave her name to the military, and she too was arrested in 1981.

She was interrogated, released and then arrested again, and spent a month in prison. After she was released, she had to report to the military every day, and they continued to threaten her.

She married, moved to Dili and started working for the clandestine movement again. In 1991 she was arrested for carrying a photocopy of a CNRM newspaper. (CNRM was the Conselho Nacional da Resistência Maubere – National Council of Maubere Resistance – a non-partisan clandestine coalition formed in 1988.) She spent three days and three nights in prison. Although she was under surveillance afterwards, she continued to work with the clandestine resistance, and helped to establish the Organização da Mulher Timorense (OMT – Organisation of Timorese Women: see chapter 3).

[Interview with Catherine Scott, June 2004]

Life for women under Indonesian occupation

The Indonesians locked up many women they suspected of participating in the resistance and imprisoned them on the island of Atauro, north of Dili. OPMT women were often singled out for more brutal treatment than other women prisoners. The Indonesian soldiers associated the OPMT with Gerwani, the Indonesian women's movement that had been unofficially affiliated to the Indonesian communist party in the 1960s.

Another reason for the brutal treatment was that many OPMT women were related to Fretilin leaders and Falintil fighters.[14] In the enclave of Oecusse, for example, the power structure in the OPMT mirrored that of Fretilin and the UDT. The cell structure of the resistance was based on trust and secrecy, so there was a tendency to rely on family connections.

There are countless stories of rapes and killings of OPMT women throughout the years of occupation. A young Timorese leader, a child at the time, remembered: 'Every night one [OPMT member] would be taken by the troops and raped, sometimes as many as three rapes per night. We children had to watch this.'[15] To avoid this fate, some women stayed in the forest.[16]

Rape and sexual violence

From the day of the invasion, sexual violence and rape became hallmarks of the Indonesian occupation. Not only did the Indonesian army visit atrocities on East Timorese women, singling out the politically active for particular humiliation, but they also forced East Timorese men into public rape and killing of women. According to Bishop Dom Martinho, former Bishop of Dili: 'One of their [the Indonesian soldiers'] favourite customs was to rape wives in front of their husbands, right there, sometimes with the children there too.'[17] Even in prisons, cases were reported of male prisoners being forced to rape female prisoners.

Wives of political activists and of the Falintil were often forced to live with Indonesian soldiers. For example, Emilia Gusmão, first wife of East Timor's president, Xanana Gusmão, was victimised by Indonesian soldiers who took over her home in Dili. Xanana's sister Armandina Gusmão dos Santos also suffered at the hands of the Indonesian special forces. Because she was personal secretary to the governor's wife, she was suspected by the soldiers of being a political link between Xanana and the governor, and after Xanana's arrest in 1992 she was detained for months, sexually harassed and raped.[18]

Children born of rape were likely to be abandoned, or handed over to church orphanages. Women victims of rape were often (but not always) ostracised by their own families and communities, sometimes ending up in prostitution as a result. Testimonies to the Commission for Reception, Truth and Reconciliation (CAVR) set up in East Timor in 2002 to address the human rights violations since 1975 revealed that some women were forced into prostitution by the army of occupation.[19] The Indonesian military also used women as sex slaves. Women living in poorer, rural areas were particularly vulnerable to enforced slavery and prostitution. Amnesty International and other human rights organisations documented many cases throughout the occupation, but these are only a fraction of the tens of thousands of incidents which have inevitably gone unreported.[20] The situation was so grave that in some instances Catholic nuns helped women to obtain abortions.[21]

Testimonies

It is truly distressing, painful and wearisome to have to speak again of my bitter suffering. Over and above the whole tragic experience of my family that I have described, I was a victim of the desires of a corrupt and murderous Indonesian major who raped me and harassed me continually to satisfy his cravings. In 1979 in Sang-tai-hoo prison, my sister was brutally raped by the prison commander.

[Ms X, a widow with two children, at the Fourth Christian Consultation on East Timor, January 1988[22]]

I will be handicapped for my entire life.... I have given birth to five children from five different fathers, all members of the Indonesian army. I have been arrested, beaten, treated like a servant, and until 1991 I had to service soldiers at night-time. This calamity will never end for me. After experiencing this shameful treatment at the hands of military forces, I have been disowned by my family, all of them condemn me. They don't want to accept that my fate was a consequence of the war situation.

[Dukai, aged 35[23]]

Rape and sexual torture is not unique to the Indonesian army, but is particular to certain forms of subjugation and attempted annihilation of one group of armed males over another. At the CAVR hearings some women testified to being raped during the civil war in 1975 by UDT and Fretilin soldiers.[24]

The UN Special Rapporteur on Violence Against Women, Radhika Coomaraswamy, explains this phenomenon as follows:

Perhaps more than the honour of the victim, it is the perceived honour of the enemy that is targeted in the perpetration of sexual violence against women; it is seen and often experienced as a means of humiliating the opposition. Sexual violence against women is meant to demonstrate victory over the men of the other group who have failed to protect their women. It is a message of castration and emasculation of the enemy group. It is a battle among men fought over the bodies of women.[25]

Forced 'marriages'

Another common practice of the occupying forces was to organise dance parties, forcing local women to join in. After the parties they often abducted women to rape them or to take them as a 'second wife' during their stay in Timor. Young, unmarried women in particular were easy prey. When the soldier left East Timor he would abandon his 'wife' and any children, often without any support. As in the case of rape victims, the family could be isolated in the community.

Some women joined religious orders to avoid rape or abduction. Other young women and girls married quickly, to avoid being forced to 'marry' Indonesian soldiers. Some married men they might not otherwise have chosen simply to obtain a little more security.

Forced contraception

Preoccupied with overpopulation in Java, Indonesian president Suharto devised a national birth control policy which was also implemented in East Timor, where it led to widespread abuse by overzealous military doctors. Many East Timorese women believe themselves to have been forcibly sterilised in the 1980s and others were injected with the long-lasting contraceptive depo provera. It has been reported that up to 62 per cent of family planning used in East Timor was of the injectable variety. Injections were frequently given without consent: women were told that the injection was a type of vaccine.[26]

According to one East Timorese woman activist, Bela Galhos:

> Every six months ... the military goes to all the high schools, seeking out the young girls for compulsory birth control. They came, closed the door, and just injected us. We didn't know, we don't have the right to ask. We don't have children any more. After visiting the schools, the military still goes around to individual villages and houses to inject the women they find. They don't know who we are, so they just inject us again. Some women get injected three times.[27]

This deterred East Timorese women from attending Indonesian clinics, with the result that other health problems, particularly during pregnancy, went undetected. Similarly, school vaccination programmes were looked on with suspicion, leading to the premature withdrawal of girls from school.[28] The Catholic church opposed these birth control practices and its traditional prohibition of the use of artificial methods of contraception may have protected some women whose health might otherwise have been damaged by these forced contraception practices.

Catholic religious orders

Some Catholic orders, such as the Canossian Sisters, had been in East Timor since the 19th century. Many of their members, and foreign priests and nuns in particular, fled the country when the civil war between Fretilin and the UDT broke out, but a significant minority, including some foreign missionaries, stayed. They saw their mission as being to remain close to the people, come what may. Their status as members of religious orders initially provided a measure of protection. Religious orders did return after the bloodiest years of the resistance war and by the early 1980s Indonesian orders were encouraged to repopulate East Timor's convents and presbyteries.

In the late 1970s a group of Roman Catholic missionaries, the Salesians, established houses in the foothills of the Matebian where hundreds of children, among them Falintil offspring and orphans coming from the mountains, could obtain shelter, food and an education. They stood up against the Indonesian army and protected the children from harassment. They provided shelter for families who supported the resistance on many occasions. The girls' boarding schools run by Salesian nuns in Laga, Venilale and Fatumaca near Los Palos became vital training institutions for orphans and girls from poor families.

The resistance
In the 1980s Falintil changed its tactics. It divided the country into four zones and started to operate in small, semi-independent units that could, if necessary, melt easily into the rural community. They used classic guerrilla tactics – hit-and-run attacks – relying heavily on the population to help with food supplies. Kinship alliances were important in this support network. Family members of the guerrillas continued to provide them, not always voluntarily, with food and other supplies.

This was not easy. The large Indonesian military presence in the resettlement villages dominated people's daily lives. They could not leave their village without the permission of the local commander. Women often had to take responsibility for the underground network because the men were all suspected of maintaining contact with the guerrillas. Thus women became the backbone of the resistance.

Women made up more than 60 per cent of the clandestine movement. Falintil had not wanted them to carry weapons, telling them: 'If we all die, you can, but for now, let us.' 'I admire the courage of the women and children,' Xanana Gusmão recalled in an interview. 'Many women, although unarmed, were braver than men carrying weapons.'[29] Some women, however, did carry arms. Mana Bisoi was one of them (see box on next page).

Mana Bisoi: a fighter with Falintil

Rosa de Camara, better known by her *nom de guerre* Bisoi ('Mana' is Tetum for 'elder sister' – a polite form of address), was a young girl when she lost her family in the war. Her uncle, Falintil commander L-Foho Rai Boot, took her with him to the forest, were she became a Falintil soldier.

After 1979, when most of the women in the mountains went back to their villages, Bisoi returned as well. But in 1983, after a massacre in the village of Kraras, where the Indonesian military killed the entire male population, many women fled back to the mountains – including Bisoi. She became a soldier again. 'In the difficult times there was no food,' she says, 'but many refused to go back to the city – they stayed put. We can be as patriotic as men, you know. We knew we could do as men did: we stayed. We wanted to show that women, too, had a strong sense of duty.'

She explains the women's role:

> When we were attacked by the Indonesian army, people died, regardless of their gender or age. The commanders encouraged us to take the children back to the city. All the men in the mountains were Falintil soldiers. Injured soldiers, the children and the sick were put in what we termed 'nucleos'. These were overseen by women who were responsible for security, and for hunting for food. Life was very basic – we were lucky to possess two changes of clothes each, and had a bath about once a month. We got our clothing quite often from the bodies of Indonesian soldiers we had killed. Uniforms were first given to the male Falintils – they fitted better, and in any case the men, especially the commanders, did not want to give us uniforms.

A Falintil attack usually had two assault groups, with women allowed only in the second. Their aim was to recover weapons lost by the first group if it met resistance. They were also supposed to scoop up booty, such as uniforms, but not bodies. They were supposed to shoot only if they came under attack.

Although women fighters acted as local representatives of the OPMT and gained a certain status within Falintil, there were no women in the command structure.

Falintil built up a reputation as a guerrilla army with widespread popular support. But Bisoi says that until 1991, they attacked Timorese villages. If the people offered no resistance, Falintil simply stole goods. If the people resisted, the guerrillas would shoot them.

After 1991, they stopped this, because the clandestine movement had been organised and was supplying them.

Bisoi calmly admits to killing several Indonesian soldiers. One day, on the Matebian, she was tired and looking for a place to sleep. She put aside her machine gun and sat, half-hidden by vegetation, filing her nails with a knife. Suddenly she found herself surrounded by about 15 Indonesian soldiers. They had been tracking her, but had not yet caught sight of her. Grabbing her gun, she sprayed them with bullets. 'I must have killed at least five, but I did not really have time to look back and see. I had to run fast,' she says.

She also killed an East Timorese spy who was giving information to a militia group in Baucau. The Falintil men handed him over to the women to kill. Did she regret it? 'This was a war,' she says. 'It's either them or you. We would confess to the Timorese priests and they would absolve us.'

Bisoi had a child by a Falintil commander who later returned to his first wife. The usual practice was for women guerrillas to place their new-borns in the gardens of village convents. If they died, it was bad luck. If they survived until morning and were found by the sisters, they would be adopted and cared for in orphanages. So it was with Bisoi's daughter, Lekas, who grew up with the Carmelite sisters.

Lekas is a little miracle, she says. When Bisoi was pregnant with her she was shot in her belly. The bullet lodged in the wrist of her unborn daughter. Miraculously, the pregnancy continued to term. The bullet remains in Lekas's arm today.

Bisoi feels that many male guerrillas fail to acknowledge the part played by women in the OPMT. She believes there is a need to tell the story of how the OPMT fought for women's rights.

[Based on interviews conducted by the authors between 1999 and 2004]

When the Indonesian military began to suspect the women, children – often as young as seven or eight – took their place as couriers bringing food supplies and messages to Falintil. The guerrilla fighters used young boys as porters to carry guns and ammunition.

The Indonesian military also recruited children to work as porters or forced them to take part in the 'fence of legs'. In this operation the Indonesian troops would take children with them to surround the guerrillas, who would be reluctant to shoot their own people and would be trapped. The tactic worked to some extent and many Falintil soldiers and village people, children included, lost their lives. In other cases, such as with families of Fretilin leaders, children were taken to the battlefield and used as bait to force their fathers to surrender.[30]

Children caught up in war

Nina was eight when her village, Laga, came under suspicion of contact with Falintil. Fearing for their lives, her mother and aunts fled to Dili, taking their elder children with them but leaving the younger ones behind with their grandparents. Nina's family was related to Falintil commander L-Foho Rai Boot, who was hiding in the hills near the village. It was too dangerous for him and his men to build fires to cook, and Nina remembers bringing him cooked rice and corn. She could not talk about what she was doing with anyone and had to claim absence from school owing to illness to sneak into the hills.

When Nina grew up she became a member of the OPMT and continued her work as a messenger. When she entered nursing college she spent her holidays with the guerrillas caring for their health.

[Interview with Irena Cristalis, August 1999]

The creation of the OPMT provided a way for women to show their courage in support of the resistance, both as fighters and in the clandestine movement. Through these activities, they built up a stronger sense of the contribution they could make to East Timor's political struggle. Those interviewed for this book concluded that women in East Timor had made progress under extraordinary circumstances during this period. They proved their bravery and capacity for service to their people. They were prepared to die for their homeland. A significant minority broke out of tight gender stereotypes in their culture. However, as Sister Guilhermina Marcal (see chapter 4) summed it up, at many levels these changes remained symbolic – the exception rather than the rule. In general women had no freedom to move and men continued to make the decisions.[31]

Notes

1 Information given to the authors by Dr Estevao Cabral.

2 For example the National Union of Timorese Students.

3 Hill, H (1978) *Fretilin: The origins, ideologies and strategies of a nationalist movement in East Timor*, MA thesis, Monash University, Australia, p159; and Maia Reis in an interview with Catherine Scott, 2004.

4 Abrantes, L, and Domingo Fernandes, M (2003) *Hakerek ho ran (Written in blood)*, Office for the Promotion of Equality, Dili.

5 Presentation by East Timorese youth at the Melaka International Youth Dialogue, 29 July-1 August 2002.

6 Abrantes, L, and Domingo Fernandes, M (see note 4).

7 Pinto, C, and Jardine, M (1997) *East Timor's unfinished struggle*, South End Press, Boston, MA, p47.

8 Information from Olandina Caeiro in an interview with Catherine Scott, June 2004.

9 Information from Olandina Caeiro (as above).

10 Interview with Catherine Scott, June 2004.

11 Interview with Irena Cristalis, May 2002.

12 Pinto, C, and Jardine, M (see note 7).

13 Abrantes, L, and Domingo Fernandes, M (see note 4).

14 See Aditjondro, G (1997) *Violence by the state against women in East Timor: A report to the UN Special Rapporteur on Violence Against Women, including its causes and consequences*, Australia East Timor Human Rights Centre, Fitzroy.

15 Aditjondro, G (as above), p131.

16 Cristalis, I (2002) *Bitter dawn: East Timor – a people's story*, Zed Books, London.

17 Quoted in Coomaraswamy, R (1998) *Report of the Special Rapporteur on Violence Against Women*, Commission on Human Rights, 54th session, Item 9a, E/CN.4/1998/54.

18 See Aditjondro, G (see note 14).

19 CAVR (2003) *Report on National Public Hearing on Women and Conflict*, Commission for Reception, Truth and Reconciliation, 5 May 2003 (see www.easttimor-reconciliation.org).

20 See Amnesty International (1995) *Women in Indonesia and East Timor: Standing against repression*, ASA21/51/95. See also Abrantes, L, and Domingo Fernandes, M (see note 4), chapters 3 and 4.

21 Information from a nun who asked to remain anonymous, in an interview with Irena Cristalis, 1998.

22 Quoted in CIIR (1989) *I am Timorese – Testimonies from East Timor*, Catholic Institute for International Relations, London, on behalf of the Christian Consultation on East Timor.

23 Fokupers (1999) *Report of a conference for female victims of war*, Forum Komunikasi Untuk Perempuan Lorosae, Dili.

24 CAVR (see note 19). Sexual violence against women appears to have been on a smaller scale during the civil war than during the Indonesian occupation.

25 Coomaraswamy, R (see note 17). See also Brownmiller, S (1975) *Against our will: Men, women and rape*, Simon and Schuster, New York.

26 Sissons, M (1997) *From one day to another*, East Timor Human Rights Centre, Melbourne.

27 Quoted in Xia, C (1995) 'Bela's story: East Timorese woman speaks out for justice' in *The activist*, Toronto, April 1995.

28 These actions violate article 1 of the Convention on the Elimination of All Forms of Discrimination Against Women (CEDAW), which Indonesia had signed.

29 Cristalis, I (see note 16).

30 As relatives of a Fretilin central committee member, Bertha Alves and her family were rounded up and arrested. Bertha's eldest son, who was 10 years old, was forced to become a porter for the Indonesian army. They took him to the battlefield and used him as bait for his father to surrender. (Interview with Irena Cristalis, August 2002)

31 Interview with Catherine Scott, June 2004.

Chapter 3
The 1990s: political and social movements

The 1990s were a crucial decade for East Timorese women. They found a voice, not only to express their grief and anger about what happened to them during the war and occupation, but also to demand a role in deciding East Timor's future. This chapter focuses on the political and social movements in East Timor and the diaspora, emphasising the role women played.

Although most male activists expected women to put the self-determination struggle first, gender considerations slowly crept into the resistance movement. President Suharto's fall from power changed the political situation in Indonesia and left East Timorese civil society with more freedom to organise. East Timorese women formed organisations that would become important voices for women's rights.

The social and political context

East Timorese political and social movements developed unevenly. Many refugees fled the territory and settled in a variety of countries around the world. The largest concentrations – in Australia, Portugal, Mozambique and Macao – became hubs of political development. Contact between the exiles and political leaders in East Timor, particularly in the first decade and a half of occupation, was difficult and infrequent. With the organisation of a clandestine movement at the beginning of the 1990s, however, and the advent of the Internet, communications gradually improved.

From the late 1980s, reforms within the Frente Revolucionária de Timor Leste Independente (Fretilin – Revolutionary Front for an Independent East Timor) led to acceptance of political pluralism in the resistance, which in turn led to greater cooperation. East Timorese activists began to recognise that it was possible to be in favour of self-determination, or even independence, without being a member of Fretilin.

The outside world seemed to have forgotten East Timor, but a turning point in international awareness came with the bloodshed that followed a peaceful demonstration at the Santa Cruz cemetery in Dili in 1991. The massacre was filmed by Max Stahl, an investigative journalist from the UK, and TV images of the Indonesian army killing young East Timorese were broadcast around the world. East Timor support networks benefited from an influx of new members. A further boost came in 1996, when Bishop Carlos Belo and diaspora leader Jose Ramos Horta shared the Nobel Peace Prize.

These trends were accompanied by the rise of East Timorese women leaders. Women in the resistance had built up a strong sense of the contribution they could make to East Timor's political struggle. Some of these women leaders had been founders of the Organização Popular da Mulher Timorense (OPMT – Popular Organisation of East Timorese Women). The younger ones were, or had been, student activists at home or in Indonesia. Others were living in exile, and working in various East Timorese political parties and organisations. They often had links to solidarity groups on East Timor as well as to the women's movement internationally.

East Timorese student activists in Indonesia came into contact with the women's movement there, and the exchanges between the two groups, and the solidarity of some Indonesian civil society organisations, were important in developing the East Timorese movement.[1]

From the early 1990s, women's organisations everywhere made increasing use of the language of women's rights as human rights, particularly after the World Conference on Human Rights in Vienna in 1993. The Beijing World Conference on Women, in September 1995, aired the themes of women's equality, development and peace, implying empowerment and participation in decision making. East Timorese women activists saw these as relevant to their own struggle, and felt emboldened to challenge the all-male leadership of the student resistance movement.

Such approaches were not always welcomed by male activists, who generally expected women to put the struggle for self-determination before gender considerations. But the women wanted to be listened to and taken seriously. (See the stories of Bela Galhos and Ivete de Oliveira later in this chapter.)

The changes in the resistance also had implications for the women's movement, both inside and outside East Timor, as they stimulated change in the way the women's movement was organised.

A united front

An important development that boosted women's participation in the resistance both inside and outside the country was the creation of an umbrella organisation for the resistance. This brought together political parties which had fought each other for years to work towards self-determination for East Timor.

The first step towards this united front was made in the late 1980s by Xanana Gusmão, whose resignation as leader of Fretilin paved the way for the Conselho Nacional da Resistência Maubere (CNRM – National Council of Maubere Resistance) which brought together Fretilin and the União Democrática Timorense (UDT – Timorese Democratic Union). This was eventually succeeded in 1998 by the Conselho Nacional da Resistência Timorense (CNRT – National Council of Timorese Resistance) which also included the other three, smaller political parties. Replacing the term 'Maubere' with 'Timorese' satisfied the other parties who associated 'Maubere' with Fretilin's communist past. Once this was done, the UDT formally recognised Xanana Gusmão as paramount leader.

This meant that the OPMT also had to adjust its structures. In 1998 the OPMT helped to spread understanding and assent to the idea of the CNRT across the country. This resulted in the formation of the Organização da Mulher Timorense (OMT – Organisation of Timorese Women), which was open to women of all political parties and none, mirroring the more inclusive CNRT. The OMT became part of the CNRT's platform for national unity. Its aims and objectives were not significantly different from those of the OPMT: it would organise at grassroots level, and support the resistance just as the OPMT had been doing.

The OMT continued to build on the original structure of the OPMT. In the second half of 1998 it had approximately 70,000 women members, organised into well over 3,000 secretariats, one in each *aldeia* or extended family hamlet.[2] This structure made it possible to mobilise supporters effectively across the country.

Each secretariat could operate independently, based on local priorities. Many initiatives arose at the local level, such as for distributing food to the resistance fighters; but directions also came from above for implementation at the grassroots (for example, informing village women about the referendum in 1999).

The OMT proved a success. Its non-partisan nature reassured women who had grown weary of the party politics that had caused them so much grief, so it attracted a wider cross-section of women than the OPMT. Given the general strengthening of the resistance movement, and the growing optimism that change was possible, the OMT was an attractive option.

After the fall of Suharto, information flow between members of the resistance improved and their work became more effective.

Women in the districts could now organise openly and conduct literacy work and informal education. In the long term, however, the OMT never completely eclipsed the OPMT: a minority remained who wanted to retain the link with Fretilin. This would lead to confusion after independence.

Women's NGOs

In the second half of the 1990s a civil society started to form in Dili. Women found the space and resolve to set up advocacy groups and non-governmental organisations (NGOs). The best known of the women's NGOs were the Forum Komunikasi Untuk Perempuan Lorosae (Fokupers – East Timorese Women's Communications Forum), the East Timorese Movement Against Violence Towards Women and Children (Gertak, later renamed ET-Wave) and the Grupo Feto Foinsae Timor Lorosae (GFFTL – East Timor Students Women's Group). (See appendix 7 for more on these organisations.) A women's section of the Centro Direitos Humanos Timor Lorosae (Centre for Human Rights of East Timor) also operated for a time.

The women behind these NGOs were often prominent figures in the resistance movement and the OPMT/OMT. But although many active in the NGOs also worked for the resistance (see, for example, Laura Abrantes' story), the NGOs' activities were not focused on the struggle for independence.

Apart from the GFFTL, these NGOs shared a strong focus on violence in Timorese society, the issue that concerned women the most in their daily lives. No woman felt safe, in the street or at home. No woman would walk the streets after dark. No woman slept peacefully at night. Much of this fear arose from the threat posed by the omnipresent Indonesian army who could act with impunity. The NGOs' advocacy was directed at the violence perpetrated by Indonesian soldiers, but they recognised, too, that violence within families was also a danger to women. Fokupers, for example, organised shelters for victims of domestic violence.

While Indonesia was in charge, the NGOs had to operate carefully to avoid antagonising the local military and civilian authorities. They had the support of Indonesian activist friends and raised funds from a few Indonesian- and Australian-based international NGOs.

The women in these organisations became spokespersons for the women in East Timor. They provided a focal point for a women's movement and an essential base for bringing women into politics once East Timor had broken free from Indonesian rule.

Laura Abrantes

Laura Abrantes went to university in Salatiga, Indonesia. She returned to East Timor after completing her studies in 1993 and worked for a church agency, Delsos, which later became Caritas Dili. There she met many people, especially women, who were involved in the resistance, and church people who came from the rural areas and told her what was happening there. Laura would translate the information and send it to the outside world, sending faxes typed on the Delsos electric typewriter to human rights organisations such as Amnesty International and the East Timor Human Rights Centre in Melbourne.

The Portuguese Jesuit, Father João Felgueiras, would tell her about human rights violations, many of which took place in the prisons where he served as a chaplain. Fr Felgueiras encouraged the Delsos staff to become active and organise themselves. A women's group was formed within the organisation. They supplied medicine to the armed resistance and passed on messages, and Laura would prepare reports for the resistance fighters and send information overseas.

The women's group also started to take an interest in maternal health, and in helping women who had been abused by the Indonesian military. It was from these activities that Fokupers, one of the leading women's NGOs in East Timor, emerged.

Laura felt a strong sense of God's blessing on her activist and clandestine activities. She feels that the souls of deceased resistance fighters and relatives willed her on and kept her safe while she did her risky human rights documentation work.

[Interview with Catherine Scott, June 2004]

Student organisations

At the end of the 1990s, after the fall of Suharto, many underground activities came into the open. New groups also emerged: for example, students at the Universitas Timor Timur (University of East Timor) set up the Dewan Solidaritas Mahasiswa Timor Timur (East Timor Student Solidarity Council).

When a European Union delegation visited in July 1998 the student council seized the opportunity to organise the largest rallies East Timor had ever seen, demanding a referendum on the future status of the territory. Anteiro da Silva, then leader of the Student Solidarity Council, encouraged female students to work at reconciliation with groups that opposed a referendum.[3] The young women organised themselves in the GFFTL – it provided an opportunity to develop leadership skills. As the rallies continued, the female students found a voice. They made speeches to the demonstrators and mediated when violence threatened to break out. They also began to challenge gender roles.

Gender comes to East Timor

Soon after its inauguration in July 1998, the Student Solidarity Council moved into a small bungalow with three rooms and a kitchen. The council's women's group, GFFTL, occupied one of the rooms, a neat office with a small table and two bookshelves.

When I visited the office for the first time one of the women was busy sweeping the floor. Another was in the kitchen preparing tea for the male students, who were sitting on the floor, deep in discussion. Nobody seemed to be embarrassed about the obvious gender roles.

But when I visited six months later, I found two of the male council members sweating over a large wok in the kitchen. The women were in their office. When I commented on the change, they pointed, laughing, at a schedule pinned up on the wall. 'We got gender here now,' one of them said solemnly. 'It is the boys' turn to cook and clean.'

[Irena Cristalis, 1999]

East Timorese student organisations in Indonesia

Timorese women activists in Indonesia who joined youth movements also manoeuvred for creative space. At a time when the struggle for self-determination was considered by many male activists to be the only priority, they sometimes drew negative responses from student leaders.

The story of one such woman activist, Ivete de Oliveira, illustrates these tensions. Ivete studied at Gadjah Mada University in Yogyakarta, Indonesia, from 1993 to 1998. At that time many East Timorese students formed organisations, underground and open, to respond to the political situation in their homeland. Ivete worked as an organiser in a politically fraught and dangerous climate, and dared to be independent of her male peers.

The largest student body was Ikatan Mahasiswa dan Pejalar Timor Timur (Impettu – East Timor Student Association, based in Indonesia), an organisation formed by the Indonesian government to exercise some form of social control over East Timorese students studying there. All East Timorese students were obliged to register with Impettu.

However, East Timorese students started an underground organisation in 1988, the Resistência Nacional dos Estudantes de Timor Leste (Renetil – National Resistance of East Timorese Students). This was a group of pro-independence activists, and by its nature it had to operate in secret. Renetil decided to subvert Impettu, which was much larger. Once Renetil members had won key positions in Impettu's leadership (including the presidency) Impettu became less subservient to the interests of the Indonesian government.

Ivete was a member of Impettu but not of Renetil, where recruitment was conducted in a clandestine fashion, with traditional blood oaths and initiation ceremonies. The group tended to behave in a rather exclusive manner, and was open only to the likeminded. Its members argued that the political situation made this inevitable.

In her time as a student Ivete met Indonesian women activists and felt she should speak out about the violence against women from the military in both their societies. She and her friends set up Le-Zeaval, a cultural group which used dance and art to change views about East Timor and encourage understanding. In a short time they had 125 members from different political backgrounds, including Renetil members as well as the sons and daughters of East Timorese families which supported Indonesian rule in East Timor. Ivete believed it was important 'to create a neutral and independent space, and not be under control of either Renetil or Impettu'.[4]

Her approach was creative, and started from a less political standpoint. Yet essentially she was contributing to the resistance struggle constructively in her own, perhaps more inclusive way. She was more prepared to give people the benefit of the doubt, less suspicious, and less inclined to coercive tactics and hierarchies.

Le-Zeaval's campaigning proved effective. It reached out to universities, embassies, ordinary people, and the middle and upper classes in Jakarta.

One day Renetil members informed Ivete that their Jakarta-based leadership was irritated with her failure to cooperate. Ivete was surprised, so she contacted Joaquim Fonseca, a leader of Renetil. He denied any intention to close down Le-Zeaval. But a number of Renetil members in Le-Zeaval left without explanation. Many of them were women. The men who stayed on found themselves isolated within Renetil.

Some time later Impettu's committee asked Le-Zeaval to a dialogue. Ivete consulted the other members of Le-Zeaval, who said they wanted to remain independent. They nominated her to express their wishes.

The Impettu women led the debate. Ivete made clear that she wished to work with the students who supported Indonesian rule, not isolate them. Her interlocutors saw her point, and caused no further problems.

Such occurrences are not uncommon in activist communities, particularly in climates of danger and secrecy. Perceptions of the activities of others, and the way that these are either supported or undermined, hinge on levels of interpersonal trust between leaders and groups.

Ivete comes from a family which had a number of pro-autonomy members. This may have added to the suspicions of her male counterparts in Renetil and Impettu. Probably gender politics also played their part in the response to her initiatives. Her story offers an interesting insight into the experience of women trying to exert leadership positions in a field dominated by young men brought up in a deeply patriarchal culture.

Joaquim Fonseca points out that possibly only 20 per cent of the East Timorese students studying in Jakarta at the time were women, and does not deny that a patriarchal culture prevailed.[5] But it would not be long before women in student organisations began to raise gender issues.

The international stage
Meanwhile, East Timorese women in Australia, North America and Europe organised no less determinedly, and in the midst of the self-determination struggle began to draw attention to women's rights.

The women in the diaspora took part in many international conferences, forums and symposiums. An important one was the 1995 United Nations (UN) World Conference on Women in Beijing. It was not the first stimulus, but was nonetheless a spur to East Timorese women's search for self-expression. Six East Timorese women went to Beijing, where they spoke about their country's plight, the struggle for self-determination and independence, and violence against East Timorese women. They came back fired with ideas from the conference Platform for Action.

While in Beijing, they publicised a letter from a woman in the East Timorese clandestine resistance which gave graphic details of the indignities suffered by women under the occupation. It appealed to women of all nationalities and Indonesian women in particular:

We hope for human solidarity and believe in the solidarity of this world. We appeal to you … to act in your own countries, in all your capacities, power and strength, for the dignity and freedom of the people of East Timor, for the dignity of all East Timorese women.[6]

During the years of occupation, courageous East Timorese, including some women, were prepared to step forward and recount their stories before the UN Commission on Human Rights, which meets in session for six weeks every spring in Geneva. Complaints about the sexual abuse of women in East Timor were a recurrent theme.

In 1997 Milena Pires coordinated an East Timorese women's lobby of the UN Special Rapporteur on Violence against Women, Radhika Coomaraswamy. They arranged for her to hear testimonies from abuse victims and their advocates gathered together in London. Making the necessary financial and logistic arrangements was not easy for the Timorese resistance, and resources for women's initiatives were particularly difficult to obtain. The initiative bore fruit, however. The Special Rapporteur subsequently visited East Timor, and reported back to the United Nations at the Commission on Human Rights in March/April 1999.[7]

Bela Galhos

Throughout the East Timorese diaspora, women worked to draw attention to the sufferings of their people in East Timor, but they also began to challenge the hegemony of the male political leaders.

Isabel Antonia da Costa Galhos (Bela) was studying at UNTIM when she was selected in 1994 for an exchange programme for students from all 27 Indonesian provinces initiated by the Canadian government.

First she had to go to Jakarta, where she was interrogated for a month. The Indonesian government was, not surprisingly, reluctant to send East Timorese students abroad where they could join the Timorese activists. The intelligence officers asked many questions about the resistance. As she knew little about the clandestine movement in Dili she could easily claim ignorance. At one point, Bela recalls, she was asked to put on a military uniform and had to march up to an Indonesian flag and kiss it. She did as instructed, with tears in her eyes. She also had to place her hand on the Koran and swear that she was a good daughter of Indonesia.

Finally, satisfied with her loyalty to the Republic of Indonesia, the authorities gave her luggage a final check and took her to the airport. When she arrived in Canada, two representatives of the Indonesian embassy took her ticket and passport away.

Bela contacted her uncle, Constancio Pinto, who was studying in the United States. A well-known activist, he had escaped East Timor soon after the 1991 Dili massacre. Within a week, the Canadian East Timor Alert Network (ETAN) had arranged to fly her to Vancouver, where she hid with a Canadian family while applying for refugee status. This was granted within six months, during which she learned English.

ETAN organised a speaking tour for her which took her across Canada and spurred the growing solidarity movement in North America. Bela became the CNRT spokeswoman in Canada. She joined the East Timorese diaspora circuit, and noticed that only five per cent of the activists were women. The women were often put in charge of the catering – 'looking after the coffee and the cookies. They were not taken seriously and their issues were not discussed.'

Although the women appealed to their political leaders to open up opportunities for women in the decision-making process, they felt that they were invited to public meetings simply as 'window dressing'. On one occasion, Bela remarks, José Ramos Horta flew her over to New York 'to save them the embarrassment of not having any women present'. Bela thought his replies to questions about women's involvement in the struggle were untrue, and when it was her turn to speak, she told how she was called in at the last possible moment.

Despite all the efforts of women activists in the diaspora to make women's voices heard, theirs was an uphill struggle. In general they met with opposition or at best, lack of interest. Bela became disillusioned. The resistance leaders' attitude to women's inclusion, she said, was that women should endorse the men's decisions, rather than that the leaders should listen to women's ideas.

[Interview with Irena Cristalis, August 2002]

The All-Inclusive Intra-East-Timorese Dialogue

Throughout the 1990s, while negotiations continued between Portugal and Indonesia on the future of East Timor, the only mechanism for consulting East Timorese opinion on the matter was a series of meetings called the All-Inclusive Intra-East-Timorese Dialogue (AIETD). This was supposed to be a representative forum composed of pro- and anti-integration East Timorese, invited to discuss strictly non-political issues as a way to facilitate peace, stability and a resolution of the East Timor question.

The first meeting was held in Chepstow, Wales, and the Indonesians controlled it. Then the UN took over, to give the process greater authenticity. The participants were chosen by hard bargaining between the two factions (pro- and anti-integration East Timorese), supervised by the UN.

The AIETD met four times in all. The first meeting had only one female participant among more than 30 men. UN personnel charged with overseeing the selection of candidates made little effort to put into practice UN resolutions and conventions affirming women's right to equal participation. Nor did the East Timorese advisers to the UN officials make an effort to recommend women who could participate. The UN claimed it had been unable to identify 'suitable candidates' – effectively denying East Timorese women a say in the only forum where East Timorese could express their views.

The first AIETD was held in December 1994. The last meeting was held in October 1998. The UN and the political elite, under fire from East Timorese women activists, had more than enough time to rectify the gender imbalance. Yet very few improvements were introduced. It was disappointing, if predictable, that East Timorese men would be slow to change their political habits, but women felt let down by the UN. Inês Almeida, an East Timorese woman living in Australia, was the only woman to be included in all four AIETDs. No other women attended the talks until the fourth and last session, when Inês was joined by three others.

The UN's failure to facilitate women's participation continued in 1998, when it conducted a consultation on the future of East Timor. For example, in December 1998 a meeting with students and alumni was organised in the garden of one of Dili's hotels. The meeting was held after sunset, a time when women and girls would be too afraid to leave their homes, and so no women were present.

Challenging the CNRT

In the first half of the 1990s a handful of women were elected to official positions in the party structures of Fretilin and the UDT.[8] But women were grossly under-represented in the umbrella structure of the CNRM, and later the CNRT. Women activists close to the leadership did their best to raise women's issues, but found that their male colleagues asked for their presence on diplomatic missions only when it was politically expedient to do so (as happened to Bela Galhos – see box on previous page).

A push for change came in 1998. An East Timorese National Convention in the Diaspora was held in Portugal on 23-27 April, bringing together activists from East Timor as well as those living in exile. For the organisers (who were male), the priority issues for discussion were political: the need to unite disparate factions and the window of opportunity afforded by the end of the Suharto regime. However, they designated a working group to discuss the 'feminine condition'.

In the meantime, a group of 13 East Timorese women activists from both Fretilin and the UDT, spearheaded by Milena Pires, an East Timorese activist then working in Europe, wrote to the organisers to propose mechanisms to facilitate the direct participation of women in making decisions at the convention. They demanded copies of all the relevant planning documents, and proposed that women activists should meet immediately before and after the convention. More audaciously still, they requested that a portion of the congress budget be ring-fenced for women participants.

The convention established the CNRT, with Xanana Gusmão as its elected president. A 'Magna Carta' on freedoms, rights and duties, and guarantees for the people of East Timor was adopted, which would later serve as a key formative document for the constitution of an independent East Timor.

But the convention was a great disappointment to the women's lobby. In the words of Inês Almeida: 'It did not give the women's proposal due respect and consideration, nor did it follow up on the initial proposal. The women's conference did not take place'. Almeida complained that although the Magna Carta itself embraced the Convention on the Elimination of All Forms of Discrimination Against Women (CEDAW), maternity and widow's rights, and repudiated all forms of discrimination, the way the male political elite organised the meeting ensured that women did not have a say. For example, the convention dropped the proposal for the CNRT to have a women's department and set up an Institute for Women's Affairs instead. This would be a think-tank under the direct control of the CNRT political commission, and was not a suggestion from the women themselves. Almeida concluded: 'The rights of Timorese women as a part of basic human rights must be pursued further in order to democratise our society and our politics.'[9]

The Dili spring
In 1998 Indonesia's president Suharto was forced out of power in

the wake of a South East Asia-wide financial crisis. The press became freer, and mass demonstrations became a daily occurrence all over Indonesia and also in East Timor, where this period was known as the 'Dili spring'.

Nevertheless, thousands of Indonesian soldiers remained in East Timor, so it was a courageous act for women's groups to organise the Conference on the Image of East Timorese Women in November 1998. Women activists flocked to the conference from all over East Timor and from the diaspora. They talked openly about the crimes against women by the Indonesian military: rape, sexual torture and humiliation. And they talked about domestic violence, the difficulty of raising children in single-headed households and the problem of polygamy.

Although much of the discussion concerned the tribulations of the past and present, some more far-sighted participants also thought about strategies for the future. Olandina Caeiro, founder of ET-Wave, advised women to seize every opportunity to develop themselves politically and economically. Clearly some women were already doing this. In 1998, however, the women were unaware of quite how urgent that need would turn out to be. They would soon have to lend all their skills to the shaping of their newly independent country. They would need to draw upon all their reserves – physical, intellectual and spiritual – and it is to the latter that we turn in the next chapter, where we explore how faith inspired many East Timorese women to keep going in adversity.

Notes

1 Indonesian women's organisations which influenced the East Timorese included Solidaritas Perempuan and Kalyanamitra. Mixed groups such as Solidamor and Fortillos were also influential, as were a number of individual Indonesian women from the churches and NGOs.

2 De Fatima, M (2002) 'Mobilising women for the sustainable rebuilding of East Timor', paper contributed to the Sustaining our Communities conference organised by Adelaide City Council in March 2002.

3 Interview with Irena Cristalis, July 1998.

4 Interview with the authors, May 2003.

5 Interview with the authors, June 2003.

6 Open letter to women activists gathering at the Beijing conference civil society forum by Ira Lafai Lighur, dated 6 September 1995, quoted in *Timor Link*, November 1995, p5.

7 See Coomaraswamy, R (1999) 'Integration of the human rights of women and the gender perspective: Violence against women', addendum to *Mission to Indonesia and East Timor on the issue of violence against women*, United Nations Economic and Social

Council, E/CN.4/1999/68/Add.3.

8   See Scott, C, and Pires, M (1998) 'The feminine face of the resistance' in Retboll, T (ed) *East Timor: Occupation and resistance*, International Work Group for Indigenous Affairs, Denmark, p147.

9   See Almeida, I (1998) 'Convention offers little to Timorese women's movement' in *Timor Link*, August 1998, p6.

Chapter 4
Faith and women's empowerment

This chapter looks at how faith empowered women to cope with extreme violence and repression during the Indonesian occupation, and how the relationship between lived faith and religious structures may gradually reshape itself in independent East Timor. It draws attention to female religious leaders who, in the spirit of early East Timorese religious emphasis, provide an alternative locus of leadership and an example. Although a few Protestant churches and a small Muslim community exist in East Timor, the chapter will focus on the influence of Catholicism.

Influences on religious beliefs

On the feast day of Our Lady of Fatima, a long procession winds its way along the streets of Dili, with a statue of Our Lady of Fatima held reverently aloft for all to see. Large crowds join the procession and many more people watch from the roadsides, where some people have built small shrines with more statues surrounded by lit candles. People dress in their Sunday best. The people hold a special devotion to this feast day, in which they ask Mary to intercede on their behalf to God the Father. The popularity of the procession demonstrates the strong Catholic faith held by many East Timorese.

Religious practice in East Timor was influenced by foreign missionaries, both Protestant and Catholic, from the 16th century onwards. Yet traditional spiritual beliefs, rituals and myths co-exist alongside these later influences and continue to shape East Timorese cultural and ceremonial life.

The pervasiveness of these traditional beliefs and use of religious symbols drew a warning from Bishop Basilio do Nascimento in 2003, who told the East Timorese that they could not and should not mix up these beliefs and their associated symbols with the practice of Catholicism.[1] The Bishop once remarked that although the quantity of faith in East Timor is high, the quality is lacking.[2] In reality, as long as the mix helps people to cope in their daily lives, it is likely that the two influences will continue side by side.

Catholicism in East Timor

Roman Catholicism was brought to East Timor by Portuguese colonisers in the 16th century. Only in 1940 was Catholicism formally integrated within the Portuguese colonial system by a concordat between Rome and the Portuguese dictator, António Salazar. According to Robert Archer, 'For much of the colonial period, the Church was the main, often the only, indication of Portuguese authority in many of the rural areas of East Timor.'[3] The church ran the education system and was responsible for propagating Portuguese culture. Nonetheless, at the time of the Indonesian invasion, only about one-third of East Timorese had joined the church.

The invasion wrought a decisive change in the East Timorese Catholic church. From 1975 to 1989, when East Timor was closed to the outside world, the church remained the only independent institution with international links. Through a succession of three bishops, who chose to identify with and speak out about the suffering of their people, the church became a voice for the voiceless in the darkest days of isolation. It stood up for the people, denouncing human rights abuses and telling the world of their suffering.

Catholicism in East Timor has been heavily influenced by the nature of the Portuguese Catholicism from which it originated. The clergy in East Timor were composed of indigenous priests and foreign missionaries, and many of the older clergy were trained at Portuguese seminaries.[4] Given the timing of the Indonesian invasion, the radical changes introduced into the church by the Second Vatican Council of 1962-65 had scarcely arrived when the territory was closed, freezing the church's ecclesiastical, theological and pastoral development.

Thus the style of Catholicism, although now gradually bringing itself up to date with Vatican II reforms,[5] remains fairly conservative. Liberation theology has had little influence on the life of the church community in East Timor, although it has inspired a number of the clergy. The emphasis, consistent with pre-Vatican II theology, appears to be on the private and personal relationship with God and on personal piety, rather than a more community-oriented approach. This was undoubtedly reinforced by the occupying forces' prohibitions on religious gatherings outside scheduled mass times. There is a strong devotion to the Virgin – in the guise of Our Lady of Fatima – and even young people can frequently be seen bedecked with crosses, medals and rosaries, a symbol at once of faith and national identity.

In an interview in 1993, Bishop Carlos Felipe Ximenes Belo was asked how East Timorese people were able to worship. He was frank about the nationalist dimension:

> There are many ways [East Timorese people can express their faith]: their presence in the church, in the Eucharist, in the chapels; they pray in their own homes; the rosary; they organise processions with a statue of the Virgin, which they carry from house to house. This is allowed. In fact other kinds of group meetings, to sit down together to read the Bible and to pray, are not allowed because the military doesn't trust them. They think that they will discuss politics – this is not allowed. But really, the Catholic faith for the people is a kind of symbol to unite them. It is a way to express the fact that they are Timorese, they don't like any other religion, they don't like Indonesia.[6]

Although Indonesia is a secular state, in the 1970s the minister for home affairs urged Indonesian citizens to choose one of the five major religions (Islam, Hinduism, Buddhism, Catholic Christianity, Protestant Christianity). For the East Timorese, becoming Catholic was one way to manifest their difference. It was an expression of nationalism not to join the majority Indonesian faith, Islam.

Faith and resistance

In discussing East Timorese Catholicism and women's relationship to it, it is important to distinguish between faith as a lived experience and the church as hierarchy and structure. There are of course strong connections between the two, but there are also limits to these connections. The Catholic church is a highly gendered entity in which males, and ordained males in particular, hold the power. Nevertheless, to a considerable degree women mould and shape the structures with which they are connected to suit both their practical and their spiritual needs. In East Timor both the church as structure (quite literally) and faith as resource appear to have helped empower women in the face of adversity.

Structure as protection

Convents offered an alternative career for young women, and nuns escaped the rape and sexual abuse meted out by the Indonesian military. Women would on occasion take refuge in convents when they felt vulnerable to attack. Convent boarding schools provided extra protection to vulnerable girls.

Priests would often shelter men, women, students and children in church premises in times of heightened danger. Bishop Belo himself regularly drove people home after bad experiences at the hands of the military, and sheltered people in his home in times of disorder.

By the time of the violent denouement of the occupation in 1999, not even the church could provide sanctuary and it was targeted for a series of extremely violent and bloodthirsty attacks, resulting in hundreds of deaths and disappearances, including those of priests and members of religious orders.

Protected by the rules
The Catholic church's strict teachings on artificial methods of birth control, confirmed by the papal encyclical *Humanae Vitae* (1968), is viewed as an authoritarian imposition by many Catholic women across the world. Paradoxically, it gave a measure of protection to many East Timorese women from the Indonesian government's coercive family planning programme. Some women were forcibly injected with the long-lasting contraceptive drug depo provera (see chapter 2). The church campaigned against this programme and many women refused to be injected. However, a more negative effect was that women began to avoid ante-natal care in state-run clinics, for fear of being sterilised. The result was that many medical problems went untreated.

The inviolability of the soul
Most East Timorese, women included, live in poverty. Women suffered deeply throughout the 24-year occupation from rape and other assaults on them personally, and also from the loss of their loved ones in circumstances of extreme violence. An insidious system of paid informers and spies divided communities, leaving individuals isolated. Women turned to Catholicism for comfort. As CIIR put it in 1996, 'The Catholic church has been for East Timorese a source of both spiritual solace and continuity in a society which has suffered a profound trauma.'[7]

Whatever the ingredients which form the lived faith of East Timorese women, its expression can be spontaneous and has assisted in situations of high tension. Religious symbols hold for them meaning and comfort, as the following example of a woman reflecting on her experiences during the invasion illustrates:

A few days later soldiers came back. They were shooting into the air. People were scared inside their houses, and wouldn't come out. The children were crying. We were all praying. The Indonesians wanted us to come out, but people were too frightened. My niece says, 'Oh mother, carry this statue of the Holy Family and put your rosary around you, and go out and then we'll follow you.'[8]

In dealing with the horrors of rape, disappearance, massacre, imprisonment of sons, husbands, and so on, faith, according to Maria Domingas Fernandes and her sister-in-law Merita Alves, was a powerful resource.[9] They said that the greatest fear women had was the prospect of being raped. Even then, they stated, 'They can take our bodies, but they do not remove our souls, our identity, our integrity.' The two women spoke of the impossibility of women organising themselves publicly to resist these abuses. Often Indonesian soldiers would be assigned to live in their homes, giving the military total control over their families. Any attempt to organise or hold meetings was construed as political, and prevented.

When foreign visitors asked what kept them going, women spoke of the importance of the church, of being able to pour out their unhappiness to the priest, of their faith, and of their determination not to give in to the oppressor.[10]

The defiant spirit the women expressed was striking. In the face of rape, they retained the inner strength to preserve both dignity and honour. Clearly, the faith they shared – the ability to make a clear distinction between body and soul – was important as both resource and defence.

Traditional beliefs
Often, traditional religious elements mix with Catholic beliefs. For many East Timorese, a distinction is not necessarily made between the spirits of their ancestors and the Christian notion of the Holy Spirit.

The belief in the magical powers of *biro*, a traditional medical talisman, is widespread. According to Mana Bisoi, a former fighter with the Forças Armadas de Libertação Nacional de Timor Leste (Falintil – Armed Forces for the National Liberation of East Timor), the *biro* is different for different people, but no one could betray their own *biro*. 'A *biro* is like a miracle,' she explains. 'Some carry samples of sacred earth from Mount Ramelau and Mount Matebian mixed together. For others, it is a piece of wood of an *uma lulik* [the sacred house of a clan], or a piece of bone from an animal. If you put it around your neck, you cannot touch people.' Everyone has their own set of beliefs attached to the *biro* – it is a kind of eternal vow which cannot be broken without bringing bad luck upon oneself. Many women who lost their *biro* in the jungle died. The *biro* is the link with the spirit world.[11]

Mana Bisoi belonged to a group called Sagrada Familia, an underground organisation influenced by traditional beliefs overlaid with Catholicism. Its leader, her uncle Commander L-Foho Rai Boot, is believed to have strong spiritual and magical powers.

Faith and empowerment

It is hard to explain the strength that East Timorese women derive from this mix of traditional beliefs and traditional Roman Catholicism in terms of empowerment models drawn from development literature (such as the model of empowerment explored by Jo Rowlands, which considers empowerment as a three-stage process consisting of personal empowerment and group empowerment followed by political empowerment).[12] Lack of education and extreme lack of freedom prevented East Timorese women from discussing and reflecting on their faith in the community style of El Salvador or the Basic Christian Communities that proliferated in Latin America and the Philippines in the 1970s and 1980s. Although women did train as catechists alongside lay men in Dili diocese, the environment was not conducive to group empowerment. Apart from the smaller Protestant communities, East Timorese did not generally meet for Bible study. Rowlands' 'process' model of empowerment seems to take us only to the first stage – where faith enables women to find personal strength.

It is at the psychological level that the empowerment evident in East Timorese women's religious faith needs to be explored. This should be seen in the context of a people under threat of annihilation. Women's faith simply helped them to survive: to go on resisting, however bad things became. It defended the people's individual dignity and cultural heritage, and provided sanctuary and comfort in the midst of their isolation. As Father Patrick Smythe puts it: 'Self-sufficiency and courage have been raised into the Christian hope for the ultimate triumph of justice.'[13]

Jeanette Rodriguez, in her study of the Mexican devotion to Our Lady of Guadalupe, explains this in terms of power:

> The word 'power' comes from the Latin *posse*, to be able. In our patriarchal society, we learn to think of power in terms of having power over someone or something. But the ultimate source of power and empowerment is having 'power with':

having one's dignity and humanity accepted in the world, having the capacity to be in relationships, having the power of memory, sharing the power of expressed feelings. In Christian tradition, God embraces that which the world has rejected.[14]

Like the East Timorese, the Aztec Indians to whom the vision of Our Lady of Guadalupe first appeared were under intense pressure from their Spanish colonisers:

If we question the humanity of an entire people, one is implicitly allowing licence to exploit those people and to tame 'the animal'.... At the time Our Lady of Guadalupe appeared to Juan Diego, the Aztec nation found itself in a situation of subordination, alienation, suffering and oppression. [In the words of Concha Malo:] 'The image of Our Lady of Guadalupe cannot be understood without the cries and sadness of the Indians and of all the poor of Mexico and Latin America. It is from there that it gathers meaning.'[15]

Religious faith, perhaps embodied in Nossa Senhora di Fatima (Our Lady of Fatima) as in Our Lady of Guadalupe for the Aztec Indians, helps East Timorese women retain their dignity despite rape, torture and death.[16]

The power of memory has been one of the most subversive that East Timorese women possess. The memory of lost sons, daughters and husbands drove them to keep on asking questions, to demand the bodies, and not to rest until explanations were offered. Catholic ceremonies are constructed around memories – the memory of Christ's passion and resurrection – hence the solace they bring to the bereaved.

Rodriguez's definitions of religious faith hold the key to understanding how East Timorese women were empowered by their faith. Religious faith enables them to continue believing in themselves. It staves off despair, from which total subjugation would quickly follow. As a symbol of their culture and identity, it restores, like Our Lady of Guadalupe to the Aztec Indians, a sense of humanity, worth and dignity to a people who have been stripped of everything. It increases their internal strength. It restores relation where brutality has destroyed the ability to trust, helps to promote reconciliation among neighbours, strengthens the surviving members of families. It is crucial as inspiration, resource, and lifeline; and in this way, it has served to empower women.

Women, faith and the church after independence

The church in East Timor is now adapting to a new pastoral challenge. As it reintegrates into the wider church in the world, a process of modernisation will gradually take place as new ideas take root. The church in East Timor will have to grapple with the same challenges that face the rest of the worldwide body: difficult issues such as child abuse scandals and women's and lay people's rights in the ecclesiastical community.

The church will gradually cease to be a symbol of nationalist resistance. If it fails to rise to the challenges, it could lose its influence. Already some young people are demonstrating a sceptical attitude and have stopped going to mass. The priesthood, mostly indigenous and nationalist, enjoyed a relatively high status during the occupation. As priests are now encouraged by their superiors (and Rome) to adopt a more pastoral and apolitical approach, those who in the past enjoyed a measure of political as well as priestly power will have to adjust.

Provided church structures behave with the transparency and honesty they have prescribed for East Timor's government, the church is likely to continue to exert considerable influence in the immediate future. There is a strong role for church leadership in peace building. Bishop Belo, who resigned in 2002, led the church in East Timor in taking a strong stance for peace and reconciliation, and also for justice for the victims of human rights violations. Bishop Ricardo da Silva has indicated his willingness to continue in this tradition. In February 2005, the governments of Indonesia and East Timor established a Truth and Friendship Commission which human rights activists fear will allow perpetrators of the killing and destruction of 1999 to evade justice. In response, the bishop called for international standards of justice for East Timorese victims of human rights violations.

The more educated Catholic women are waking up to the realisation that in their church as in their society, despite Biblical and papal assurances of equality, they are expected to cook, clean, and be quiet. There is growing awareness that women will need to assert themselves in the church as well as the state, and they have begun to do so, with mixed results. Women such as Maria Lourdes Martins Cruz, Maria Dias and Sister Guilhermina Marcal (see boxes) are important role models, who have set an example of women's leadership.

They receive little acknowledgement from the church as religious leaders, although to all intents and purposes that is what they are. Perhaps they will find inspiration in the figure of Pastora Maria

Gomes, the much respected leader of one of the main Protestant denominations, the Assemblies of God. The Pastora has led the church since her husband, who founded it, died in 1991. While the other main Protestant denomination in East Timor, the Igreja Protestante Timor Leste, has yet to recover from the departure of much of its congregation in 1999 when the Indonesians left, the Assemblies of God seems to have been growing. It now has 43 churches throughout the country, and is particularly strong on Atauro island. Christian Solidarity Worldwide has pointed out that Pastora Gomes and Maria Lourdes Martins Cruz could play a powerful role in promoting ecumenical relations in independent East Timor.[17] This is particularly important given the huge Catholic majority.

East Timorese women's non-governmental organisations and international organisations have lobbied the Catholic church to promote gender equality and speak out more clearly against domestic violence. In the past the church was reluctant to do this, but in late 2004, after a year of wrangling over the wording, it gave its approval to a brochure on domestic violence produced by the United Nations Family Planning Association; the brochure will be distributed nationally.

Faith will remain a motivating and nurturing force in the lives of many, though not all, East Timorese women as they build their country over the coming decades.

Maria Lourdes Martins Cruz

Maria Lourdes Martins Cruz does not see herself as a priest, but in many ways, she exemplifies some of the better qualities of 'priesthood' if this is seen in terms of ministry, service and faith leadership. Mana Lou, as she is called by her friends, is the founder of Maun Alin Iha Kristu – a secular institute based in Dare, in the hills above Dili. She entered the novitiate of the Canossian Sisters in the 1980s, but the restrictions of religious life did not suit her. She left before her final profession.

Inspired by the liberation theology of Gustavo Gutiérrez and others in Latin America, and the pedagogical methods of Paulo Freire, she founded her secular institute. Her aim was simple: to train young women to work and bear witness to the poorest of the poor in remote East Timorese villages, and to teach practical skills such as healthcare and animal husbandry. It is a vision to which she remains dedicated today, doggedly arguing with those of her novices who want to soften and adapt the image of the order.

Her mission extends beyond her sisters, however. She was one of the few religious leaders who, in the aftermath of the mass displacements and destruction that followed the 1999 referendum, went across the border to try to bring the militias back to God and reason. Given the mass killings, rape and arson for which they were responsible, this was a brave act. She worked with the Besi Merah Putih, a militia army which had terrorised the Liquiça area and committed a massacre in the Catholic church there in April 1999. She explains:

> The militias knew that I always talk about Jesus. They encouraged others to listen. Some told me that at first they felt angry. But they said: 'Then our minds and hearts opened, and we understood that we had been the victims of politics.' I tried to explain to them that God does not condemn.... He loves his children and waits for them to convert. I relied a great deal upon the Bible stories. Isaiah 43 was fundamental because it talks about bringing people home.

Mana Lou's secular institute was not well understood at first by those who should have understood it best – the local church hierarchy. Some East Timorese clergy regarded her as a nuisance – a nun 'trying to be a priest'. It took a peace prize from Pax Christi International (awarded in 1996) for the East Timorese church to wake up to the jewel in its midst. Gradually, hostility waned. Mana Lou today helps to train priests. Young seminarians are sent to her centre in the countryside to experience her work with the poor, travelling with her young novices for two weeks' pastoral work in remote areas. They then have a week or two reflecting on their experience – a chance to discuss faith and commitment and benefit from Mana Lou's unique spiritual direction.

If someone has a calling, asserts Mana Lou, she should 'answer to the reality of the people':

> Like Moses, and St Paul, we have to adapt and follow God's lead. If people respond to the needs of their society, they are also responding to God. In this way, we can develop our spiritual life, and through prayer, become a friend of Jesus – meet him in the gospel.

'We see that Jesus was very simple,' says Mana Lou:

He was impassioned – always ready to do something, ready to act.... I sometimes get the impression that we Christians don't know who Jesus is. Social status becomes more important.

[Interview with Catherine Scott, June 2002]

Maria de Fatima Ximenes Dias

Maria Dias, now 38, was educated in Dili and Ainaro in church schools. She then worked at the Motael clinic before joining the Carmelite novitiate. The Carmelites sent her to Spain for three years, where she trained as a nurse. On her return, however, she decided to leave the convent. She felt she was too outspoken to keep quiet about the political problems of East Timor.

When she came back to East Timor, she decided to work with people who needed her help – the poor and the sick. She started work in a hospital, visiting the sick who had no relatives or friends to visit them. She also worked with Fr João Felgueiras, a Portuguese Jesuit who was a prison chaplain, and she visited political prisoners.

Maria would sometimes hide young people from the military if they were in trouble. Gradually she gained a reputation for nursing sick clandestine workers and Falintil guerrillas. Falintil members would be sent from the mountains secretly to be treated by her.

Maria also began working with Forum Komunikasi Untuk Perempuan Lorosae (Fokupers – East Timorese Women's Communications Forum) caring for rape victims. At this point, Fokupers did not even have premises, so Maria set up a clinic in her mother's house. The military never found the clinic. Eventually, with financial support from agencies such as Caritas and Timor Aid, the clinic was able to move out of her mother's house. For a while she also ran one of Mana Lou's projects: a hostel for sick people, where she treated patients with TB, polio, leprosy and burns.

Maria also sent news about human rights violations out of the country. She sent information to Amnesty International through a priest she met in Spain who was active on human rights issues.

Maria's religious formation has been a very big influence on her life. She tries to make it clear to those who run the church in East Timor that women have a big role to play in the church as well as in the world. Many women are working in the church, but Maria says they are afraid of the priests, most of whom have pre-Vatican II attitudes to women. She hopes the new bishop will use his power to challenge the church's conservatism and make decision making at parish level more democratic.

She is concerned that the church is encouraging people to compartmentalise their lives and their faith, and experience them separately. In her view, the work one does in the public sphere is the church's work too: faith must be worked out through daily life in its problems and challenges, rather than as a set of external rituals. It must be connected to the lives of the people, otherwise it runs the risk of being superficial and unrooted.

[Interview with Catherine Scott, June 2004]

Sister Guilhermina Marcal

Sister Guilhermina comes from Same, where her father was a local leader of the UDT. He was killed by Fretilin after the Indonesian invasion and Guilhermina, then 15, inherited the responsibility of looking after her baby brother. She fled to the mountains with a large group of refugees.

She came down from the mountains in 1978, with around 5,000 women and children, to surrender to the Indonesians. Three battalions – a total of 3,000 soldiers – came to receive 5,000 civilians. It was a peaceful surrender and no-one was killed, although they were interrogated. She went back to her village to find nothing was left of it.

Guilhermina went to work for the Indonesian government, while studying for her high school diploma. Once she had got her younger brothers through primary school, she entered the convent. After two years she made her first profession. She worked with young boys and girls in Baucau and also contacted Falintil. Youth leaders were oppressed by the Indonesian soldiers and she too must have come under suspicion, because she was interrogated three times. She believes she was on a blacklist, and that the Vatican embassy in Jakarta must have heard about her, because the Provincial (the head of the order) moved her to Jakarta.

But she kept her clandestine links with Falintil. She used to receive faxes for Xanana Gusmão, who was in Cipinang prison in Jakarta; she would smuggle them in to him and relay messages out on his behalf.

Sister Guilhermina feels strongly that women have been the backbone of the resistance, and that many of them are endowed with extraordinary courage. In her experience, she says, women are far more likely to stay and resolve problems, and to defend home, family and children, whereas men often run away. She felt that in the church there were often instances when priests would take credit for the work of the sisters.

She believes that since 2000, the church has started to look at the position of women and how it can change. But even simple innovations meet with disapproval. She once tried to energise a meeting of a religious order by playing a pop song and encouraging the sisters to dance and clap their hands. It met with strong disapproval from Bishop Belo. She believes that the attitudes to power must change among the clergy – but that they are frightened to relinquish it. She places her hope in the few radical priests and nuns in the East Timorese church.

Sister Guilhermina now works at the national university in the education department and practises as a student counsellor. She also teaches English and gives training in human rights, classroom management and teaching.

[Interview with Catherine Scott, June 2004]

Notes

1   Catholic News Service, 'Bishop says moral, spiritual darkness haunts East Timor's Catholics', 24 April 2003.

2   Cristalis, I (2002) *Bitter dawn: East Timor – a people's story*, Zed Books, London, p66.

3   Archer, R (1995) 'The Catholic church in East Timor' in Carey, P, and Carter Bentley, G (eds) *East Timor at the crossroads: The forging of a nation*, University of Hawaii, Honolulu, pp120-133.

4   Many missionaries, especially the Portuguese, fled in 1975. After 1975, Indonesian missionaries began to come in, and now compose around one-third of the church's personnel. Indigenous priests could no longer be trained in East Timor after the invasion because the seminaries were destroyed. They were sent to seminaries in Indonesia.

5   The Second Vatican Council 1962-65 introduced sweeping reforms in Roman Catholicism, including the translation of the mass into local languages from Latin.

6   Interview with Catherine Scott, September 1993.

7   CIIR (1996) *East Timor: The continuing betrayal*, Catholic Institute for International Relations, London, p14.

8   Quoted in Turner, M (1992) *Telling East Timor: Personal testimonies, 1942-92,* New South Wales University Press, Sydney, p108.

9   Interview with Catherine Scott, April 1996.

10 Interviews with Catherine Scott, April 1996.

11 Information from interviews with Mana Bisoi by the authors. Quote from interview with Catherine Scott, July 2002.

12 See Rowlands, J (1997) *Questioning empowerment: Working with women in Honduras,* Oxfam, Oxford.

13 Smythe, Fr P (1995) *The crucifixion of East Timor*, MA dissertation, Leeds University, p25.

14 Rodriguez, J (1994) *Our Lady of Guadalupe: Faith and empowerment among Mexican-American Women*, University of Texas Press, pxxi.

15 Rodriguez, J (as above), p14.

16 The story of Our Lady of Fatima has particular resonance for the East Timorese. The story is that the Virgin Mary appeared six times to three shepherd children near the town of Fatima, Portugal, between May and October 1917. She told the children that she had been sent by God with a message for every man, woman and child living in the century. Coming at a time when civilisation was torn asunder by war and bloody violence, she promised that Heaven would grant peace to all the world if her requests for prayer, reparation and consecration were heard and obeyed. (See www.fatima.org)

17 Panter, M, and Rogers, B (2001) *Report on a visit to East Timor 28 April-5 May 2001*, Christian Solidarity Worldwide, Hong Kong/Australia.

Chapter 5
The transition to independence

This chapter explores how the women's movement consolidated its new platform as East Timor entered its transition to independence. The referendum in 1999 was followed by a transition period from 2000 to 2002, preparing the way for full independence which was proclaimed on 20 May 2002. During these two years women activists from both inside the country and the diaspora worked ever closer together as they struggled to find the most effective ways to secure their rights and freedoms. The chapter assesses the contribution and role of the United Nations (UN) in promoting gender equality and women's participation in politics, reconstruction and development. It looks at how women have sought to assert their interests in the emerging political and governmental institutions.

Historical context

1999 was to prove a watershed year for East Timor. Indonesian president Suharto's strong links with the Indonesian army meant that any discussion of policy change on East Timor was not possible. His successor, president B J Habibie, had no such links and was prepared to take a broader view and discuss options. More crucially still, at the end of 1998, Australian prime minister John Howard wrote to Habibie, indicating that Australia was changing its policy on East Timor. It would no longer recognise Indonesian sovereignty, and favoured an eventual act of self-determination. Under pressure also from the International Monetary Fund (IMF), in the wake of the Asian financial crisis, Indonesia was about to lose its staunchest ally in the region.

Habibie appeared to take the pragmatic path. Defying military opposition, he decided to negotiate with Portugal. If the East Timorese people rejected his offer of special autonomy, he would ask the People's Consultative Assembly to consider 'letting East Timor go'. For the first time in 24 years, it looked as if the East Timorese could look forward to independence in earnest.

Scenarios were shifting for East Timorese women too. Although the majority of women in East Timor continued to live in poverty and danger, by 1999 East Timorese women's organisations and activists had laid down an agenda for change. They had been raising their concerns both at home and internationally and registered a particularly powerful protest against all forms of violence against women. Increasingly, women's issues were gaining attention, and the Conselho Nacional da Resistência Timorense (CNRT – National Council of Timorese Resistance) was at last beginning to take heed.

The road to independence

In April 1999, shortly before the negotiations between Indonesia and Portugal began, key East Timorese intellectuals met in Melbourne to put together a strategic development plan for an independent East Timor. They discussed every conceivable area of concern, from health to education to governance.

Diaspora activist Milena Pires argued the case for gender mainstreaming – that is, considering gender in all areas of policy and throughout East Timor's new institutions:

> East Timorese women have been marginalised in East Timorese society, in the political and the socio-economic context. Assessing the relationship between Timorese men and women, their respective place in East Timorese society and how these are constructed by gender is an essential step in ensuring that all of East Timor's population can enjoy their full rights and partake fully in society. Failure to do so, in this crucial juncture, is tantamount to emphasising, reproducing and legitimising the oppressive policies prevalent during the Indonesian military occupation which has kept the East Timorese population in servitude....
>
> The indivisible, interdependent and universal nature of human rights must be reflected in development policies, so as to avoid the convenient exclusion of rights to already marginalised groups in society which may pose a threat to the status quo.[1]

The development planners organised themselves into longer-term working groups and went away to refine their ideas, not anticipating just how much reconstruction would later be needed.

Soon after, negotiations between Indonesia and Portugal began under UN auspices in New York. An agreement signed on 5 May 1999 provided for a referendum on Indonesia's offer of autonomy for East Timor. A vote against autonomy would mean a vote for independence. The drawback was that Indonesia would retain control of security arrangements up to, during and directly after the referendum.

The UN machinery spun into motion and the United Nations Assistance Mission in East Timor was assembled to conduct the referendum, originally scheduled for June 1999. But the Indonesian military, determined to prevent East Timor breaking away, drew up a plan to terrorise the population into voting for continued integration – and to wreak systematic and total revenge if the vote went against them. For some time, the Indonesian army in East Timor had been forming militia groups, which could be used to foment trouble and provide a pretext for repressive military action. They set about consolidating these and forming new ones in every district – groups of 200-1,500 pro-autonomy mercenaries recruited locally and imported from the Indonesian islands.

The violent aftermath of the referendum, which eventually took place on 30 August 1999, and the dramatic arrival of the Australian-led intervention force (InterFET) have been well documented elsewhere.[2] As it became clear that the population had voted overwhelmingly for independence, the militias, directed by the Indonesian army and police, began their retaliation. Up to 250,000 people were forcibly displaced, mostly across the border into West Timor, although some were taken as far afield as Bali, Sumatra and Java. Property was burned, smashed and comprehensively looted. The fires were so intense that they were picked up by weather satellites 500km above the earth. Amnesty International believes that as many as 1,400 people lost their lives in the months preceding and immediately after the ballot.[3]

As the dust settled and InterFET moved in to restore order, CNRT cadres assembled in Darwin to assess the damage and plan for the future governance of their shattered country. The demands on this small group of individuals were great: they would have to adapt almost overnight from resistance to reconstruction. Moreover, CNRT figures inside East Timor had been hunted down and some had been murdered. Others were only just emerging from hiding. Leaders from the diaspora had to wrench themselves away, probably indefinitely, from lives and livelihoods which had been well-established elsewhere in the world.

In these early weeks the CNRT often found its efforts to set priorities overtaken by events. There was a pressing need to reconcile a variety of approaches among a diverse group, but the fault-lines were particularly marked between three sets of protagonists: insiders and diaspora people, the younger and older generations, and men and women.

After agreeing a transition structure for the CNRT, its leaders were required to amalgamate this with the UN Transitional Administration in East Timor (UNTAET), set up under Security Council Resolution 1272 to administer East Timor through the transition to independence. The influx of international humanitarian non-governmental organisations (NGOs) and UN agencies, and the continued presence of InterFET, further complicated the picture. Through lobbying, women activists had persuaded the CNRT to establish a gender equity commission as part of the transition structure. But it was abandoned when the joint CNRT-UNTAET structure was established because the UN did not see it as a priority.[4]

The women's movement

Civil society organisations too were adapting to the new circumstances. In March 2000 a new women's network was founded. Rede Feto Timor Lorosae (the East Timorese Women's Network) brought 16 disparate women's organisations together under one umbrella to lobby for common interests. Its spokesperson, Filomena dos Reis, described the network as being 'representative of a broad cross-section of society as there are mass-based organisations with national membership down to the village level, cultural, income-generating/small business and rights based organisations, as well as organisations affiliated with political parties'.[5]

The network took upon itself the task of representing East Timorese women to the joint UN/CNRT administration. It lobbied for women to be included in a consultative body, the National Council, which was set up to pass legislation before the Constituent Assembly elections scheduled for August 2001. Thirteen out of 33 seats on the National Council went to women, including one for Rede Feto, whose representative Milena Pires was elected deputy speaker. This was not without controversy as 'insiders' disliked the appointment of a former exile, irrespective of her abilities. The reaction highlighted a problem which besets East Timorese civil society organisations and the government itself. The misunderstandings between the exiles and those who had stayed behind, and the rivalry over accounts of their relative contributions to the self-determination struggle and consequent claims to office, caused some tensions in these first few years of post-conflict reconstruction. Such attitudes could continue to affect politics in the future unless individuals and groups consciously decide to move on.

In early 2001 Rede Feto developed a partnership with the UN women's development organisation Unifem (United Nations

Development Fund for Women), which began its time in Timor by investing resources and personnel in building up the capacities of the network.

Freedom from occupation brought the freedom to explore new ideas and address the whole range of women's concerns. In June 2000 activists organised their first major women's congress. The two-day congress, held in Dili, drew up a national plan of action for women's rights based on the 1995 Beijing Platform for Action[6] and the commitments outlined in the 'Magna Carta' issued by the CNRT conference in Portugal in 1998 (see chapter 3).

The CNRT held its own congress shortly afterwards. Armed with their newly formulated plan of action, women had the confidence to speak out. The congress unanimously passed a resolution on women (see appendix 3), and also pledged a future government to sign the key UN covenants protecting women's rights.

The CNRT dissolved itself before the Constituent Assembly elections – although the Organização da Mulher Timorense (OMT – Organisation of Timorese Women) set up as its counterpart has continued. However, many of its members returned to their first party of affiliation, Fretilin, and the allied OPMT (Organização Popular da Mulher Timorense – Popular Organisation of East Timorese Women). As a result there are now two national grassroots women's organisations vying for influence, members and funding. Although many women activists outside these two organisations are anxious to contain their rivalry and bring them to collaborate in the interests of women, there are strong and differing views on how to resolve the impasse.

Manuela Leong Pereira and Fokupers

Manuela Leong Pereira is director of the Forum Komunikasi Untuk Perempuan Lorosae (Fokupers – East Timorese Women's Communications Forum), one of East Timor's leading women's NGOs. The main focus of its work is violence against women.

Manuela started working for Fokupers in 1998, as a volunteer in a women's shelter. The following year, as violence intensified in the run-up to the referendum, the organisation sent women out to work in the districts. 'The Indonesian troops used to think we were doing church work,' she says. The Fokupers staff had little training. Manuela says they just listened to the stories of victims of violence and wrote them up. But listening was one way of giving support. It was also a way of teaching women about their rights, and an opportunity to inform people about the referendum.

In the mayhem that followed the vote, the Fokupers office was destroyed, the computers were looted and all the data was lost. But all the staff survived (although some lost their husbands in the violence) and they re-established the organisation.

It was a time to address new issues and new ideas. Manuela explains: 'We rebuilt and reconstructed. We were really strong in that first year.... The UN and international NGOs were both supportive.' But she feels that some NGOs became too dependent on external support, and that support faded as time went on. 'Some of the women's NGOs have been good at getting external funding, others such as OPMT and OMT less so, despite their mass base,' she says.

Fokupers has continued to work with women victims of violence, but in the transition it has expanded its remit. It took part in the campaign for a 30 per cent quota for women candidates in the elections to the Constituent Assembly (see 'The campaign for quotas' below), worked with the Women's Caucus to produce a charter of women's rights (see below), and helped choose the three independent women candidates who ran for the assembly.

[Interview with Catherine Scott, June 2004]

The United Nations

At their congress in June 2000, women activists issued a declaration demanding resources for the advancement and empowerment of women, as well as demands that 'UNTAET fulfil the United Nations commitment to gender equity...'. The pressure on the UN was necessary. Throughout the UN engagement with East Timor, it was pressure from East Timorese women that kept the UN focused on gender. While the UN undoubtedly played an important role in East Timor in this regard, it would not have succeeded without the encouragement and support of East Timorese women.

The late Sergio Vieira de Mello, the Special Representative of the UN Secretary General in East Timor, announced UNTAET's plans for governance and public administration in early 2000. 'In the interests of economy,' he said, plans for a gender unit had been scrapped.[7] But women refused to give in and eventually a separate Gender Affairs Bureau was set up under the deputy Special Representative of the UN Secretary General for Governance and Public Administration, and allocated a modest budget.[8]

During its short life, the bureau fought a number of tough battles with different sections of UNTAET, and with elements in the East Timorese political leadership, to ensure gender considerations were taken seriously throughout the administration. The unit's personnel encountered little understanding of the concept of gender mainstreaming or of its practical implications.

At election time, mindful that the Gender Affairs Bureau would have only six more months in East Timor, its concern was to try to safeguard the progress made. To this end, it circulated a paper explaining why a women's ministry or office on the status of women should be located in the office of the prime minister – an idea supported by Sergio Vieira de Mello. He, and the head of the Gender Affairs Bureau, wanted to see senior gender advisers placed at the highest level, where they would be in a position to ensure that gender would be addressed in all areas of policy. They felt that it would also be necessary for the international community to assist the women's ministry or office practically and financially, offer moral support, and provide training and expertise to the East Timorese staff.

The first task of the women's equality office would be to ensure that the post-independence government signed and ratified the Convention on the Elimination of All Forms of Discrimination Against Women (CEDAW) – and that the new constitution reflected its articles. Once CEDAW was ratified, the government of East Timor would be required to report regularly to the UN on implementation of the convention. This would serve as an important yardstick for measuring progress and an opportunity for East Timorese women's organisations to lobby for improvements at an international level.

The campaign for quotas

For those seeking to enshrine rights for women in an emerging nation, an important first step is to ensure that women gain sufficient political representation to press their concerns and interests. Women had traditionally played a minor role in East Timorese politics and activists on women's issues recognised that this would have to change.

One of Rede Feto's campaigns in 2001 was therefore to win the inclusion of mandatory quotas for women in the rules formulated by the National Council for the elections to the Constituent Assembly. Drawing on the 2000 Congress Platform for Action which called for a minimum of 30 per cent representation in government employment, membership of appointed bodies, etc, in January 2001 Rede Feto proposed 30 per cent as a reasonable quota of women. This would level the playing field and fast-track women's participation in politics. The proposal gained initial backing from the delegates, but was slated for discussion and a vote three weeks later.

East Timorese women campaigned for national and international support. They were optimistic. But opponents of the move emerged. Women activists observed what seemed to be collusion to oppose quotas between a group of mostly male East Timorese politicians and UN employees, also male, mostly from the Division on Electoral Affairs in New York.

A variety of reasons for rejecting a quota for women were aired in the National Council debate on 8 February 2001. Socialist leader Avelino Coelho said his party would support only a 50 per cent quota. Others claimed that women 'lacked the capacity' to serve in the Constituent Assembly.

Fretilin leader Mari Alkatiri told a CIIR election monitoring team in August 2001 that he favoured a 30 per cent quota for women in the Constituent Assembly elections, but Fretilin feared that a mandatory quota would prevent the smallest parties from taking part in the election. 'That is why Fretilin disagree,' he said. 'We made it clear that it should be a commitment of the biggest parties first to really give the example of how to involve women in the whole process and not really to create some legal mechanism....'[9]

But women MPs in Fretilin, such as Cipriana Pereira (see box below), said later that they were misinformed or put under huge pressure to reject the quota proposal.

The vote went against quotas and women activists were forced to rethink their strategy for ensuring that women would be represented in the assembly. Rede Feto urged political parties to put female candidates high on their party lists, so that women would have some guarantee of gaining seats. They also had some key allies, including Sergio Vieira de Mello, who decided to deny airtime to parties which had not fielded women candidates in winnable positions.[10] Xanana Gusmão and José Ramos Horta also publicly supported the women's campaign.

In the run-up to the elections, UNTAET's Gender Affairs Bureau, with the assistance of Unifem, mounted a series of women's leadership training workshops aimed at strengthening women's capacity and resolve to stand for office.

From these workshops a group called the Women's Caucus emerged to take forward some of the crucial debates. It drew up a women's charter of rights (see appendix 4) and lobbied for them to be included in the new constitution. The charter included clauses on political, social and labour rights, as well as rights to education and health, and called for the prohibition of prostitution and slavery. Much of it was incorporated into the constitution, the notable exceptions being the clauses on prostitution, polygamy and *barlaque* (bride price). Activists hoped that these would be addressed later through legislation.

The Constituent Assembly elections

The election was organised on the basis of a mixed system. Both individual candidates and political parties were invited to submit lists of candidates arranged in order of priority and 75 of the 88 seats in the assembly would be allocated according to proportion of votes. The remaining 13 were reserved for the 13 districts on a first-past-the-post basis.

In addition to campaigning for quotas for the political parties, Rede Feto decided to field three independent candidates of its own. In Dili some prominence was given to women's issues. Rede Feto's candidates received media coverage, and seemed to be well-known. However, in the countryside, particularly beyond the reach of print or radio media, awareness was much lower, and few people knew about the women candidates.

An observer mission organised by CIIR noted that levels of awareness of the implications of the vote varied considerably, among both women and men.[11] Some had clearly benefited from civic education programmes. One woman in Maubara on polling day said that democracy was about 'transparency'. Other women, especially in villages, complained that they did not really know anything about the political parties' programmes. Few in the villages seemed to understand that the Constituent Assembly would be responsible for drafting the constitution which would set out their rights and duties as citizens in the fairly near future.

Rede Feto's three independent national candidates were Olandina Caeiro, Teresa Carvalho and Maria Domingas Fernandes. Two women also ran for the assembly as the district candidate in Oecusse: Etelvina da Costa and OPMT leader Appolonia da Costa. All these candidates had been prominent women activists, some of them in party-related women's organisations, for many years. They decided to run as independents so that they would be free of party policies, and could make a priority of women's issues.

Without a party machine behind them, however, all of them suffered from under-resourced campaigns. Like the parties, they received funding from the United Nations Development Programme, but had no independent sources of funding. They had little more than their own women's organisations to give them support.

Many voters assumed that only women without family responsibilities could participate in politics, and such women would be
unable to understand the concerns of ordinary women voters. One
woman candidate said that people accused them of looking for
'jobs for the girls'.[12] In fact, all three independent women candidates had either children or elderly relatives, and came to creative
arrangements with other family members to enable them to run for
office.

Rede Feto was unable to rally support behind the candidates and
none of the women was elected. It seems that without party backing, it is extremely difficult to campaign as an independent.[13]
Socialist leader Avelino Coelho suggested that the women's organisations should have united behind a single candidate if they wanted to compete at the national level, rather than splitting their support three ways.

Political representation after the elections

Although 26 per cent of candidates elected to the Constituent
Assembly were women – one of the highest proportions in the Asia-
Pacific region – this was very much a first step. Women activists
knew that numbers alone would not be enough to secure women's
strategic interests in the legislature. As Terezinha Cardoso of the
Women's Caucus said: 'It is not enough to elect women if they do
not speak out.'[14] Women would need to be able to form their own
alliances, act independently on occasion, and benefit from
capacity-building support.

So far, little progress has been registered. Political parties which
were only too happy to express their deep concern for women's
issues during the campaigning period have found it difficult to put
their promises into practice. Women in parliament found they
were having to toe the party line and some were disappointed to
find their party's commitment to women's rights faded after the
elections.

The Women's Caucus is continuing to educate women to participate in politics at both local and national level. It encourages
women to take part in politics and run for elections, mentors promising candidates, builds their skills and shows them how they
might play a role representing others. It also works with the political parties to persuade them to adopt and nurture women candidates. According to Terezinha Cardoso, the response has been
mixed: 'Parties are becoming more open , but need a lot of encouragement, and the women need a lot of support and training.'[15]

A woman in parliament: Cipriana Pereira

Cipriana Pereira was elected to the Constituent Assembly as a Fretilin representative, after serving as a member of the National Council. Born in Laga, Baucau, she has been involved in politics since she was 12 years old. She joined Fretilin in 1974. After the Indonesian invasion, she became an armed combatant with Falintil (Forças Armadas de Libertação Nacional de Timor Leste – Armed Forces for the National Liberation of East Timor). In March 1979 she went back to the city to become a political organiser.

Defending women's rights in the Constituent Assembly was not easy, she found:

> If I want to fight for women's rights, I have to fight against my party.... We have been discussing women's protection measures in the parliament. But women are more affiliated to their political parties than they are to fighting for women's interests.

As a member of Fretilin, she was obliged to oppose the 30 per cent quota for women in the Constituent Assembly elections. Now she feels let down. 'Fretilin's view of equality is just words: there is no implementation,' she says.

> If I raise my voice in protest ... I am simply isolated.... The other Fretilin women are scared and don't say anything. They are fixing it in the parliament so that women can only say yes or no. I have been a faithful member of the Fretilin party, but it has not practised what it preached. The Fretilin I joined always defended equality, independence and democracy. Now I see that women's equality is getting nowhere, I feel betrayed.

She is still under pressure from the party and fears that if she continues to speak her mind on democracy and women's rights, the party may expel her. If that happens, she intends to become an academic:

> I will not join another party. But if I go out, I will look for a way to change Fretilin.... We must be able to admit our mistakes. Fretilin is a historic party, but we need to deal with the leadership which does not accommodate people's views.

[Interview with Catherine Scott, June 2002]

The Office for the Promotion of Equality

As the period of UN administration drew to a close, there was a debate as to which form of national machinery would best suit women's interests and at the same time receive support from Fretilin, the largest political party which was expected to win the elections. Women's ministries elsewhere have failed because they were under-funded, marginalised and ignored, and women's concerns have therefore met a similar fate. The approach of placing women's or gender advisers in central decision-making locations such as the office of the prime minister was considered by gender experts to be more effective and this is what happened in East Timor.[16]

The Office for the Promotion of Equality (OPE) was set up in the Office of the Prime Minister, and a well-known woman activist, Maria Domingas Fernandes (one of Rede Feto's independent candidates) was appointed as its head and gender adviser to the prime minister. The OPE is responsible for implementing the Beijing Platform for Action and a national plan of action for gender mainstreaming. With the help of foreign donors it recruited seven staff (the Human Rights Unit, in the same office, had only one).

In addition, each district has a designated person – either a government employee or an activist – who serves as a 'gender focal point' charged with helping to implement gender mainstreaming strategies at district level, in line with OPE policy.

Reviewing the work of the OPE a year into its mandate, Maria Domingas Fernandes noted some successes.[17] These included awareness-raising on domestic violence and the preparation of draft legislation on domestic violence for the Constituent Assembly. She also felt that good progress had been made in mainstreaming gender through government ministries, despite problems caused by poor communication between government departments. However, she thought the real challenge in protecting women would not be legislation but implementation, which would require more far-reaching social change. She felt the unit had insufficient resources to undertake all the research needed for monitoring and planning.

The OPE has had to defend its staff, its budget and its very existence, but its leader's greatest frustration was the lack of decision-making power or influence over government decisions. Her mandate has no legal status – she is dependent on the office of prime minister Mari Alkatiri. He has been supportive, but there is no guarantee that this would continue under subsequent prime ministers.

Maria Domingas Fernandes thought that the gender and development framework has had more success than the rights-based approaches employed by some women activists, in particular those from the diaspora:

> We have found it easier to approach gender from the perspective that women should be included in development and able to participate and contribute, instead of saying it's women's human rights, which is harder to discuss. Men react by saying: 'What about us?'

She felt that the rights-based approach has provoked a backlash and reinforced discrimination.

Financial support for the OPE has come from foreign donors, but the office needs the support of East Timorese civil society if it is to be effective. Maria Domingas Fernandes thought that women's organisations were doing their best to support the work of the OPE. However, until women begin claiming some power of their own, she said, progress in challenging cultural attitudes would be slow:

> Women have to believe that they can change their society, change mentalities. They have to be agents of change in society. That means being constantly active – and not giving up.

The OPE will remain a key focal point for advancing gender equality in East Timor. East Timorese women activists believe that it has done good work so far and want to ensure that it maintains an independent voice. Manuela Leong Pereira, director of Fokupers, feels the office has made considerable progress, but needs more support from government and from civil society:

> I don't really trust the government to support the OPE to the extent that is needed. There is always the danger of a women's department becoming a bucket for women's problems and of its focus on gender mainstreaming being lost or undermined.[18]

An agenda for the future

Gathered at their second women's congress in July 2004, women from East Timorese civil society organisations reaffirmed CEDAW, the Beijing Platform for Action and UN Security Council Resolution 1325 on women, peace and security as the basis for their work. They drew up a new national plan of action (see appendix 6), building on the plan drawn up at the first National Congress in 2000. It shows a range of concerns and approaches, including cultural change as well as demands for resources and new legislation. Key areas of concern included education, health and livelihoods.

Education

Many activists also see education, for both men and women, as key to bringing about changes in cultural attitudes to gender relations. Improving girls' access to educational opportunities was a central demand of the women's platform of action drawn up at the June 2000 East Timorese women's congress. Four years on there was still much to do. Adult literacy rates are estimated at only 42.8 per cent for women, and 43.1 per cent for men.[19]

The entire educational infrastructure was devastated by the destruction of 1999. Access to education beyond primary level under Indonesian rule was low. According to Unicef (the United Nations Children's Fund), only three per cent of teachers have been formally trained and a typical primary class has 60 or more pupils.[20] The curriculum under Indonesian rule did not correspond to the needs of the pupils and was gender-biased, with girls sent off to vocational schools to learn to cook and sew.

The reintroduction of Portuguese as a national language has considerably raised the costs of the new system. The national development plan aims to increase primary enrolment and reduce drop-out rates, improve teaching quality and literacy rates, and further the teaching of Portuguese.

The ratio of girls to boys in high school and university remains very low. In 2001-2002 the ratio of male to female enrolment at the University of Dili was four to one. In education studies, 77 per cent of students were men.[21] This means that few women will enter the teaching profession, thus perpetuating the problem because there will be few role models for girls. Women activists say there is a need to challenge the custom of early marriage and pregnancy with positive role models, offering alternative visions of women's lives. Most UN agencies and international NGOs supporting the educational sector are emphasising girls' education.

Laura Menezes Lopez Belo: challenging patriarchy

Laura Lopez Belo was a child when the civil war came, but she saw a great deal of violence. A schoolgirl during the Indonesian occupation, she worked for the clandestine movement as a messenger.

One of the main reasons for her involvement in politics, she says, was her concern about how the invasion affected the lives of women. She wanted to take part in the struggle for freedom. She feels that the majority of women who took part in the resistance had two principal objectives: freedom from occupation and freedom from illiteracy. The notion of freedom from patriarchy, she says, only really came with independence: 'It was only in this period that we began to really understand women's rights, even though there are still big obstacles to be overcome to realise them.'

For Laura, being in the women's movement means bringing change into her own family. She is trying to influence her husband to be more gender sensitive. She explains:

It's been a big struggle as he's from a very patriarchal background. There is a strong tradition of customs and ceremonies which reinforce discrimination against women. As a wife, I'm expected to work – clean and cook – and eat later. But now I wonder which customs we should still respect: ones that discriminate against women or ones that help women? ... A lot of women still don't believe that they have rights. They still think that we are supposed to respect men's decisions and simply obey. They still think that if a man hits his wife it is to teach her a lesson. It's still a big struggle for women activists because most women still accept men's behaviour.

Laura believes traditional culture needs to be changed, although it is often used as an excuse for other objections to equality. She adds:

There is also a need to look at masculinity Timor-style and try to get men more involved in initiatives to promote women's issues and interests. Their contribution to this needs to be more valued. The high levels of domestic violence are not because of Timor's high levels of poverty, but because of the controlling power of men.

[Interview with Catherine Scott, June 2004]

Livelihoods

A household expenditure survey conducted in September 2001 defined the national poverty line in East Timor as US$0.55 per person per day.[22] Forty-one per cent of people fell below it. During the Indonesian occupation most urban workers were employed as civil servants and earned on average three times as much as rural people. However, the new civil service is much leaner and unemployment rates have risen starkly.

Today, 85 per cent of the poor live in rural areas.[23] The population lives daily with the consequences of poverty: degradation of land and forests, inability to save and invest, and rising crime. Economic necessity forces most East Timorese to live off the land and to find creative ways of generating income.

For women, solutions are often to be found in small-scale income-generating projects, mostly in the informal sector. Women are running restaurants, raising pigs and chickens, running bakeries, producing peanut butter and jam, fish-farming and weaving.

These provide an independent income to buy food and pay for schooling for children. Such projects, funded by micro-credit and revolving loan schemes, have been promoted by both local and international NGOs. The best of these inculcate business management skills in their beneficiaries, and sometimes help to create trading networks and cooperatives, thus increasing self-sufficiency. These projects may also lead to women gaining more respect from their husbands, as they prove their ability to provide for the family – perhaps reducing the likelihood of domestic violence. One woman told the authors that sometimes, when women gain paid employment, they find that their husbands stop beating them.[24]

Health

Diseases such as tuberculosis, malaria and respiratory tract and childhood infections are common in East Timor. Life expectancy is 57 years, and the infant mortality rate is 80 per 1,000 live births. Less than a quarter of births are attended by skilled birth attendants and 420 women die for every 100,000 live births.[25]

The statement of the Second Women's Congress expresses concern at the lack of 'adequate, appropriate, and affordable health care' for women, and for sexual and reproductive health care in particular.[26] It notes women's vulnerability to sexually transmitted diseases (STDs) and HIV and AIDS at a time when it appears that trafficking of women and girls for sexual services both into and out of East Timor is a growing problem. Women's organisations are calling for preventative programmes of education on family planning and reproductive health, STDs, HIV and AIDS, professional midwifery training and general health education. They have also emphasised the need for community health centres and called for additional services for those traumatised by war and violence, the mentally ill and victims of sexual violence.

This chapter has charted a period of immense change for East Timorese women as well as men. Although women face the same problems in 2005 as they did in the past, the new context means that progress is more likely. Violence against women has been one of the most important issues for the women's movement in East Timor and for this reason it is examined in depth in the next chapter.

Notes

1   Pires, M (1999) 'Towards a gendered approach to post-conflict reconstruction and development', unpublished paper for a conference on a strategic development plan for East Timor, Melbourne, 4-9 April 1999.

2   See CIIR (2001) *East Timor: Transition to statehood*, Catholic Institute for International Relations, London; and Cristalis, I (2002) *Bitter dawn: East Timor – a people's story*, Zed Books, London.

3   Amnesty International (2004) *Indonesia and Timor Leste: Justice for Timor Leste – The way forward*, AI Index ASA21/006/2004, Amnesty International, London.

4   José Ramos Horta's address to the CIIR AGM 1999, quoted in *Timor Link* No 48, December 1999.

5   Address to donors' conference on East Timor, December 2000.

6   United Nations World Conference on Women, Beijing, September 1995.

7   Quoted in *Timor Link* No 50, August 2000, p4.

8   For further information see Whittington, S (2000) 'The UN Transitional Administration in East Timor: Gender Affairs' in *Development Bulletin* 53.

9   Interview with a member of the CIIR observer mission to the East Timor Constituent Assembly election, August 2001.

10 Sergio Vieira de Mello also used affirmative action in recruitment to public administration, adopting a 30 per cent quota. Although the target was not realised, 18 per cent of newly recruited staff were female. The same policy was adopted for the police force, with the result that 40 per cent of the first batch of recruits were women.

11 Unpublished report of the CIIR observer mission to the East Timor Constituent Assembly election, 30 August 2001.

12 As above.

13 One male independent candidate from Oecusse was elected. However, he was a Fretilin member who had been late in registering as a party candidate and had been forced to stand as an independent. He presumably had access to party support.

14 Interview with Catherine Scott, June 2004.

15 As above.

16 For a thorough analysis of national machineries for women in development, see Byrne, B, et al (1996) *National machineries for women in development: Experiences, lessons and strategies for institutionalising gender in development policy and planning*, Institute of Development Studies, UK.

17 Interview with Ivete de Oliveira and Emily Roynestad, June 2003.

18 Interview with Catherine Scott, June 2004.

19 UNDP (2002) *National Human Development Report*, United Nations Development Programme, p24.

20 O'Keefe, C, and Whittington, S (2002) *Women in East Timor: A report on women's health, education, economic empowerment and decision-making*, Office for the Promotion of Equality/Ireland Aid, Dili.

21 OPE (2002) *Women in East Timor,* Office for the Promotion of Equality, Dili.

22 UNDP (see note 19), p16.

23 As above.

24 Information given to Catherine Scott by Ivete de Oliveira, June 2004.

25 UNDP (see note 19), p14.

26 Statement of Second National Women's Congress, East Timor, July 2004.

Chapter 6
Violence against women

This chapter looks at gender-based violence in East Timor, both as an endemic problem and as a legacy of the Indonesian occupation. It examines the challenges facing post-independence society in dealing with gender-based violence, and shows how East Timorese women's organisations addressed it. It also looks at East Timorese men's views on the issue, and describes efforts by one group of men to confront traditional attitudes.

Raising the issue

In May 2002, José Ramos Horta gave his first official speech as foreign minister of East Timor at the United Nations (UN) Security Council meeting in New York. Among the major challenges facing post-independence East Timor, he put tackling domestic violence as number one. This was a frank admission, and is certainly backed by the statistics – 40 per cent of all reported crime in East Timor in December 2001 related to domestic violence.[1] Yet relatively few foreign ministers would have been prepared to mention it, despite its worldwide prevalence.

Contrast this with the reaction to Bela Galhos, an exiled East Timorese feminist who dared to raise the issue of domestic violence at a solidarity conference on East Timor held in Portugal in the 1994. Galhos was harangued and denounced – not by political opponents, but by East Timorese male activists, who were angry and embarrassed. They felt the emphasis should be on acts of Indonesian aggression against East Timorese of both sexes. Women's issues were rarely discussed by East Timorese resistance leaders, who were almost exclusively male.

In the few years separating these two events perceptions about gender justice and the legal protection needed to underpin it changed enormously at international level. These advances have been achieved thanks to the efforts of a highly effective international group of women activists who raised women's rights, and gender and development issues, at the UN and other international forums. The case has been made for all government institutions to take gender into account, and for gender-differentiated responses to the causes and consequences of conflict and to development and peace building.[2] This was increasingly reflected in the outputs and statements of UN conferences in the 1990s (see appendix 2), and it nurtured the confidence of East Timorese women to raise the issues in relation to East Timor's struggle for self-determination.

Ultimately, East Timorese political leaders had to pay attention to this mounting pressure. Throughout the 1990s and even before, East Timorese women's organisations had highlighted violence against women as their most important concern. Women activists continue to seek justice for violent crimes against women committed by the occupation forces and their militias. They are also demanding protection from violence in the new East Timor. Manuela Leong Pereira, director of the non-governmental organisation (NGO) Fokupers (Forum Komunikasi Untuk Perempuan Lorosae – East Timorese Women's Communications Forum), summarises their position:

> Women are not the property of men; a woman's value is beyond monetary price. Women have the right to control the major decisions in their lives and to decide with whom and when they will marry, how many children they will have, and when they want to have sexual relations with their husbands. Women have a right to develop themselves, to learn new skills. Women have a right to make decisions in their family and to work outside the home. Perhaps more important, women have a right to talk about the violence they face and look for a solution. Domestic violence is not simply an individual or family problem as so many people think, it is a societal problem that we must identify as ... one that needs immediate attention. There must be mechanisms to support survivors of violence ... women living with violence must have the courage to speak and the strength to leave the violence.[3]

Gender-based violence in the transition to independence

The pattern of gender-based violence during the Indonesian occupation – mostly but not exclusively perpetrated by the Indonesian army (see chapter 3) – grew worse during the referendum year. During the mayhem following the ballot on 30 August 1999, many women were subjected to humiliation and abuse. Fokupers documented some 180 cases of gender-based human rights abuses during this period, despite its own office being attacked, looted and burned on 5 September 1999.

The Fokupers research revealed the close relationship of the militias with the Indonesian army:

We found that women were not only raped during the chaos that ensued, where families were separated and gangs of marauding men acted with impunity. Instead, many of these acts of violence were planned, organised, and sustained – militia and soldiers conniving together to abduct women and share them like chattel; or, in some cases, forcibly taking women across the border into West Timor where the women were raped daily and made to perform household chores. Out of the 31 cases of rape documented so far, eight counts of rape were conducted by TNI [Indonesian armed forces] soldiers and eight counts of rape were conducted by militia. Out of the findings to date, at least 50 per cent of the rapes were conducted by state actors.[4]

Many of the rapes were perpetrated in front of the victim's family, including children, who were particularly traumatised by the experience. Some women saw their husbands or other family members killed. A number of rape victims were subsequently rejected by husbands, boyfriends or families and blamed for their fate. Fokupers was critical of the failure of the UN multinational force, and later UNTAET (the UN Transitional Administration in East Timor), to provide justice for the victims of sexual violence:

> It has become evident that gender-based human rights violations are not seen as a priority. Survivors find difficulty in speaking with UN investigators, who are predominantly male civilian police. The lack of female translators and other female support staff further impedes effective work with these survivors. There seems to be a lack of interest in working with national women's NGOs on these cases.[5]

Tens of thousands of East Timorese women ended up in squalid refugee camps in West Timor after the mass displacement of September 1999. In many camps the living conditions were appalling, with little privacy. The camps were often run by armed militia men and violence against women, including rape, prostitution and wife-beating, was reported regularly. In one study alone Tim Kemanusiaan Timor Barat (TKTB – the West Timor Humanitarian Team, composed of religious leaders, community leaders, and women activists) documented 163 cases of violence against 119 women. This would have been the tip of the iceberg. The TKTB study noted the impact on women's health:

What the TKTB documentation most clearly supports in terms of women's health vulnerability is the damage caused by physical violence. Incidents of severe beatings, rapes, and threats on women's lives have led women to experience miscarriages, attempted abortions, seek medical attention for injuries, suffer extreme trauma resulting in emotional and mental instability, and more.[6]

Violence against women in post-conflict East Timor

Domestic violence is common in East Timor, although it was rarely discussed during the Indonesian occupation. During the transition to independence, from 2000 onwards, it appeared that incidents of domestic violence had increased dramatically. Research by the International Rescue Committee (IRC), an international NGO which ran a programme on gender-based violence in East Timor from 2001 to 2003, suggests that growing awareness of the issue had increased the likelihood of its being reported.[7] Also, women under the occupation would have been less likely to report such crimes to the Indonesian police.

Whatever the reality, it is a well-documented feature of post-conflict societies that domestic violence levels can rise even when peace has been re-established. Often men, and even older women, who depend for their living on the work of their daughters and daughters-in-law, seek to return social norms to the pre-war status quo. In practice, this presents problems, particularly when conflict has been a part of life for several generations: the brutalising aspects of war on human behaviour are difficult to eradicate. War also changes gender roles, and women often find themselves fulfilling roles previously assigned to men, who find their former role as breadwinner usurped. Unemployment may cause bitterness and frustration, which may find expression in alcohol abuse and violence in the home. As Tina Sideris notes:

> The overall social destruction inherent in dirty wars leaves men with few opportunities to implement traditional roles as providers. Thus war leaves men with either an eroded sense of manhood or the option of a militarised identity with the attendant legitimisation of violence and killing as a way of maintaining power and control.[8]

East Timorese society has suffered high levels of physical and psychological violence for several generations. Inevitably this legacy will affect how its people adapt and adjust to peacetime.

Justice for serious crimes under international law

After the liberation of East Timor from the Indonesian army, it was recognised that those who had committed crimes against humanity in East Timor would have to be brought to justice. This was the finding both of the Indonesian Commission on Human Rights (Komisi Nasional Hak Asasi Manusia – known as Komnas Ham) and two separate UN enquiries conducted towards the end of 1999. Both recommended that an international tribunal should deal with the criminals. Instead, the UN Security Council decided to allow Indonesia the chance to prosecute the military perpetrators itself, through a new human rights court.

The quest for justice continued along three parallel lines. Jakarta tried a number of key generals and military figures indicted for war crimes; the UN set up a Serious Crimes Unit in Dili with special panels of international judges to deal with perpetrators who remained in East Timor;[9] and a Commission for Reception, Truth and Reconciliation (Comissão de Acolhimento, Verdade e Reconciliação – CAVR) was set up by the East Timorese government to deal with the lesser crimes, to document people's stories and to facilitate community reconciliation.

More than five years on, it is clear that real justice will remain elusive. There have been deficiencies in all three processes, but the Jakarta trials in particular were ineffective: even the few defendants who were convicted were later freed on appeal.[10] In addition, the East Timorese leadership, and in particular Xanana Gusmão, have been anxious to build close relationships with Jakarta, and not to antagonise them by calling for an international tribunal. Despite this a coalition of NGOs, the East Timorese Alliance for Justice, has been set up to campaign for this goal. Women's organisations are vocal members of the coalition.

The CAVR was set up in 2002 to deal with lesser crimes committed since 1974, during the Indonesian occupation and the civil war. In April 2003, 14 women gave testimony about gender-based violence before the commission. They reported intra-East Timorese violence during the civil war, as well as crimes by the Indonesian army against women in East Timor. Because the hearings were also attended by a team from the Indonesian National Commission on Violence Against Women, a submission was also made about the violence committed in Indonesia against Chinese women in 1998 (anti-Chinese riots broke out in Indonesia following the financial crisis in 1997). Representatives on the team from both Aceh and Papua made comparisons with the violence committed against Acehnese and Papuan women by the Indonesian army.

The Dili special panels have been described as a 'state of the art system for prosecuting international crimes ... grafted onto the fledgling criminal justice system of East Timor',[11] perhaps in the hope that the Serious Crimes Unit could provide political leverage in dealing with Indonesia. However, the international community's under-investment in mechanisms for justice in East Timor and the low priority accorded to it suggest that the UN was not serious about achieving results.[12]

International legal mechanisms for the prosecution of war crimes have improved greatly over the past decade, and are better equipped now than they were to address crimes relating to gender-based violence. Article 5(g) of the International Criminal Court Statute states that rape is a crime against humanity. Both the International Criminal Tribunal for the Former Yugoslavia and the International Criminal Tribunal on Rwanda have successfully convicted defendants for gender-based crimes such as rape. In East Timor rape of women had become so commonplace it was perceived almost as ordinary. Few women have been prepared to bear the shame and horror of recounting their appalling experiences, and the 14 women who did find that courage before the CAVR were both brave and exceptional. So the ability of East Timorese victims of rape to gain justice remains low.

The biggest problem is that while charges for crimes against humanity are currently pending against a total of 313 accused, 279 of them remain at large in Indonesia, which has refused to hand them over to the UN's jurisdiction.

The case of Leonardus Kasa shows the difficulty of winning justice for crimes against women under the Indonesian occupation.[13] Kasa was an alleged member of Laksaur militia from Cova Lima district, arrested and indicted in December 2000 on one charge of rape of a woman in Betun village, West Timor, in September 1999. The Special Panel of the Dili District Court declared that it held no jurisdiction in the case because the rape had been perpetrated in West Timor. This precluded trials in all further cases of women who had been forcibly removed from East to West Timor, despite the principle of universal jurisdiction.

Indeed many cases seem to have been addressed by the pre-existing legal arrangements – such as the Penal Code of Indonesia and UNTAET regulations – rather than international law, leading to unsatisfactory court decisions.

In September 2002 the Special Panel handed down its first conviction for rape. Francisco Soares, a former militia commander, was sentenced to four years' imprisonment for raping a woman taken from the TNI 744 base in Becora in September 1999 (Case Number: 14/2001). The maximum penalty was 12 years.

The first crime against humanity case in East Timor to include charges of rape alongside charges against superiors based on the actions of their subordinates was the Lolotoe case.[14] The three defendants – militia commanders José Cardoso Ferreira and João França da Silva, and former Guda village chief Sabino Gouveia Leite – were accused of waging a campaign of deadly terror in the Lolotoe area near the border with West Timor in 1999.

The two militia commanders were accused of illegal imprisonment, murder, torture, rape, persecution and inhumane treatment of civilians. They were alleged to have maintained a 'rape house' where three women related to suspected Falintil guerrillas were raped repeatedly from May to July 1999. On 5 April 2003, Cardoso was convicted of murder, torture, imprisonment and other inhuman acts and sentenced to 12 years' imprisonment.

Domestic violence

Domestic violence legislation has been drafted and put before parliament (at the beginning of 2005 it had not yet been passed because it was awaiting the finalisation of East Timor's penal code). East Timorese women see the development of this legislation as a major success, although its implementation will take time to enforce even when it does pass into law.

Another legal initiative which has helped reduce violence is the banning of the sale of local wines along the roadside. Women argued convincingly that alcohol consumption had contributed to the rise in domestic violence since the referendum.

One important problem is pursuing the few prosecutions that are brought to a conclusion. Even if the victim tells the police (and most cases still go unreported[15]) she may relent if she decides the imprisonment and humiliation of her breadwinner are not in her long term interests. A church worker in Viqueque told researchers:

In one case, a wife was beaten by her husband and injured badly. They really needed our help to resolve their situation, but when we were ready to send the case to court, the wife refused and wanted to resolve the situation in a traditional way. She told us that this was because there would be no one to take care of the children or provide support for the family if the man went to jail....[16]

Village communities remain inclined to settle domestic incidents through *adat*, or customary law. In these cases the perpetrator compensates the offended male relatives of the female victim with gifts of livestock or other goods. Sometimes the female victims take the matter to court regardless, because they do not feel that *adat* has compensated them personally for their injury and humiliation.

Research by the IRC revealed that many men regard their wives as possessions because they have paid a bride price, which can be as high as US$1,900.[17] This, coupled with male responses to female insubordination, could be enough to spark beatings. The IRC cites one case of a man who had recently beaten his wife and tried to have her arrested for disobedience. He was horrified to find that the UN civilian police force arrested him instead.

In one particularly notorious case, the Dili District Court decided that health minister Dr Sergio Lobo, indicted on several cases of wife battery, had, for reasons of culture, the right to control the actions of his wife. He was released, placing the victim in danger of repeated attacks.

NGOs, women's organisations, the police, health services and churches have launched a range of initiatives to address domestic violence at district level all over the country. All sectors interviewed by IRC researchers seemed to lack the training and background knowledge to work effectively, and there is clearly a need to improve coordination between them. Church workers in particular seemed at a loss when faced with the needs, and welcomed a group approach. Given that many people first turn to the church for help with their problems, it is encouraging that church workers are frank about their limitations and accept assistance. In Baucau, diocesan training sessions on domestic violence have been organised for *chefes de sucos* (village heads), and the issue is raised during the course of marriage preparation for couples.

Legal redress

The weakness of East Timor's justice system makes it well-nigh impossible for women to obtain appropriate remedies in the formal justice system, for the time being at least. The Judicial System Monitoring Programme (JSMP), an NGO in Dili which monitors the operation of the courts and justice system, has identified some of the problems. The JSMP notes that only a few East Timorese nationals are legally qualified, and few of them are women. Delays in appointing judges have been exacerbated by their long absences to attend training in Portugal, and contracts for international judges have been short term. Despite UNTAET's efforts to support the fledgling justice system, it has proved more difficult than expected for international advisers to transfer their skills. Legislation is sometimes incomplete or inadequate. The judicial sector also suffers from incomplete and inappropriate legislation, a lack of administrative skills and poor planning.[18]

It remains largely unclear how East Timor will harmonise its existing Indonesian-based legal system with international legal norms and treaties, and how customary law, which has regulated local disputes for centuries, will relate to either.

The inexperience of the judiciary was highlighted by the Lobo case (see above), which not only gave the impression that the judiciary condoned domestic violence, but also that government ministers could influence the impartiality of the judges.

For two months in 2003, the JSMP monitored the progress of all cases involving women before Dili District Court.[19] It found that:

- Cases involving women represented the majority (55 per cent) of all criminal hearings scheduled during those two months. In all these cases, the women were victims and not perpetrators.
- Seventy-eight per cent of cases relating to women were serious cases of sexual violence, including multiple rape.
- Despite the frequency of domestic violence complaints received by the UN-established Vulnerable Persons Unit in 2003, not one domestic violence case was scheduled for a court hearing.
- Very little progress was made in any of the cases involving women. Hearings went ahead in only 16 per cent of cases, and very few of those made any progress towards resolution.
- The court reached no decisions in any case involving women.
- In interviews with the JSMP, court officials displayed gender-biased views that could prejudice effective and sensitive handling of the cases.
- The JSMP believed that certain low-cost policy initiatives could improve the treatment of female (and potentially male) victims of violence.

After the JSMP published its report, in May 2004 a judge at Dili District Court delivered a conviction in a case of sexual assault by an adult male against a girl under the age of 15. This was the first such decision by the court and indicates some progress in delivering justice for women. However, the JSMP noted some problems with the process:[20]

- Consistent, unreasonable delays in the court process (in more than 13 months, only two hearings proceeded in which evidence was heard).

- The lack of thorough questioning at all stages of the criminal and court process caused confusion as to what offence had actually occurred.
- The inappropriately high value placed on the medical evidence, as opposed to the testimony of the victim and the accused, appears to have led the prosecutor and judge to charge and convict the accused of a lesser offence.
- Inadequate regard for Section 34.3 of the UNTAET Transitional Rules of Criminal Procedure (Regulation 25/2001).
- Failure to charge and convict the accused with rape because of the limitations of the Indonesian criminal code and lack of awareness of the definition of rape in international law.
- The short sentence imposed did not reflect the seriousness of the crime.

Part of the problem in achieving justice for rape victims is the law itself. Under UNTAET Regulation No 1/1999, Indonesian law applies unless and until either UNTAET or Timorese legislation exists, or Indonesian law contradicts international legal standards.

Article 285 of the Indonesian Penal Code sets out four elements essential to prove rape:

1. the offence occurred with violence or the threat of violence
2. the offender was a man and committed the offence against a woman, without her consent
3. the woman was not the offender's wife
4. the offence involved sexual intercourse.

Sexual indecency under Article 290(2) provides a maximum sentence of seven years for a person who 'commits obscene acts with someone who he knows or should reasonably presume has not yet reached the age of 15 years or, if it is not obvious from her age, is not yet marriageable'.[21] There are no articles that specifically address domestic violence.

These provisions have not yet been replaced by East Timorese laws, although a new penal code is being drafted. Article 152 of the Draft Penal Code of East Timor defines rape as oral, anal and vaginal non-consensual forced sex (including with an object other than the penis), and includes rape of a spouse. Article 153 provides that if the victim was under the age of 16, the accused would be punished with a penalty of three to 12 years, rather than the two to 10 years provided for otherwise. Article 157 provides for a penalty of two to 10 years if sex with a minor was consensual. Article 151 defines sexual coercion and lays down a sentence of one to six years, which Article153 extends to two to eight years if the victim is under the age of 16.

These provisions are more compatible than the Indonesian legislation with the definitions adopted by the International Criminal Court.

Male attitudes

Ending sexual assault and domestic violence requires more than legislation and law enforcement, important though these are. It also requires a shift in attitudes and prejudices that accept violence against women.

A minority of men have benefited from educational opportunities, but most have not. With a few exceptions, the governing rules and customs among East Timor's diverse ethnic groups are patriarchal and East Timorese traditional cultures make a sharp distinction between the expected functions and roles of males and females. Traditionally, the political sphere has been reserved for men, although this has been challenged over the past decade.

There is no such thing as a single East Timorese 'culture', but rather a variety of traditional attitudes, practices and customs which have grown up over the centuries and which differ from region to region. The unifying influence of Portuguese and Indonesian colonialism and the spread of Roman Catholicism have had at least as powerful an influence on the consolidation of patriarchy as traditional indigenous cultural practices.

Efforts to prevent exposure of domestic violence (as well as the successful mobilisation against the quota campaign – see chapter 5) show that traditional attitudes are alive and well. There is a fear of and resistance to feminist ideas. Such attitudes have been reinforced by the Catholic church, which fears that the feminist agenda will destroy families, undermine marriage, and fragment 'culture'.

Some East Timorese priests have been critical of women's organisations such as Fokupers, which has encouraged women to prosecute violent husbands in the law courts rather than relying on traditional conflict resolution methods. The women's organisations have countered that these customs, with their compensation rates measured in head of buffalo, reinforce the image of women as men's property.

'Culture' is frequently cited as a reason why women could not or should not participate in politics, or why it is difficult to press for women's rights in East Timor. In 2001 a CIIR fact-finding team found that men used culture to justify the status quo, as did some women.[22] Older politicians said that they respected women 'even more than men' and that was why women had to be protected from unsuitable environments such as the world of politics. Most seemed to think that it would take a long time to effect cultural change.

The presence, during the transition to independence and beyond, of a large community of expatriates with lifestyles that most East Timorese could only dream of has also fed resentment and frustration.

Some men blame the United Nations for importing 'foreign' feminist ideas. East Timorese women activists have cogently argued against cultural relativism, but resistance and suspicion remain strong. Some East Timorese men have issued ominous threats along the lines of 'Wait until the UN goes, then we will get our power back....'

Inspired by Nicaraguan groups such as Puntos de Encuentro ('common ground/meeting points') which have encouraged men to explore the roots of violence and *machismo* in their social conditioning, an East Timorese men's group, Mane Kontra Violencia, was formed in 2002. Its leader, Marito Araujo, believes that the group has made inroads into changing the opinions of men on gender issues.

Marito Araujo: men against violence

Marito Araujo is one of the founders of Mane Kontra Violencia. He traces his concern for gender issues to his childhood, when his mother struggled to put him through school after his father died:

> One of the things she had to do was to confront our relatives about her inheritance rights. My uncles wanted to deprive her of her share of our family's coffee plantations and she had to fight them to get her share. She won – but she had to battle.

Marito acknowledges that some men feel threatened by talk of women's rights, but he believes that men's attitudes are changing for the better, particularly among the more educated. He attributes this to the new constitution, the efforts of international aid agencies to encourage a focus on gender in development policy and projects, and to East Timorese organisations that work on gender. He is optimistic that further change will come. Mane Kontra Violencia has about 18 active members.

They travel to rural areas to encourage villagers to examine the consequences of violence against women and their exclusion from decision making. They speak first to the head man in the village and win support from the village leaders. In general their efforts have been well received. For example, says Marito:

> Some of them ask us to teach them not to beat their wives. We ask: 'Well, why do you want to beat your wife?' They respond: 'Because I am angry.' Often the anger stems from the bride price paid for the wife, or from the inability to pay a bride price.

This can lead to a discussion of why these customs are established if they cause anger and frustration leading to violence.

Marito estimates that 90 per cent of East Timorese marriages use the *barlaque* bride price system. The way to change it, he believes, is from within families. He himself refunded the bride price paid for his niece. He says:

> It is good for East Timorese to engage other East Timorese in discussions about their local customs. It is up to them to change their culture. In many places the domestic violence legislation has been accepted as well as sanctions for men if they break its rules.

[Interview with Catherine Scott, June 2004]

Notes

1   UNTAET Press Office (2002) 'Fact Sheet II: Gender equality promotion', United Nations Transitional Administration in East Timor, April 2002.

2   See International Alert (2000) *From kitchen table to the negotiating table*, International Alert, London.

3   Pereira, M (2001) 'Domestic violence: A part of women's daily lives in East Timor' in *La'o Hamutuk Bulletin,* Vol 2 No 5, August 2001.

4   Fokupers (1999) *Gender-based human rights abuses during the pre and post-ballot violence in East Timor: Preliminary report, Jan-Oct 1999*, unpublished report, Forum Komunikasi Untuk Perempuan Lorosae, Dili.

5   Fokupers (as above).

6   TKTB (2000) *Violence against IDP/refugee women: Report of TKTB*, Tim Kemanusiaan Timor Barat, Kupang, West Timor, pp7-8.

7   IRC (2002) *Gender based violence: Challenges and ways forward – A report of focus groups in four districts,* International Rescue Committee, Dili.

8   Sideris, T (2001) 'Rape in war and peace' in Meintjes, S, Pillay, A, and Turshen, M (eds) *The aftermath: Women in post-conflict transformation*, Zed Books, London, p152.

9   The regulations for the special panels state that they have universal jurisdiction for genocide, war crimes, crimes against humanity and torture (UNTAET Regulation 2000/15

on the establishment of panels with jurisdiction over serious criminal offences, REG/2000/15, 6 June 2000). The Serious Crimes Unit was set up to conduct investigations and prosecutions of these crimes. Crimes of murder and sexual offences remained under the provisions of the Indonesian Legal Code. (Amnesty International and JSMP (2004) *Justice for Timor-Leste: The way forward*, Amnesty International/Judicial System Monitoring Programme, Dili, p7.)

10 See ICTJ (2003) *Intended to fail: The trials before the ad hoc human rights court in Jakarta*, International Centre for Transitional Justice, New York.

11 Linton, S (2001) 'Rising from the ashes: The creation of a viable criminal justice system in East Timor' in *Melbourne University Law Review* Vol 25.

12 See Martinkus, J (2002) 'Beyond justice' in *The Bulletin*, 11 June 2002.

13 *The General Prosecutor of the United Nations Transitional Administration in East Timor v Leonardus Kasa*, Dili District Court Special Panel for Serious Crimes case number 11/CG/2000, 9.5.01.

14 *The General Prosecutor of the United Nations Transitional Administration in East Timor v João França Da Silva alias Jhoni Franca, José Cardoso Fereira alias Mouzinho and Sabino Gouveia Leite*, Dili District Court Special Panel for Serious Crimes case number 4/CG/2000 ('The Lolotoe trial').

15 In 2003, 361 cases were reported to the police – see JSMP (2005) *Statistics on cases of violence against women in Timor Leste*, Judicial Systems Monitoring Programme, Dili.

16 IRC (see note 7), p43.

17 IRC (see note 7), p31.

18 See JSMP (2004a) *An analysis of a sexual assault decision from the Dili District Court, Dili, East Timor, July 2004,* Judicial Systems Monitoring Programme, Dili, p9. See www.jsmp.minihub.org.

19 JSMP (2004b) *Women in the formal justice sector,* Judicial Systems Monitoring Programme, Dili, p4. See www.jsmp.minihub.org.

20 JSMP (2004a – see note 18), p23.

21 See JSMP (2004a – see note 18).

22 Unpublished report of the CIIR observer mission to the East Timor Constituent Assembly election, 30 August 2001.

Chapter 7
Mozambique: war, peace and women's movements

By Isabel Casimiro, Ximena Andrade and Ruth Jacobson

There are close affinities between the historical experiences of Mozambique and East Timor. This chapter looks at the role and position of women, gender relations, and the development of women's movements in Mozambique from the 1960s to the present.

Historical background

Mozambique's newly independent government was one of the first in the world to recognise the new Democratic Republic of East Timor in 1975. After the Indonesian invasion, it opened its borders to Fretilin (Frente Revolucionária de Timor Leste Independente – Revolutionary Front for an Independent East Timor), and many East Timorese militants continued their resistance struggle while living and studying in Mozambique, including Mari Alkatiri (who became prime minister of East Timor after independence) and Ana Pessoa Pinto (who became minister of justice). In 1988, Ana Pessoa Pinto joined Isabel Casimiro and the lawyers Isabel Chicalia and Noemia Francisco (now a judge of the Mozambican Supreme Court) in founding the Women and Law in Southern Africa research project.[1]

Mozambique has also lived through successive phases of war. The armed struggle for national liberation against Portuguese colonialism began in 1964, led by the Frente de Libertação de Moçambique (Frelimo – Mozambican Liberation Front). This came to an end only with the 'carnation revolution' in Portugal in 1974, which enabled the establishment of a transitional government in Mozambique from 20 September 1974 to 25 June 1975. Having achieved independence for Mozambique, Frelimo converted itself into a one-party government under the leadership of president Samora Machel.

The new government immediately encountered opposition from the Resistência Nacional Moçambicana (Renamo – Mozambican National Resistance), an armed force backed by the apartheid regime of South Africa. This war of destabilisation (referred to by some analysts as the civil war or the struggle for democracy) started practically at the moment of independence in June 1975 and continued until 1992. It came to affect almost the entire country, causing a million deaths, displacing an estimated six million people and destroying the country's economic infrastructure.[2] This second phase of war came to an end with the signing of the Rome Accords between Frelimo and Renamo on 4 October 1992.

So except for a few months, the people of Mozambique lived in a war environment from 1964 to 1992. Although the population did not experience an invasion as in East Timor, the war similarly affected the entire country, and virtually every family, in some way. Unlike East Timor, however, Mozambique also experienced a structural adjustment programme imposed in 1987, at the height of the war.

The Rome Accords opened a new era of peace, supervised by a United Nations (UN) peacekeeping force. Constitutional reform, approved in November 1990 by the National Assembly, opened the way for multi-party government, and presidential and legislative elections followed in October 1994. The peace process in Mozambique is widely considered to be the most successful of all UN operations in the 1990s. The guns fell silent on 4 October 1992 and have remained so, despite the many threats from various dissatisfied former soldiers.[3] The clash of weapons has been replaced by the exchange of words in the National Assembly.

The new Mozambican constitution has established the principle of freedom of association and organisation, the separation of legislative, executive and judicial powers, and free elections (on the western model). It also incorporates the principle of equal rights for women, replacing an earlier version which discriminated against women married to foreign nationals who wanted to pass on their Mozambican nationality to their children. The change was a result of pressure from women representatives in the legislature. The government became a signatory to the Convention on the Elimination of All Forms of Discrimination Against Women (CEDAW) on 16 April 1997, and ratified it without reservations on 16 May 1998. With the revision of the 1990 constitution, approved by the last parliamentary session before the 2004 presidential and legislative elections, women now formally enjoy full citizenship rights for the first time in the country's history

Profile of Mozambique

The population of Mozambique is very diverse, with over a dozen major linguistic groups and more than 150 dialects. More than 200 varieties of religious faith are registered with the government. Most of these are from the established Christian churches but they include Islam and independent African churches. The majority of the population profess to be followers of traditional African religions.

The majority of the population live in rural areas, and approximately 90 per cent of women work in subsistence agriculture. It is women who ensure that the people of the country are fed. The rural population is very widely dispersed, making it difficult to provide basic social services, but there is also severe pressure on the infrastructure of the capital city and the larger towns. The large number of young people creates further pressures on health and education services, and on jobs.

Mozambique stands out among many countries (including those of the west) in the representation of women in the legislature. The proportion of women in parliament in 2004 was 30 per cent, and decision-making posts which are or have been held by women include prime minister, minister of planning and finances, and minister of mineral resources and energy.

However, Mozambican women politicians themselves recognise that this is only part of the picture. In 2002 only 31.4 per cent of the female population over 15 was literate, and the average length of journey to a health post was 30 km. Women continue to experience high rates of maternal mortality (around 403 per 100,000 live births) and infant mortality (125 per 1,000). The fertility rate remains high, with around 5.4 children for each woman of reproductive age.[4]

The colonial inheritance

The impact of Portuguese colonialism remains evident today. The colonial power's drive to accumulate capital led to the creation of three distinct socio-economic regions in Mozambique. The provinces of the south provided labour for mines and farms in neighbouring South Africa and for the capital city of Lourenço Marques (today's Maputo). The central region was dominated by grand plantations and the north by smaller farms, also owned by colonialists.

As elsewhere in sub-Saharan Africa, women were specifically affected by colonialism, particularly the 80 per cent who depended on small-scale agriculture. Colonial policies restructured the economy and introduced forced agricultural labour. As capitalist relationships developed, women's essential work in production became systematically undervalued and they also lost access to land. The combined impact of missionary and colonial forces meant that the western ideological model of the 'male breadwinner, female homemaker' family became dominant, even when it was far from the reality.

Cumulatively, Portuguese colonialism contributed to a shift in gender relations. Large-scale male migration all over the southern African region and the introduction of a monetarised trading system transformed 'work' into 'waged work'. Within the family unit, women's economic contribution came to be systematically undervalued.[5] The division of labour was demarcated more rigidly on the basis of sex and age, and although the concept of reciprocity remained, tensions arose between women and men over the control and distribution of material goods. Historical research shows that the colonial system intensified women's dependency and increased their work burden.[6] This 'overloading' of women with responsibilities was not matched by any investment in social welfare by the Portuguese.

Women's lives and livelihoods in post-conflict Mozambique

Women's lives today are still marked by this colonial inheritance, as well as decades of war and intervention by the international financial institutions, major institutional donors such as the European Union, and international non-governmental organisations (NGOs).

The demobilisation process carried out by the UN provided sufficient incentives in cash and material benefits for ex-combatants to encourage male combatants to return to civilian life. However, the needs of women who had played important supporting roles in the two opposing forces, for example accompanying military commanders into the field, were largely ignored. This marginalisation in part reflects lack of awareness within the UN and the international community. At the beginning of the 1990s, activists in the international community were only beginning to consider gender issues in armed conflict and its aftermath.

The most important local effect on women's lives and livelihoods was the international peacekeeping forces' demand for sexual services, which extended to girls below the legal age of consent.[7]

Women continue to struggle against poverty and insecurity. Although some women have found paid work in administration and services, in general women are concentrated in the worst paid and least secure sectors. They are also more likely to have been dismissed as a result of the impact of structural adjustment programmes. Many more people work in the informal economy than in formal employment, and in the informal sector women are the majority. So although the risk to life from armed conflict is gone and women have the same rights as men, they continue to experience very high rates of day-to-day insecurity. There is also unmistakable discrimination on the basis not only of sex, but also of class and colour.

Thus although women made up 30 per cent of Mozambique's national legislature in 2004 (among the highest proportions of women in parliament in the world and the highest in Africa), this has not resulted in the transformation of political, social and economic life.

Changing roles

Different types of armed conflict – for example national liberation struggles, Cold War-era proxy wars, and resource wars – can affect women in different ways. Nevertheless, in Mozambique, East Timor, and any other country which has lived through armed conflict, it is women, children and the elderly who suffer most directly. Yet the impact on women's lives and the activities they may be forced to take on can constitute important avenues for their liberation, despite the overload of work, pervasive violence and discrimination. With the transformations brought about by African independence in the late 1960s, many women believed in the possibility of a 'new world order' to be achieved through nationalist and armed struggle in their countries.[8]

In contrast to several other national liberation movements,[9] Frelimo saw women's emancipation as a crucial element of revolutionary struggle. It thus attached central importance to the visible participation of women in military, social and cultural activities. Many of the women who took part in the independence movement identified the struggle for national independence as a way to defend their interests as women. This represented a transformation of their political role and status. For the first time, they could operate as citizens. The debate over gender and women's emancipation, moulded by the experience of armed struggle, highlighted the social contradictions in women's role. For example, the armed struggle depended on women transporting arms, provisioning Frelimo's forces and ensuring the support of local communities through their grassroots health and education campaigns. These activities could be interpreted as traditional 'support roles' or as breaking through patriarchal expectations.

Once Frelimo had taken power it established a one-party state on the Leninist model and attempted to replicate the experience of its liberated zones in the rest of the country. Initially this meant mobilising women in an instrumental way, but it did create spaces for women. Its political project was avowedly to construct *O homem novo* – the new (generic) Mozambican person – in a country that was to be transformed from an overwhelming dependence on peasant farming to a state-controlled economy, a mixture of large-scale agricultural production and new industrial sectors. The sphere of personal relations was to be taken over from the churches and transformed through education in schools and through the party's ideological campaigns. The role of indigenous civil society in development was thus extremely constrained.

In this first period, aid took the form of government-to-government agreements for technical aid, the integration of solidarity workers into the state machinery and assistance from a handful of (western) NGOs.

For women, the transformation was to be achieved through a programme which drew on the thesis of Friedrich Engels that gender inequality stemmed from property and production relations, extending from the public to the private domain. Women's transformation was to be achieved by: (1) abolishing the system of private property relations in which women were chattels of their husbands; (2) the entry of women into wage labour, producing goods for general social consumption; and (3) transforming domestic labour into a public industry.

Frelimo's ideological discourse covered the first of these, addressing the entrenched system of bridewealth and polygamy for example. It also stressed the need for women to take part in 'production': one very commonly disseminated image was that of women as tractor drivers on state farms, who were to be role models.[10] The economic reality of women's ceaseless work tilling small family plots, grinding staple foods, carrying water and so on, was not deemed 'productive'. Moreover, discussion of power relationships within the home or of male sexual conduct was out of bounds: it was regarded as a manifestation of undesirable, western-derived feminism.[11]

However, despite these constraints, the discourse of transformation did bring material results. The state was committed to preserving the gains of the armed struggle. Retrospective condemnations of 'non-democratic rule' have failed to take into account the positive outcomes of this phase: much of the improvement in female literacy rates, and in maternal and child health, was due to the dedication and commitment of Frelimo's cadres, female and male. For example, state-led primary health campaigns aimed at reducing infant mortality and promoting birth spacing brought the aim of controlling family size closer.[12] Girls who had enrolled in schools and market women who had benefited from adult literacy campaigns could argue for citizenship and equality.

Interpreting the changes

There were distinct periods in women's experiences of armed conflict and thus it is not possible to give any single evaluation of the changes. The anti-colonial struggle was a historic transformation for women across the African continent. Even though their participation was controlled and sanctioned by men, their entrance into the public sphere in the second half of the 20th century represents a transition from the patriarchal epoch into an era of visibility. Of course, this change was never without controversy, because it involved rethinking other social relations, not only with the men who had taken over the state, but with brothers, husbands, other family members or friends.[13] One problem which remains today is that the majority of women have not yet received recognition for their participation in the national liberation struggle.[14]

During the second phase of armed conflict (late 1970s-1992), the potential for transformation was closed down. As destabilisation took hold, the hopes of the earlier period were dashed and sheer survival became the priority. Ideas about socio-economic progress gave way to the demands of humanitarian crisis. The forms of gender-based violence during this phase are all too familiar from other wars: massive displacement and loss of livelihood, widespread sexual violence against women, forcible recruitment of male and female adults and children by both sides,[15] and psychological torture of young boys as a way to enforce obedience.[16]

For the great majority of women, the demands of day-to-day survival took precedence over any form of strategic organising during this phase. Many women found themselves heading their households, and thus acquired new roles and responsibilities.

It was only after the 1992 cease-fire was consolidated by the 1994 elections that women could turn their full attention to the possibility of living in peace. Of course, virtually all Mozambican women – and men – welcomed the end of armed conflict. They then enthusiastically started on the process of 'national reconstruction' – often literally, by rebuilding destroyed houses. Despite the traumatic losses suffered by families across the country, there has been a remarkable restoration of the social fabric. There was a marked emphasis (among women and men) on 'letting the past be the past'. However, one outcome was that women's gendered experience of armed conflict was once again obscured, this time in the interests of national reconciliation.

Trajectories of change: the Organização da Mulher Moçambicana

During the liberation struggle and the first post-independence phase, the only 'official' national women's organisation was the Organização da Mulher Moçambicana (OMM – Organisation of Mozambican Women). It was created in 1973, in Tunduru, Tanzania, during the armed struggle for national liberation, as a 'mass democratic organisation'. Its task was to mobilise and organise all Mozambican women to fight for national independence, through the emancipation of the working class and the liberation of women.

After Frelimo's rebirth as a Marxist-Leninist party in 1977, OMM's Third Conference defined its principal objective as 'the principle of women's emancipation, as defined by the Frelimo party and consecrated in the Constitution'.[17] At that point, the conference considered that the best way to create the conditions for women's emancipation in rural areas was through communal villages and cooperatives.

Although the OMM was the most active and creative of the mass movements of the post-independence period, it was beset by contradictions. Some of these were linked to the liberation struggle, others to the necessity of working within the infrastructure inherited from the colonial state. It was difficult to operate as an 'umbrella' organisation for women while at the same time being a Party organisation. The OMM's programme also failed to take into account that women are not a homogenous group, and that they have different interests which change over time.

In the early 1980s Mozambique had few people with the training and experience to prepare and implement strategies to improve women's situation, and decision makers held stereotypes that consigned women to a secondary position. The OMM began to lose the initiative.

Despite these tensions, between 1982 and 1984 the OMM undertook a ground-breaking national study of economic, social and political conditions in preparation for its Fourth Extraordinary Conference. The study recognised that Mozambican society as a whole was concerned about the transformations that had taken place: older people felt that they had lost control over the youth, men were worried about the prospects that had opened up for their wives and families, and there was a general sense that the revolution had led to a vacuum, without supplying credible alternatives. The study identified a wide range of issues of concern to women: family relationships, initiation rituals, premature and forced marriages, inheritance by widows and ceremonies of widowhood, adultery and *amantismo* (having multiple sexual partners) among men, divorce, separation and abandonment of families, bridewealth (*lobolo*), matrimonial compensation, polygamy, single mothers, prostitution, and women in production (as peasants, cooperative farmers, government officials, market sellers, housewives or industrial workers).

After the conference, debate continued on some of these topics, but the economic and political instability caused by the war prevented the OMM from taking them further. Instead, the principal activity of the 1980s was the creation of 'Circles of Interest' – places to meet and learn, dependent on the voluntary labour of women.

In the late 1980s and the 1990s political changes allowed the emergence, or re-emergence, of a range of organisations. Although the OMM remained the only women's organisation with a national base, it had to live with a diversity of women's organisations, often created by its former members. In 1990, when the new constitution introduced a multi-party system, the OMM had to change its own status. Initially, it declared itself to be a non-party, autonomous organisation and open to all. It could therefore be defined as an NGO. The 'Circles of Interest' continued, with 35 spread over the country offering training courses in English, leadership, democracy, information technology, family planning and sexually transmitted diseases, among other things. However, it was generally thought the OMM had lost its direction and was living too much in the past, unable to adjust to its new situation. Moreover, the organisation was encountering major difficulties in funding its activities.

In 1996 the OMM claimed a membership of 1,774,379. The members were of all ages, and although most of them lack formal education, many have gained some qualifications thanks to the OMM's programme over the past 25 years.

In June 1996, at the OMM's first Congress, the delegates voted to return to being a party organisation. Contrary to expectations, transformation into an NGO had not increased the number of members, and some felt the organisation was at risk of losing its history as part of Frelimo's armed struggle.

The obvious question this raises is, will the OMM be able to guarantee its independence as an organisation that fights for women's emancipation, now that it is a women's group within a political party?

Women's movements today

It is problematic to refer to 'the' women's movement in Mozambique, given the diversity of objectives of the wide range of women's organisations. In Mozambique (and East Timor) the majority of women's associations do not consider themselves to be 'feminist', whatever their actual practice. Despite this qualification, they share certain overarching characteristics:

- a substantial growth in the number and visibility of women's groups that have been influenced by the global feminist movement
- a (belated) recognition of the importance of traditional women's organisations
- the recognition that everyone has an 'identity' made up of multiple elements, some of them in conflict, which are in a constant process of transformation[18] so that women often experience conflict within themselves, as well as with powerful external forces
- a reconceptualisation of women's bodies, not just as physical entities, but as having psychological, discursive and political dimensions. If women are in a position to control their own bodies, this establishes the conditions for their liberation. But it is on women's bodies that male power can be exercised most dramatically through rape and other forms of violence
- a revaluing of the meaning of democracy, calling attention to the diverse ways in which women's participation can be realised
- a movement towards politicisation of daily life, for example greater willingness to look at inter-family relationships, including male violence against women and children.

During the 1990s, women's groups also moved into the legislative sphere, using the multi-party system and drawing on developments in the international community. For example, the processes leading to the Fourth World Conference on Women in 1995 and the ensuing Platform for Action gave activists access to international resources and legitimacy which had previously been denied them in the name of 'traditional' gender relations. As a result, in the early post-conflict period, women political representatives (including those from the parties formerly at war) could work with Mozambican women lawyers and international advocacy groups against proposed legislation on land and property. Thus women and their organisations were active participants in the Land Campaign, in which about 100 diverse associations lobbied political and legislative bodies against privatisation and for protecting the rights of women – and men – to land.

The proposed legislation would have threatened women's access to land, and excluded the women's farming cooperatives that had been established in the 1980s. These cooperatives produced fruit and vegetables for the urban market, and were a mainstay for women heads of household, especially those who had fled from rural areas, or had been widowed or abandoned. As a result of the campaign, the final legislation was amended to incorporate at least some safeguards for women.

Another facet of the women's movement in Mozambique is the so-called traditional or 'endogenous' groups. Based on cooperation, they also have an important role in defending not only women's rights, but the entire community.[19] Colonialism and urbanisation had combined to devalue associations where membership is based on birthplace, age, sex, parenthood or territorial affiliation, rather than personal choice. In traditional African society, the members of these groups played a central part in agriculture and also had political and social functions. In some societies they ensured the fulfilment of obligations and social norms, and were central to a sense of cohesion among women. As a result, it is still possible today in Mozambique to see a 'women's culture' in traditional ceremonies invoking the spirits of ancestors, the knowledge of healing plants, and postpartum and female initiation rituals.

Traditional women's groups

A living women's culture is visible in Mozambique in the traditional ceremonies that evoke the ancestors and the ancestral spirits, in the knowledge and practices of women healers, and in women's knowledge as a whole. They know which plants can be eaten in difficult times, which have medicinal powers, which to use in various ceremonies and rituals. Another example of this culture is the dance groups called *tufo*, found in the northern provinces of Cabo Delgado and Nampula, and in some neighbourhoods of Maputo. These groups are linked to the Muslim faith.

In Nampula province, a ceremony called *mukeya* is presided over by the *pwyamwene*, a traditional female authority-holder, normally the sister of the *mwene* or chief. The ceremony invokes the ancestors and seeks their protection in family affairs and for the community as a whole.

All these ceremonies and practices are associated with a feminine culture that emphasises the relationship between the physical body and the soul, the living and the dead, the individual and the community. It contrasts with the notion of development 'transferred' through project-based activities which emphasise only the physical body, the living population and the individual. This form of development has resulted in a gradual destruction of the feminine culture.

The sheer existence of women's organisations is evidence that Mozambican women never passively accepted discrimination and injustice. However, the majority of women continue to suffer disadvantages in employment, education, health, access to justice and political representation, and they are absent from the most important areas of decision making.

Mozambican feminists feel that, although the violence of armed conflict has ended, violence against women in all spheres of post-conflict life has not only continued, but has acquired new dimensions. The phenomenon has become more visible as a result of the activism of women's organisations. Such violence continues regardless of the end of armed conflict because at its root are gendered relationships of unequal power, combined with unprecedented levels of poverty and unemployment. These are in turn associated with the armed conflicts that have raged since 1964, with the colonial inheritance and with a model of 'development' based on a fundamental inequality which affects women much more than men.[20]

This intensifying violence is inextricably linked to the impact of neoliberalism: for example, the effect of the structural adjustment programme was to halt and in some cases reverse the advances made in primary health during the 1970s.[21] Although economic restructuring was accompanied by a formal democratic transition, institutional authoritarianism remains pervasive. In this climate, the vision of equality and full citizenship has come under intense pressure, for men as well as women.

Domestic forces

The role of domestic actors cannot be considered in isolation from the external forces which imposed a neoliberal economic model on Mozambique. This imposition took place in the 1980s, before the transition from war to peace.[22] Fifteen years of destabilisation left the country one of the poorest in the world, in a state of social and economic crisis. So 'women's participation' came to mean their status as being poor and having urgent basic needs, rather than their human rights as citizens. To an extent, the effects of the war opened up some political spaces for women at community level and at the intermediate leadership level, but they remained excluded from all major national decision making. At the same time, the version of democracy that was imposed along with neoliberalism disrupted the identities that women had been creating in their communities and replaced them with the anonymous process of voting in a male-dominated system.

Neoliberalism in Mozambique, as elsewhere, has translated into an attack on the state. Thus the second period of armed conflict saw a marked decline in the capacity of the government to meet the needs of its citizens.[23] As a result, by 1992 other domestic forces had taken on important roles. But none of them were able to resolve the huge infrastructural problems affecting rural life – for example the reconstruction of a commercial system of feeder roads. The resulting growth in unemployment, disintegration of family structure and persistent inflation are all obstacles to the achievement of gender equity.

Civil society and women's organisations

NGOs and social networks proliferated from the mid-1980s onwards. They included youth and student groups, socio-professional associations, faith-based groups and human rights organisations. Women's voluntary associations included the Mozambican Association for the Development of the Family (Amodefa), the association of businesswomen and executives (Activa) and the rural development organisation AMRU. These organisations concerned themselves with aspects of women's lives arising from the sexual division of labour, social and power relationships, or women's reproductive health. Muleide, the first organisation for women's human rights, was started in 1991.

The first women's umbrella organisation, Forum Mulher (Woman's Forum) was set up in 1993 and given legal status in 1994. Forum Mulher is a network of organisations including women's sections of political parties, state and research institutions, trade unions, national and international donors, and external NGOs. All work on behalf of Mozambican women or help them participate in the nation's political, social, economic and cultural life. In 2004, Forum Mulher had 61 member organisations, of which 48 per cent were NGOs, 25 per cent were state institutions, 16 per cent were international development organisations and 11 per cent were international NGOs. It is run by a female executive director supported by a directing council of five representatives of member organisations, elected for a period of three years. The president of the council must be a woman, but the other members can be female or male.

Forum Mulher is important as a motive force and a space for debating fundamental national questions related to women. After the first multi-party elections in 1994, it led the debate on a state mechanism to address women's issues. It also put pressure on the political parties to select women for positions of power. It led the participation of Mozambican civil society in the Fourth UN Conference on Women in Beijing and played a key role in advocacy for revision of the land law and, more recently, of family law. It has helped train women to build provincial networks and worked with the government to elaborate a national gender strategy. It has also helped formulate legislation against domestic violence. Despite these achievements and Forum Mulher's best endeavours, however, it has had difficulty in maintaining a high level of participation from such a wide range of member organisations.

Post-war civil society organisations have operated on the basis of liberal politics, for example extending periods of maternity leave, creating creches and infant schools, and campaigning for equal pay, laws against sexual harassment, and improvements in health, education and justice. However, few organisations have demonstrated the capacity to sustain themselves, so many depend on external donors.

Political parties
When it comes to promoting women's interests, Frelimo is the most progressive party, both in theory and in terms of putting women in positions of political power.[24] In contrast, the major opposition party, Renamo, emphasises the family role of women and until 2004 has had a significantly lower percentage of women representatives.

Faith-based groups
The Catholic church is not the single dominant faith in Mozambique as it is in East Timor. In 1992, 195 religious groups were registered with the Ministry of Justice, and this had grown to about 300 by 1995. Among the most notable are the Islamic Congress of Mozambique and the Christian Council of Mozambique which encompasses 22 Protestant faith communities. Faith groups have taken part in advocacy on land and are contributing to various anti-poverty campaigns, such as the G20.[25]

A substantial proportion of women invest their time and energy in these groups. Some of their activities are specific to their faith, for example weekly prayer groups, but many others are community based. Women have actively supported campaigns against the hoarding of weapons from the war, the arms control campaigns, and the Tools into Ploughshares programme. Almost all religious groupings have women's organisations that educate children, instruct couples intending to marry, participate in campaigns to prevent or treat illness (increasingly HIV and AIDS), and attempt conflict resolution.

1: *An East Timorese woman in traditional dress (photo Irena Cristalis)*

2: Olandina Caeiro (photo Irena Cristalis)
3: Maria Domingas Fernandes (photo Irena Cristalis)
4: Teresa Carvalho (photo Irena Cristalis)
5: Ivete de Oliveira (photo Irena Cristalis)
6: Milena Pires (centre, answering media questions following the loss
   of the vote on quotas for women candidates in the Constituent
   Assembly elections, February 2001) (photo Catherine Scott)

7: *Laura Abrantes and Maria Dias (photo Catherine Scott)*
8: *Maria Lourdes Martins Cruz (Mana Lou) (photo Irena Cristalis)*
9: *Mana Bisoi (photo Irena Cristalis)*
10: *Mana Bisoi pictured with her uncle, Falintil resistance army
    commander L-Foho Rai Boot (photo Irena Cristalis)*
11: *Falintil women sewing insignias onto uniforms at the guerrilla
    training camp in Waimori, 1999 (photo Irena Cristalis)*

12: *A Falintil family (photo Irena Cristalis)*
13: *A woman in the Falintil resistance army with her child (photo Irena Cristalis)*
14: *Falintil women working as nurses, sitting in front of a makeshift clinic at the guerrilla training camp in Waimori, 1999 (photo Irena Cristalis)*
15: *Young women members of Renetil singing the Falintil song at the 24th anniversary celebrations of Falintil at the guerrilla training camp in Waimori, 1999 (photo Irena Cristalis)*
16: *East Timorese student activists in Semarang, Java, Indonesia, demonstrating in 1998 in support of independence for East Timor (photo Irena Cristalis)*

17

18

19

17: *Women at a remembrance ceremony in 1998 for victims of the 1991 Santa Cruz massacre (when Indonesian troops opened fire on a peaceful demonstration in Dili, killing more than 270 East Timorese) (photo Irena Cristalis)*

18: *Widows at a mass in commemoration of the victims of a massacre by a pro-Indonesian militia group at the Catholic church in Liquiça in April 1999 (photo Irena Cristalis)*

19: *Women collecting tin sheets to use to make shelters following the destruction by the Indonesian military and militias after the referendum in August 1999 (photo Irena Cristalis)*

20: *A woman holds a picture of Fr Hilario Madeira during a memorial service held in Dili in 1999. Fr Hilario was one of three priests killed in a massacre at Suai church in September 1999 (photo Irena Cristalis)*

21: *Two generations join together to oppose violence against women at a demonstration organised by Fokupers and other organisations in Dili, November 1999 (photo Irena Cristalis)*

22: *Women at the demonstration against violence, Dili, November 1999 (photo Irena Cristalis)*

23: *Men prepare to join a march against violence against women on International Women's Day in March 2001 (photo Catherine Scott)*

24: *Women at a Fretilin rally in 2001 (photo Irena Cristalis)*

25: *A debate between women candidates in the run-up to the Constituent Assembly elections in 2001 (photo Irena Cristalis)*

26: *Olandina Caeiro addressing a rally prior to the Constituent Assembly elections, flanked by (left) Maria Domingas Fernandes and (right) Teresa Carvalho (photo Irena Cristalis)*

27

28

29

27: *Appolonia da Costa, one of two independent women candidates in the district of Oecusse (photo Irena Cristalis)*
28: *A young supporter of Olandina Caeiro (photo Irena Cristalis)*
29: *A young supporter of Maria Domingas Fernandes (photo Irena Cristalis)*
30: *Women in Lequidoe queuing to vote in the Constituent Assembly elections (photo Irena Cristalis)*
31: *Women in Lequidoe queuing to vote in the Constituent Assembly elections (photo Irena Cristalis)*

32

33

34

32: *Fretilin supporters the night of independence, 20 May 2002 (photo Irena Cristalis)*

33: *A woman holding a statue of Jesus (photo Irena Cristalis)*

34: *The procession for Our Lady of Fatima in Dili, 1999 (photo Irena Cristalis)*

35: *Children in traditional costume welcoming Bishop Basilio do Nascimento to a remote mountain village (photo Irena Cristalis)*

36: *A primary school in Aileu, 1999 (photo Irena Cristalis)*

37: *A woman weaving at a project in Dili run by the Organização da Mulher Timorense (photo Irena Cristalis)*

38: *A woman in Ermera district picking coffee beans (photo Irena Cristalis)*

The role of the international community

The impact of international institutions on women's lives has been unmistakeable. In 1989 there were 180 non-Mozambican agencies operating in Mozambique, providing US$78 million to the emergency relief effort. After the Rome Accords this grew considerably. By 1997 there were 204 overseas organisations, with 60 agencies operating in the health sector alone.[26] Their impact was mixed. For example, the international community provided funds for the demobilisation process at a level which has not been matched in any subsequent conflict in Africa, yet the needs of women combatants and soldiers' dependants were largely ignored.[27] Only recently has international attention been drawn to this kind of gender discrimination in peacekeeping.[28]

Donor institutions have also proved reluctant to implement their own mandates with regard to gender. Major infrastructural rehabilitation projects such as the Feeder Road Programme, funded by various western governments, had a nominal commitment that 25 per cent of the labour force would be female, but achieved only 14 per cent. Evaluation reports note that recruitment was carried out by word of mouth, with women being discouraged from applying for jobs for which they would be well qualified.[29]

The western-based international NGOs working in Mozambique have ranged from very large development organisations such as Oxfam and World Vision to much smaller ones working on a single issue such as child soldiers. From 1994 onwards, the international NGOs gradually shifted their priorities to development, while the number of Mozambican NGOs committed to rebuilding their country's social fabric grew rapidly. The two groups have also worked together on environmental concerns and gender relations, including the needs of rural women, and publicly raised the issue of violence against women. This means that the impact of the international community has been crucial in enabling the global shifts in the gender debate to be reflected in Mozambique. The long term economic effects of wartime destruction and the impact of neoliberalism, however, have made the relationship between international and domestic actors complex. Genuine efforts at partnership co-exist with conditionality and dependence.

Conclusions

Mozambican women have acted in a variety of ways to alter unequal gender relations and have achieved positive outcomes, although several challenges remain. The most obvious is the impact of armed conflict, which deprived women of the opportunity to engage with the post-independence programme of socialist modernisation. It is possible, however, to assume that even without the impact of war, women would have confronted major difficulties.

The current, post-conflict phase has facilitated alternative or more emancipatory institutions of power, and the possibility of a more participative citizenship. However, conflict has also been followed throughout southern Africa by the rise of international criminal syndicates engaged in arms and drugs trafficking, and sex tourism.

From the early days of the liberation struggle, women's organisations in Mozambique have included men. Thus although women realise the patriarchal, androcentric and eurocentric nature of contemporary citizenship, they are trying to create a new environment in which the biological differences will become politically irrelevant.

In Mozambique in early 2005,[30] people are raising their voices against the sharpening of social inequalities and the polarisation of income, against war, corruption, lack of transparency, the ecological crisis, discrimination based on sex, skin colour, religion and ethnic group. There are calls for justice and equality, for greater material well-being, more democratic freedoms, more information, equality of opportunity and rights for all women and all men. A struggle is being fought for the right to a human and dignified existence.

In this part of Africa, the individualism of the neoliberal project has not yet completely corroded individual and collective relations between citizens. Forms of solidarity, mutual aid and passive resistance persist, often silently protected and preserved by women.

Over the years women's organisations have produced knowledge based on research, held dialogues with various sectors of society, worked to improve people's living conditions, addressed problems and confronted taboos. Expressions of solidarity have arisen, as have possibilities and spaces for work, study and reflection, for dialogue and for a new descriptive language. Above all, there is new awareness and new social practices which amount to expressions of the active citizenship of Mozambican women. Increasingly women are beginning to drop their fear of being subversive. They are continuing their work of building alternatives to political patterns of exclusion, and declaring that they too have a right to citizenship.

Notes

1   Between 1999 and 2001, Women and Law in Southern Africa researched formal and customary systems affecting women, looking at maintenance rights; inheritance and succession; families in the context of change; administration of justice; violence against women; women in parliament.

2   Of a population estimated at between 12 and 15 million in the mid-1980s, one million died as a result of the war and the ensuing destruction of health services; more than four million were displaced inside the country; and nearly two million fled to neighbouring countries. See Hanlon, J (1986) *Beggar your neighbours: Apartheid power in Southern Africa*, James Currey and Indiana University Press.

3   Recent research by one of the authors revealed that there are still soldiers who have not been demobilised. This is the case with some women from the *Destacamento Feminino* (Women's Brigade) of Renamo. Some weapons also remain hidden. (Isabel Casimiro, interviews with Jacinta Jorge, coordinator of the organisation PROPAZ and former officer in the government forces, and with Flora Alberto Ngoma, former member of the Women's Brigade, 12 January 2005.)

4   Sources: UNDP (2001) *Mozambique: Gender, women and human development – an agenda for the future*, United Nations Development Programme; INE (1998) *II recenseamento geral da população 1997: Resultados definitivos*, Instituto Nacional de Estatística, Maputo; INE (2001) *Questionário de indicadores básicos de bem-estar*, Instituto Nacional de Estatística, Maputo; INE (no date) *Projecções anuais da população por província e àrea de residência, 1997-2010*, Instituto Nacional de Estatística, Maputo; INE (2000) *Mulheres e homens em Moçambique*, Instituto Nacional de Estatística, Maputo.

5   See Hay, M, and Stichter, S (eds) (1995) *African women south of the Sahara*, Longman, London, 2nd edition, pp164-186.

6   See Mafeje, A (1992) 'Agregados e perspectivas de relançamento da agricultura na África ao sul do Sahara' in CODESRIA *Ciências sociais em África: Alguns projectos de investigação*, CODESRIA, Dakar, pp231-281.

7   See Jacobson, R (2005) 'Gender, war and peace in Mozambique and Angola: Advances and absences' in Mazurana, D, Raven-Roberts, A, and Parpart, J (eds) *Gender, conflict and peacekeeping*, Rowman and Littlefield, Oxford.

8   See Jirira, K (1995) 'Our struggle ourselves: Shaping feminist theory in our context – The Zimbabwe scenario' in *SAFERE* (Southern African Feminist Review), *The gendered politics of land*, Vol 1 No 1, SAPES Books, Harare, pp77-8.

9   See Mama, A (1995) 'Feminism or femocracy? State feminism and democratisation in Nigeria' in *Afrique et Développement*, Vol XX No 1, CODESRIA, Dakar, pp37-58; Gaidzanwa, R (1992) 'Bourgeois theories of gender and feminism and their shortcomings with reference to southern African countries' in Meena, R (ed) *Gender in southern Africa: Conceptual and theoretical issues*, SAPES Books, Harare, pp92-125.

10 Urdang, S (1988) *And still they dance: Women, war and the struggle for change in Mozambique*, Earthscan, London.

11 Jacobson, R (see note 7).

12 See Cliff, J, Kanji, N, and Muller, M (1986) 'Mozambican health holding the line' in *Review of African Political Economy*, Vol 13 No 36, Summer 1986, pp7-23.

13 See McFadden, P (1997a) 'Challenges and prospects for the African women's movement into the 21st century: Workshop on feminist theory and practice in Africa' in *Report of the First African Women's Leadership Institute*, AWLI, Kampala, pp26-34, 43-49; McFadden, P (1997b) 'Culture and sexual harassment' in *SAPEM*, Sept 15-Oct 15, pp27-29.

14 McFadden, P (1997a – see above), pp26-27.

15 For example, a girl of 11 was captured and raped, and by the age of 12 she had become a member of Renamo's Women's Brigade (authors' interviews, see note 3).

16 See Gersony, R (1988) *Summary of Mozambican refugee accounts of principally conflict-related experience in Mozambique*, US State Department, Washington; Jeichande, I (1990) *Relatório da consultoria OMM-Unicef sobre mulheres deslocadas em Moçambique*, Unicef, Maputo.

17 Casimiro, I (2004) *'Paz na terra, guerra em casa': Feminismo e organizações de mulheres em Moçambique*, Editora PROMÉDIA, Maputo.

18 For example, both Mozambican authors of this chapter are women, mothers, wives, feminists, teachers and researchers, activists, members of political parties and so on. One of us has been a deputy in the Assembly of the Mozambican Republic, while the other was originally from Chile and is now a Mozambican.

19 Wipper, A (1995) 'Women's voluntary associations' in Hay, M, and Stichter, S (eds) *African women south of the Sahara* (see note 5), pp164-186.

20 Elson, D (1997) 'Gender analysis and economics in the context of Africa' in Ayesha, I, Mama, A, and Sow, F (eds) *Engendering African social sciences*, CODESRIA, Dakar.

21 Hanlon, J (1986 – see note 2).

22 Hanlon argues that the objective of the international financial institutions operating in Mozambique was to demonstrate the necessity of following the 'free market' path without question, regardless of local conditions. See Hanlon, J (1996) *Peace without profit: How the IMF blocks rebuilding in Mozambique*, Irish Mozambique Solidarity and International African Institute in association with James Currey and Heinemann.

23 See Hanlon, J (1996), as above.

24 The presidential and legislative elections of December 2004 saw the same number of Frelimo women returned as in previous years, and in early 2005 women replaced men in key ministries, including foreign affairs and labour.

25 The G20 includes the Episcopal Conference of Mozambique, the Islamic Council of Mozambique, the Christian Council of Mozambique, along with trade union, business and commercial associations and a range of national NGOs including Forum Mulher.

26 Hanlon (1996 – see note 22), p3.

27 Most women combatants were not demobilised in accordance with the positions they achieved in the war. These women soldiers complain that even their demobilisation 'kits' of clothing were put together to meet only the needs of men (interviews with Isabel Casimiro).

28 See Mazurana, D, Raven-Roberts, A, and Parpart, J (eds) (2005 – see note 7).

29 See, for example, Baden, S (1997) *Post-conflict Mozambique: Women's special situation, population issues and gender perspectives to be integrated into skills training and employment promotion*, Training Policies and Systems Branch, International Labour Organisation, Geneva.

30 These reflections are based on two papers by Isabel Casimiro: 'Are women citizens?' in *Agora*, No 8, February 2001, Maputo, pp36-37; and 'Feminism and women's human rights' in *Boletim Outras Vozes*, No 3, English language supplement, Maputo, July 2003, pp26-28.

Chapter 8
Namibia: liberation, politics and women's rights

By Caroline Roseveare

The experience of women in the new Namibia and even newer East Timor is remarkably similar in many respects, even though they are separated by vast geographical distance and have been influenced by different cultural and political forces. Their shared heritage includes deep-rooted paternalism, authoritarianism and military occupation, diversity exploited to 'divide and rule', and widespread, almost routine impunity for human rights abuse. This chapter looks at the development of the women's movement in Namibia, and the challenges that confront it today.

Historical background

Namibia's population of around two million people is spread across a land area the size of western Europe. It is one of the wealthiest countries in Africa, with abundant deposits of minerals, fertile coastal fishing grounds and abundant ranching land for stock-raising.

At independence in 1990, however, Namibia exported most of what was produced locally and imported most of what it consumed. In addition, it had one of the most unequal distributions of income and wealth in the world. The majority of black Namibians lived in poverty with most women confined to ethnically based 'tribal homelands', or to black and 'coloured' urban locations. Under the policy of apartheid adopted by South Africa with increased fervour from 1948, separate schools and health facilities were created and access to superior services was reserved for the white settlers and the predominantly white business elite.

First colonised by Germany, Namibia (then known as South West Africa) was surrendered to South African troops following the outbreak of World War One. In 1920 South Africa was mandated by the League of Nations to 'promote to the utmost the material and moral well-being and the social progress of the inhabitants of the territory'.[1] But in 1945, when the United Nations (UN) took over trusteeship of League of Nations mandated territories, South Africa refused to relinquish control.

Initially the South West African People's Organisation (SWAPO), founded in 1960, relied on diplomatic pressure in the effort to achieve political independence and sovereignty. This strategy was complemented from 1966 by armed struggle launched by the People's Liberation Army of Namibia (PLAN).

In 1971 the International Court of Justice declared South Africa's occupation illegal and in 1973 the UN recognised SWAPO as the 'sole and authentic representative of the Namibian people'. UN Security Council Resolution 435 of 1978 specified the terms under which Namibia was to gain independence through UN-supervised free and fair elections. However, as in East Timor, it took more than a decade for the aspirations endorsed by Resolution 435 to become a reality.

South Africa was bent on establishing alternative administrations in Namibia. Its first attempt collapsed in disarray in 1983, but the Multi-Party Conference was unilaterally installed in its place in 1985. SWAPO was to remain excluded from the internal political process until 1989, despite UN efforts to make South Africa comply with the terms of its mandate and the imposition of international sanctions and trade boycotts.

The impact of war on women

Namibia's 24-year liberation war caused untold hardship and suffering and forced many thousands of Namibians into exile in neighbouring countries.[2] A majority of the exiles lived in 'health and education settlements', run by SWAPO and funded through massive international aid, in Angola and Zambia. The armed struggle was waged from bases in Angola. Although the party portrayed women as 'freedom fighters', relatively few women were engaged in direct combat. The majority remained in the settlements where they bore the main responsibility for childcare and day-to-day camp maintenance.

At the peak of the illegal occupation Namibia, just like East Timor, was heavily militarised with large numbers of troops on the ground. It was estimated that there was one armed soldier for every five men, women and children, making it one of the most highly militarised territories in the world. Conscription coupled with internal and regional recruitment drives by the South African Defence Force meant that the military machine in Namibia increasingly assumed a 'black face', and an almost totally male one.[3] On both sides, the armed struggle epitomised militarised masculinity with little direct participation by women. Their roles in the South African military machine were, as in SWAPO, confined largely to support services, such as health, telecommunications, reconnaissance and lower-level administration.

The impact of war for men and women was very different, and women were harassed and sexually abused by male combatants on both sides. The South African security forces, including ethnic battalions, paramilitary police units and the counter-insurgency *Koevoet* ('crowbar' in Afrikaans), were responsible for widespread violence and abuse, targeting civilians with impunity. The brunt of this was felt by communities in the operational military zone, where a majority of female-headed households supported large numbers of dependants because of the contract labour system and the drain of younger men into exile.

Often it was the black soldiers of the security forces who were the most visible in the terror campaigns, as a woman living near the Angolan border described in 1983:

> Often soldiers from the Ovambo battalion come to the women in their gardens posing as SWAPO fighters. They tell us: 'We are hungry, please give us food.' Unless we know who they really are what can we do? We don't want to see our children starving. This happens many times and our people, especially the women, suffer for it. We are learning to be more careful, to know whom we should help and whom not, but we still make mistakes sometimes.[4]

Incidents of rape and sexual harassment were widespread, as another woman who had herself been the victim of such an attack said:

> Since 1979 incidents of sexual harassment and the rape of young women by the South African soldiers have increased dramatically. If people report these things to the police or the military, they have to live with the fear that they will be murdered.[5]

According to Amnesty International, 'The security forces had virtually unlimited powers of arrest and detention: people were held without charge, often in secret, torture was routinely used and many prisoners died or were deliberately killed.'[6] Female nurses were particularly vulnerable to detention without trial because of their ready access to medical supplies. One young nurse who was arrested while on night duty and accused of giving medical supplies to PLAN shared the painful details of her arrest, interrogation and torture. She was three months pregnant at the time. She recounted that after extensive sessions of torture and interrogation:

> I bled for eight days alone in my cell.... On the ninth day they came and took me to the army doctor.... From there I was taken back to my cell where I stayed for a further six days without treatment. On the seventh day the police came to fetch me again for more torture. I was tied upside down with my feet in rubber stirrups.... The following day they took me to make a statement and forced me to sign a paper saying that I had done this and that, and that I supported SWAPO.[7]

On release from detention these women were prime targets for future arrests. One urban woman activist said that she was detained three times: 'In 1978 I was detained for three weeks at Otavi army camp, two weeks in Gobabis prison and then a further four months in Gobabis.'[8] Labelled 'SWAPO terrorists', these women also suffered loss of income because they were unable to secure paid jobs.

Namibia's national liberation movement led by SWAPO also meted out its share of violence to people who came under suspicion of collaborating with 'the enemy'. According to Amnesty International, SWAPO in exile had:

> ... [a] security service headed by the Deputy Commander of PLAN, [which] was responsible for the arrest of increasing numbers of SWAPO members who were suspected of spying for South Africa. Prisoners were tortured and forced to incriminate themselves and their friends or acquaintances. A number reportedly died as a result of torture or harsh conditions of detention and the fate of many others remains unknown.[9]

The SWAPO detainees are thought to have included much larger numbers of women than those detained by the South African regime. As one report stated:

> Women are said by some interviewees to have made up as much as 40 per cent of the detainees. The women were kept in the same camps as men, but in separate dungeons. One female detainee interviewed spoke of being detained with about 100 other women at a base with three dungeons, each accommodating about 38 women and 18 to 20 children aged between eight months and three years ... some were said to have been sexually abused.[10]

In 1987, after an Amnesty International report was published, SWAPO gave the UN High Commissioner for Refugees access to some of its camps. A full investigation was prevented, however, by the signing of the Geneva Peace Accord in December 1988, which paved the way for a cease-fire and Namibia's transition to independence. Under the UN Independence Plan, in May 1989 SWAPO announced the release of 201 detainees from its military bases in Angola. Some months later, following their repatriation to Namibia, the Commission on Justice and Peace of the Catholic church issued its first public statement acknowledging the abuse the detainees had suffered and calling for national reconciliation. Hitherto even the churches had made no public response to the persistent allegations that women, organised in the Parents Committee, had made about the ill-treatment of their exiled children.[11] Some months later the South African authorities released all uncharged detainees whose arrest had been acknowledged.

It is not known how many Namibians 'disappeared' while in the custody of the South African Defence Force and many questions continue to surround the fate of people known to have been detained by SWAPO who never returned to Namibia. In September 1989 a delegation of officials appointed by the UN Special Representative to Namibia visited 22 SWAPO camps in Angola and eight in Zambia, with a view to finding out about 1,100 people named as having been detained by SWAPO and not released. It found that 263 men and women could not be accounted for.[12]

Since independence, calls by the Namibian churches and others for a truth and reconciliation commission have not been heeded. Few of the alleged perpetrators have been indicted to stand trial either in Namibia itself or in South Africa, as part of the truth and reconciliation proceedings there. Various civil society initiatives have attempted to raise the issue, including a mass meeting convened in Windhoek in June 1999 to mark the 10th anniversary of the SWAPO detainees' return to Namibia. The issue remains unresolved and continues to create cleavage and dissonance in society.

Women's organisations during the struggle

During the period of armed struggle women organised themselves inside the country and in exiled communities.

For women exiled under the umbrella of SWAPO, the only choice was membership of the SWAPO Women's Council (SWC) which was born out of SWAPO's Consultative Congress held in Tanzania in 1969.[13] There were no real efforts to mobilise women inside Namibia until 1976, when meetings were held in different parts of the country to discuss 'how to mount political education campaigns which would draw women more centrally into the struggle for liberation and which would also educate the men about the problems unique to women'.[14] A year later SWAPO elected its first SWC secretary in Namibia. A number of women activists identified 1976 as a significant turning point in their history of self-organisation, but as in East Timor the opportunities for a women's movement to develop were limited by the political context.

Constraints on women's organisation

The efforts of women in the SWC and the Organização Popular da Mulher Timorense (OPMT – Popular Organisation of East Timorese Women) alike were repressed by the occupying forces. A woman living in the south of Namibia explained the constraints that the SWC faced in the decade before independence:

> Between 1976 and 1980 the SWC established centres in every town in the south. Since the government closed down the SWAPO headquarters in Windhoek it has been impossible to organise SWC activities. Even if the SWC is able to organise small gatherings in people's houses, these have to be underground. The women want to be active, but the South African government has blocked everything with its laws.[15]

Another major constraint was that communications between the SWC internally and in exile were not well developed, as an SWC leader, at the time under house arrest, emphasised:

> One of the things we find most frustrating inside the country is that we cannot get any information about what is happening politically either here or outside. Those of us who support SWAPO are very isolated because of this. We need to have news about what is going on internationally.[16]

The SWC did not have the benefit of easy communications through the Internet and e-mail which women in East Timor used to their advantage in the late 1990s. However, this was not the only obstacle. SWAPO in exile did little to encourage the free flow of communication. Its preoccupations with security and the risks of infiltration grew, and allegiance to the Marxist-Leninist model of women's emancipation solidified. Clearly the end of the Cold War and gradual breaking down of divisions between this model of feminism and 'western feminism' was a benefit East Timorese women enjoyed in ways that Namibian women did not.

The socialist model

The SWC's allegiance to the socialist model of women's emancipation was clear in the way it defined its priorities and programme of action in exile. These centred on equal access to education and training; the provision of universal, collectivised childcare to enable women's wider participation; and cooperative projects in various spheres of production. SWAPO's draft Family Act sought to transform relations between men and women within marriage so as to create a new family (as the basic cell of society) founded on principles of equality and mutual responsibility. One of its key goals was to 'politicise all women and men in order to effectively challenge sexism and sexual discrimination on a personal as well as organisational level'.[17]

In exiled SWAPO communities the SWC brokered little discussion about gender roles and capabilities because this was seen as divisive of the liberation struggle. A minority of women, seconded by the party for studies in Europe and elsewhere, were exposed to western feminist and other ideas, but the alternative viewpoints they developed about women's equality and gender roles were poorly tolerated by the party. Hence there was little open debate. Stereotypical concepts of appropriate gender roles were challenged only rarely and resulted in small changes in individual women's roles within the national liberation movement, rather than broader-based changes in male-female relations. For example, a majority of SWAPO drivers were women because their safety record was better than that of men.[18] However, while all exiled Namibians were subject to often authoritarian party control, many women grew accustomed to living more independent lives outside the traditional limitations imposed on them by extended families.

Civil society organisation under the churches' umbrella

Inside the country the churches provided one of the few channels for organising open to women outside the ambit of the main political parties. Church women's groups provided marriage counselling and guidance and opportunities to develop handicraft projects. They organised self-help schemes for the aged and disabled, set up and managed childcare centres, and conducted pastoral activities such as bible reading and prayer. The depth and extent of women's impoverishment and the age profile of many communities made broad-based participation difficult to inspire. As a church social worker explained:

> Many women are simply not interested in the activities of the women's league. I think this is because most of them feel that

they have done their duty if they go to church services regularly, and [that] the league does not offer them anything apart
from bible reading, prayers and singing.[19]

However, church women's groups provided a meeting point where
women could share their problems and ideas, and support each
other. But even church-based groups were affected by the war,
which deprived them of much-needed support networks, as one
woman living on the Angolan border explained:

We used to hold meetings for women in the church, but they
are frightened to come, because they fear the South African
soldiers may attack them on their way. They fear that the
Boers may think that we are holding an illegal SWAPO meeting and attack. This has made it impossible for the church
women's group to meet .... The women really want to get
together, but they fear that if they leave their homes and their
children the soldiers will come and break into their *kraals*,
hurt their children. [Women are not] willing to hold meetings
in their homes because they know that if we are found meeting the whole household will suffer. The house may even be
burnt down. We cannot afford to take risks like these, so we
do not meet.[20]

Namibia Women's Voice
Despite the obstacles, however, in the early 1980s women started
to develop organisations outside party politics and the churches.
The most significant of these was the Namibia Women's Voice
(NWV) which grew out of the Association of Professional and
Business Women. Although the initial support base of the association was quite limited, it sought to advance women's rights and to
this end it lobbied the existing regional administration on such
issues as equal pay for equal work, better conditions for market
women and family planning.

The NWV shared the association's leadership and aims, but
acquired a broader, national orientation and a more inclusive support base. Its constitution called on women to support national liberation, but also emphasised the need to raise women's awareness
of their human rights. It pledged the organisation to the total erad-
ication of discrimination against women (through law, religion,
tradition or otherwise) and committed itself to forging international links between women. Unlike the SWC constitution, which
did not specifically advocate affirmative action, the NWV called for

'a minimum of 50 per cent representation of women in all decision-making processes, in recognised institutions'.[21]

Membership of the organisation was open to all and by 1986 it had established 13 branches in different parts of the country. These embraced women of different political persuasions and the SWAPO leadership grew increasingly anxious. In the words of Colin Leys and John Saul: 'as far as SWAPO was concerned, there was no room for ambiguity in the struggle – if you were not with SWAPO, or did not submit to its political direction, then you were against the struggle.'[22] In addition, the NWV was seen to be in direct competition for membership with the SWC. Its non-partisan approach and emphasis on development rather than political issues also meant that it was better placed to access international donor funds. Most importantly, however, was the challenge that 'the organisation represented to male authority in the churches and in SWAPO,' write Leys and Saul:

> While the supporters of the Voice were adamant that in theory there should be no contradiction between the struggle for women's liberation and that for national liberation, in practice, with an authoritarian and male-dominated movement leading the struggle, the contradiction was acute.[23]

Shortly before independence, in March 1989, the NWV was disbanded and its project work was subsumed under the women's desk of the Council of Churches in Namibia. Thus a promising women's organisation died largely because it was perceived to be a challenge to the male-dominated churches and leading party.

The transition to independence

A number of schisms constrained the development of a united women's movement during Namibia's transition to independence, and these divisions remain today. They include differences in experience and perception between women who were exiled and those who were not; the social and economic distance between a minority of educated, professional women and the impoverished majority; the historical legacy of diversity rooted in ethnicity and race; and to a lesser extent differences between town and countryside.

During the transition and the early years of independence the divergence of needs, experience and expectation between 'remainee' women[24] and those who had been exiled were at the forefront. Women who had lived in exile had different perceptions of themselves, although they were far from a homogenous group.

Those who had remained in the country regarded the exiles as a privileged elite with greater access to education, training, and positions of power under the new political dispensation. As a paper published by the Legal Assistance Centre, a Namibian non-governmental organisation (NGO), puts it:

> With respect to the women's movement, while both men and women in exile benefited from contact with other feminisms in other countries, at the same time they unavoidably lost touch with practical conditions inside Namibia. Returning Namibians who benefited from educational opportunities abroad have also formed the backbone of the new black elite, from whom grass roots women often feel alienated.[25]

After independence the black income elite grew rapidly, primarily because of a growth in government employment. This provided a key source of division within the women's movement and constrained the development of civil society.[26] In this Namibia's experience is very different from that of East Timor, where government salaries on independence were so low that women with education and skills often chose non-governmental employment. Similarly, in Mozambique the structural adjustment programme demanded a reduction in overall government employment, thereby encouraging the growth of NGOs.

It has been suggested that in independent Namibia: 'While the government's policy of national reconciliation was both politically and economically necessary, there is evidence that it has done much to reinforce the status quo by protecting the pre-independence gains of the minority.'[27]

The divisions that historically separated a minority of more affluent women from an impoverished majority has become more complex. The divide can no longer be explained primarily in terms of race. Growing inequalities in the income and socio-economic status of women have reinforced the pre-independence distinction that women themselves drew between 'ordinary' and 'educated' women. This is, however, understood to revolve around unequal access to economic and other opportunities, rather than class difference.

The tiny size of Namibia's population relative to its land mass, combined with patterns of poverty and its distribution, also posed immediate obstacles to communication and cooperation across groups and communities, as a report on *Affirmative action for women in local government in Namibia* highlighted:

A Namibian woman's individual experience may be shaped not only by her race and class, but also by her political affiliations, by whether she lives in Windhoek or in a smaller town or in a rural area, by whether she lives in the north or in the south, by the situational characteristics which may be unique to her region, and by the ethnic identity of her particular community. This multiplicity of experiences created an immense challenge for organisation by women's groups.[28]

The legal framework

The Namibian constitution, forged through an intensive process of inter-party negotiation, 'has been heralded as the model of democracy for the rest of Africa while the government's policy of national reconciliation has been lauded as a mark of political maturity'.[29] Just like that of independent East Timor, the constitution underlines the need for affirmative action – given the special discrimination women have traditionally suffered – to encourage their full, equal and effective participation in the political, social, economic and cultural life of the nation.[30] However, the Namibian experience suggests that while such endorsement is important, it is not enough to guarantee women's full enjoyment of their human rights.

Soon after independence, in November 1992, the government ratified the UN Convention on the Elimination of All Forms of Discrimination Against Women (CEDAW), and in May 2000 it ratified the Optional Protocol to CEDAW. Namibian NGOs, led by the Legal Assistance Centre, played a key role in preparing Namibia's initial report to the CEDAW Committee, which was submitted in December 1993. NGOs were also part of the government delegation that presented the report to the UN in 1997. The committee noted that Namibian women continued to face persistent discrimination arising from traditional and customary laws and that a majority of people living in poverty were women, which made it difficult for them to fulfil their aspirations as guaranteed by the convention. In addition, it found that a general lack of knowledge about human and legal rights was an obstacle to the implementation of CEDAW.[31]

The committee made more than 20 recommendations to the government, some of which have been implemented. Significant progress has been made in legislation, in particular with respect to rape and domestic violence. Current legislative priorities identified by the Legal Assistance Centre and others relate to women and HIV and AIDS, and child protection. However, the government of

Namibia has fallen behind with its reporting to CEDAW, and – as in many other countries undergoing transition – the impetus to push women's rights hard appears to have waned somewhat.

Rape and domestic violence
In all Namibian communities violence against women was perceived to be a widespread problem at independence. Although pre-independence statistics of reported rape are available, there are no comparable statistics for domestic violence, which was believed to be even more extensive. As a report published by the Legal Assistance Centre stated:

> Power relations are such that societal blame still focuses on women who suffer violence rather than on the male aggressors. On the other hand, violence against women has inspired the mobilisation of women at grassroots level and seems to be one of the few issues which has the power to bring women together across party-political lines.[32]

As a result of significant civil society mobilisation the Combating of Rape Act came into force in 2000. It stipulates that 'no marriage or other relationship shall constitute a defence to a charge of rape under this Act' (Article 3). It lays down the sentencing regime to be applied (ranging from five years for a first offence without the use of coercion to 20 years for a second offence with coercion) and the special responsibilities of the police and the prosecution services in dealing with rape cases.[33]

The Combating of Domestic Violence Act was passed in 2003 amid huge controversy. Several prominent political leaders held the view that the issue should 'remain in the bedroom'. However, after a national campaign by women's organisations, joined by a new group called Men against Domestic Violence, the legislation eventually came into force.[34] Its definition of domestic violence includes physical, sexual and economic abuse as well as intimidation, harassment and emotional, verbal and psychological abuse.

Political representation
Following independence the ethnic system of government was dismantled with considerable difficulty, and a framework was established for strong central government, supported by increasingly decentralised functions at regional and local levels.

Initially the number of women elected to local councils, including a number of women town mayors, was promising, but the representation of women in senior positions at central level was poor. In 1993, according to a report published by the Legal Assistance Centre:

> Although the participation of women in government structures has increased markedly since independence, women are still seriously under-represented in leadership positions.... For example, there are only five women among the 72 elected members of the National Assembly, and only one woman among the six non-voting members appointed by the president. There is only one woman among the 26 members of the National Council. Only two out of 18 ministers are women, and there is only one female deputy minister.[35]

In the 1992 regional council elections, only three out of the 95 members elected were women, representing only three per cent of regional council seats. In contrast, in the local authority elections held at the same time, of the 362 persons elected 114 were women – just under 32 per cent of the total.[36] In East Timor the representation of women at higher levels has been much more impressive.

Although progress has been slower in Namibia, in December 2004 seven women were sworn in as members of the National Council (the second chamber of the Namibian parliament), following the naming of three others as regional governors. This brought the representation of women on the National Council from a mere 7.7 per cent to 27 per cent. However, this remains short of the 30 per cent target set by the Southern African Development Community Declaration on Gender and Development and the Beijing Platform for Action. Although more than 30 per cent of the election candidates of most political parties were women, they were placed low down on the party list, and therefore less likely to win a seat in the proportional system.[37]

Women's rights campaigners have pointed out that the Namibian government is failing to meet its obligations as a signatory of CEDAW, and to implement the promise of its own national gender policy to increase women's participation at all levels of politics and decision making.

Civil society

It proved difficult to create a non-partisan and sustainable national women's organisation after independence, perhaps in part because the short-lived experience of the NWV left deep scars. Shortly after independence women attempted to form an umbrella organisation that would unite women from across the political, social and economic spectrum. Thirteen women's groups took part in these discussions and a steering committee was formed with two delegates from each. They reached consensus on the aims and objectives of the organisation, but serious disagreements emerged over its form. The women's wings of various political parties wanted an organisation based on individual membership, while Namibian NGOs preferred a federation of women's groups. The initiative failed.

Namibia's independence came at a time of sweeping political change in the international arena and in South Africa, as well as of major changes in the international economy and in aid flows to Africa. New Namibian NGOs formed on, or just after, independence were much less overtly political than some of their predecessors, and sought to play more active roles in community development.[38] This repositioning was influenced both by the reluctance of international donors to fund initiatives that were overtly political and the perception by national NGOs that they had been too closely affiliated to the leading party, SWAPO.

Many organisations focused on development in Namibia's communal areas or former black locations. Here they sought, with varying degrees of success, to meet some of women's practical problems at local and community level. Some initiatives also opened up new spaces for women to discuss strategic issues, such as domestic violence, and to organise around these. The Multimedia Campaign on Violence against Women and Children, which is an umbrella group for a range of organisations, was particularly successful.

However, after more than a decade of political independence, some concern remains about the capacity of predominantly male-led civil society organisations to advocate women's rights. Gender awareness remains patchy and the results of civil society efforts for women have been mixed, although in some campaigns women's access to land and women's rights have been quite visible. Similarly, national NGOs have pushed for legislative change on the family and women's property rights. The impressive results of this work are the Married Persons' Equality Act 1996, the Affirmative Action (Employment) Act 1998 and the Communal Land Reform Act 2002. Important and progressive legislation is still in process to improve the situation of divorced women, protect children, recognise customary marriage and increase women's participation in decision making.

Many national NGO activists are keen to challenge the social divisions which continue to permeate Namibian society. Hence there is a tendency, just as there was in the national liberation movement, to disregard gender difference rather than to challenge the forces perpetuating gender inequality and women's exclusion. Gender inequality now has life and death outcomes because of extremely high rates of HIV and AIDS prevalence, so this is of considerable concern. Moreover, few advances are likely for women if civil society continues to shrink as it has done over the past few years, through either too close a party-political affiliation or financial collapse.[39]

Conclusions and lessons

While the Namibian nation as a whole has freed itself from the colonial past and released its potential for self-determination, deep social inequalities remain. Although some gains have been made, the majority of Namibian women have not been able to participate equally in the benefits of liberation, or to play pivotal roles in determining the direction and nature of political, economic and social change. Much remains to be done to promote a process in which women's rights feature more strongly in political and civil discourse. Otherwise there is a danger, once again, that the promotion of women's rights will become lost among the welter of broader issues in the struggle for greater democracy.

The lessons from the Namibian experience that might be relevant to women in East Timor are:

- In a society where the colonial legacy is one of brutal repression and human rights abuse, it is important to heal wounds. This must be an integral part of the larger human rights and development agenda. It is necessary to look backwards as well as forwards. In East Timor the Comissão de Acolhimento, Verdade e Reconciliação (CAVR – Commission for Reception, Truth and Reconciliation) has made a start, and paid some attention to women's rights and issues of particular concern to them. Now that its work is nearly complete it will be important to build on the lessons learnt and to weave these into a longer term agenda for change.
- The introduction of new legislation and reform of inherited legislation are important to guarantee the protection and promotion of women's rights, especially in relation to such issues as rape and domestic violence. However, if it is to have real and effective impact the implementation of the new law must be supported by concerted community mobilisation, awareness raising and public education.
- When the majority of women are deeply impoverished and have

been excluded from mainstream economic and political life, the difficulties of creating a national organisation that fully represents women are immense. Much can be gained, therefore, from working from the bottom up – perhaps creating a more fluid movement embracing community-based women's and other organisations.

- It is important to develop strategic alliances across civil society that are designed to engage even those who are most resistant to the promotion of women's rights. This is needed to change dominant and entrenched ideas and beliefs, as well as to develop policy and change practice.
- It is essential to maintain the momentum of increasing political representation of women in decision making. A key target must be senior levels of the political hierarchy. But most women live in remote, rural communities so it is important for them to gain more voice at local and regional levels. Mechanisms for effectively linking women through the political system are needed if those at the top are to legitimately speak out for women in less privileged positions.

Notes

1 Quoted in Smith, S (1986) *Namibia: A violation of trust*, Oxfam Public Affairs Unit, Oxford, p15.

2 Estimates of how many Namibians were exiled during the liberation struggle vary enormously. Fewer than 50,000 were repatriated home under UN auspices during the transition to independence.

3 Allison, C (1986) *It's like holding the key to your own jail: Women in Namibia*, World Council of Churches, Geneva.

4 As above, p29.

5 Personal discussion with the author, Namibia, 1983. See also Roseveare, C (2002) *Constraints on women's civil participation and organisation: Namibia's democratic transition*, D.Phil dissertation, University of Sussex.

6 Amnesty International (1990) *Namibia: The human rights situation at independence*, internal paper, August 1990.

7 Allison, C (1986 – see note 3), pp53-56.

8 Allison, C (1986 – see note 3), p62.

9 See note 6.

10 Preston, R (ed) (1993) *The integration of returned exiles, former combatants and other war affected Namibians*, NISER (Namibia Institute for Social and Economic Research) Report, University of Namibia, Windhoek, pp845-847.

11 Leys, C, and Saul, J (1995) *Namibia's liberation struggle: The two edged sword*, James Currey, London.

12 Amnesty International (see note 6).

13 SWAPO Department of Information and Publicity (1981) *To be born a nation: The liberation struggle for Namibia*, Zed Press, London, p179.

14 As above, p289.

15 Personal discusson with the author, Namibia, 1983.

16 Quoted in Allison, C (1986 – see note 3), p68.

17 Allison, C (1984) *The situation of Namibian women in exile*, unpublished paper.

18 Personal discussion with the author, Zambia, 1984. For more detail also see Allison, C, with Ivula-Kaulinge, P (1986) 'Women in development' in United Nations Insititute for Namibia (1986) *Namibia: Perspectives on national reconstruction and development*, United Nations Institute for Namibia, Lusaka.

19 Personal discussion with the author, Namibia, 1983.

20 Personal discussion with the author, Namibia, 1983.

21 *Namibian Women's Voice: Constitution* (unpublished, not dated).

22 Leys, C, and Saul, J (see note 11), p110.

23 As above.

24 The term 'remainee' was developed by the majority of Namibians who had not been exiled in response to the focus of UN and other international assistance on repatriated groups of 'returnees'.

25 Hubbard, D, and Solomon, C (1994) *The women's movement in Namibia: History, constraints and potential*, Legal Assistance Centre Paper, Windhoek, p4.

26 As above, p3.

27 Hubbard, D, and Kavari, K (1993) *Affirmative action for women in local government in Namibia*, Legal Assistance Centre Paper, Windhoek, p2.

28 Hubbard and Solomon (as above), p5.

29 Hubbard and Kavari (see note 27), p1.

30 Constitution of the Republic of Namibia, 1990.

31 CEDAW/C/1997/II/L.1/Add.2.

32 Hubbard and Kavari (see note 27), p8.

33 Combating of Rape Act No. 8, 2000.

34 Combating of Domestic Violence Act No. 4, 2003.

35 Hubbard and Kavari (see note 27), p1.

36 Hubbard and Kavari (see note 27), p10.

37 Malestsky, C (2004) 'Our time will come' in *The Namibian*, Windhoek, 20 December 2004.

38 Allison, C, with study team (1997) *Study of Namibian NGO development*, USAID/NANGOF, Windhoek.

39 As above, p15.

Chapter 9
Cambodia: conflict, reconstruction and women's organisations

By Brigitte Sonnois

This chapter examines efforts to promote women's rights and gender equality in Cambodia after the wholesale destruction of the 1970s. It assesses the impact of armed conflict on women's roles and social status. It then looks at how Cambodian government institutions, the United Nations (UN) Transitional Authority, and local and international non-governmental organisations (NGOs) addressed women's and gender issues after the 1991 peace accords.

Recent history

Cambodia obtained independence peacefully from France in 1953 under the leadership of King Norodom Sihanouk, after 90 years as a French protectorate. Young Cambodian communists who had studied in France started a guerrilla struggle in the late 1960s. In March 1970, King Sihanouk was overthrown by a military coup and civil war broke out. In April 1975 the Cambodian communists, known as the Khmer Rouge, took over the country and established Democratic Kampuchea (DK). They closed the borders, emptied the cities, abolished money and religion, destroyed Buddhist pagodas, closed schools and hospitals, and forbade the use of modern medicine. They executed military and civil servants of the former government and people who had more than a primary education, and turned the country into an agrarian society. Estimates of the number of people who died from execution, torture, exhaustion, hunger or disease vary but are on average around two million in a population of 7.3 million in 1975.[1]

The DK army launched repeated attacks on southern Vietnam. In retaliation, in January 1979 the Vietnamese army overthrew the DK government and established the People's Republic of Kampuchea (PRK) headed by Khmer Rouge dissidents who had fled to Vietnam. This was during the Cold War, so the international community – with the exception of communist countries and India

– did not recognise the new government because it had been installed by Vietnam and continued to receive Vietnamese military, economic and technical support. As a result, Cambodia was represented at the United Nations by the Khmer Rouge/DK until 1982, and from 1982 to 1990 by a tripartite coalition based in Thailand which waged war against the PRK. The tripartite coalition was composed of the Khmer Rouge/DK, the royalist United National Front for an Independent, Neutral, Peaceful and Cooperative Cambodia (Funcinpec) and the republican Khmer People's National Liberation Front (KPNLF).

In May 1989 the PRK adopted a new constitution which restored private property, established a free market economy and declared Buddhism the state religion. The country changed its name to the State of Cambodia (SOC) and the remaining Vietnamese soldiers and advisers left the country. In 1990 Cambodia's seat at the UN was declared vacant.

The war between the tripartite coalition and the PRK/SOC government continued until the September 1991 Peace Agreements, which established the United Nations Transitional Authority in Cambodia (UNTAC). UNTAC was charged with maintaining peace, supervising the government during the transitional period, organising the return of 370,000 Cambodian refugees from camps in Thailand, and organising national elections. The governing body consisted of SOC, Funcinpec, KPNLF and the Khmer Rouge/DK, and was headed by Prince Norodom Sihanouk.

The Khmer Rouge/DK left the peace process early and did not participate in the UN-supervised elections in May 1993. It continued to control territory and to fight a guerrilla war until the end of 1998, when peace was achieved through negotiations between the government and Khmer Rouge leaders.

As a result of the 1993 elections, a new constitution establishing a parliamentary monarchy was adopted and a coalition government was formed with some difficulty. High tensions within the government led to renewed armed conflict between the Cambodian People's Party (CPP) and Funcinpec in 1997, yet elections took place as scheduled in July 1998. The CPP won, and after five months of difficult negotiations, a government headed by a CPP prime minister was formed in a coalition with Funcinpec.

The next elections, in July 2003, were followed by a year of negotiations before a new governing coalition, again headed by the CPP in coalition with Funcinpec, was formed. A third party, the Sam Rainsy Party, named after its leader, became the parliamentary opposition.

Consequences of prolonged conflict

In 1979, Cambodia started to rebuild from scratch: its physical infrastructure had been completely destroyed, family and society had been broken up, people were deeply affected psychologically and most of the educated people had been wiped out. Only a few dozen medical doctors, a handful of lawyers and a few hundred teachers and nurses had survived. Moreover, most non-communist countries and international agencies denied assistance to the country until 1991 and the country continued to suffer guerrilla warfare until 1998. To this day, Cambodia is one of the world's poorest countries and remains heavily dependent on international aid. Landmines and unexploded ordnance are still present. Public administration is weak because of a lack of qualified personnel, extremely low salaries, corruption and politicisation. Cambodia remains predominantly rural, with 84 per cent of its population living in the countryside, mainly on rain-dependent rice cultivation.[2]

The UNTAC operation brought about freedom of association and freedom of expression, which led to the creation of local NGOs, trade unions, political parties, newspapers, and radio and television stations. The UN operation also succeeded in disseminating information and raising awareness about human rights and democracy. Yet these achievements remain fragile. The UN and the Cambodian government signed an agreement to set up a tribunal to judge Khmer Rouge leaders, but at the time of writing funding for its implementation had not been secured.

Formation of women's organisations

January 1979-September 1991

This was a period of armed conflict (three resistance forces against the government), post-genocide reconstruction and international isolation.

Both sides in the conflict had their own official women's organisation: the PRK's Revolutionary Women's Association of Kampuchea (RWAK), which became the Women's Association of Cambodia (WAC) in 1989, and the coalition forces' Khmer Women's Association (KWA), based in the refugee camps in Thailand.

At international conferences on women, the KWA represented Cambodia at the official meetings, while RWAK took part in the NGO forum. In 1990 the United Nations Children's Fund (Unicef) arranged the first encounter between the WAC and the KWA in Thailand.

In July 1991 Khemara, the first local NGO in Cambodia, was established; it worked on women's issues.

September 1991-October 1993
This was the transition period, with UNTAC in operation.

The transition government signed the Convention on the Elimination of All Forms of Discrimination Against Women (CEDAW) in 1992. In March 1993, 100 women from all walks of life took part in a National Women's Summit, supported by the United Nations Development Fund for Women (Unifem) and organised by Khemara with help from international organisations. Afterwards the summit core group campaigned on women's issues on UNTAC radio and television, and in public forums. UNTAC organised training for women on constitution writing and on human rights.

In the May 1993 elections the turnout was 90 per cent of registered voters, of which women accounted for 50 per cent. The new constitution adopted in October 1993 provided for full equal rights for women.

Some National Women's Summit participants established the Women's Committee for Non-Violence in the Elections, which later became the Khmer Women's Voice Centre and the Women's Media Centre, the first local NGOs dedicated exclusively to advocacy, public awareness and research on women's issues. Altogether, 17 local NGOs focusing on women were established, most of them working on social and economic programmes.

October 1993-December 1998
This was a period of low intensity armed conflict (Khmer Rouge against government) and high tension in the newly-formed tripartite coalition government, leading to renewed conflict.

In 1993 a Secretariat of State for Women's Affairs was established. It became the Ministry of Women's Affairs in 1996. Advisers on women's issues were appointed to each of the two prime ministers in 1995.

A nationwide network of women's NGOs, Amara, was established in 1994. HIV and AIDS and violence against women – sexual exploitation, domestic violence, sexual abuse – became major issues for NGOs in this period. An NGO Committee on CEDAW was formed in late 1995, and the first NGO report on implementation of CEDAW was prepared in 1997.

In September 1995 a total of 115 Cambodians attended the Fourth World Conference on Women in Beijing (the official meeting and the NGO forum).

From end 1998

For the first time since the late 1960s, the country finally experienced peace.

The Ministry of Women's and Veterans'Affairs was established in 1998. Gender focal points were set up in line ministries in 2001, and in local councils the following year. The Cambodian National Council for Women was formed in 2002. The government completed its first report on the implementation of CEDAW in January 2004.

Priorities for NGOs now include sexual exploitation and trafficking of women, domestic violence and HIV and AIDS, but they continue to do awareness raising and education work. The Women's Media Centre has established a radio station and a weekly television programme, and legal literacy programmes are teaching women about relevant laws.

The role and status of women

Pre-colonial Cambodia was a traditional society, ruled by a king surrounded by a small aristocratic circle. The majority of the people were farmers. Then as now, women played an important economic role, which was not always recognised.

The French protectorate had the greatest influence on the small minority of women who lived in the large towns. A few urban women gained access to education, which had previously been provided by Buddhist monks only to boys. Education became much more accessible to girls in the 1950s and 1960s. Cambodia's first woman minister was appointed during this period: she was minister for education.

Women in wartime

In wartime women had to perform many of the same tasks as men in defence and production, either as a result of government policies or because many men were dead, disabled or in the army. Under the PRK, women's roles in agriculture, industry, civil service and defence received official recognition. How this affected women and social perceptions of their status, and to what extent, is a matter of debate. In general, women tend to see the painful side of having had to do men's work, rather than welcoming a proof that they could do as well as men. Performance of what were traditionally male tasks was usually not seen as a gain and Cambodian women have not used it as an argument to promote equal rights.

Under the PRK, the most powerful institution was the party: one woman was in the seven-member political bureau and five in the 31-member central committee. Five women had ministerial rank and 18 per cent of the members of the National Assembly were women. Official women's organisations on both sides of the conflict played an important role and their leaders enjoyed high status: the president of the RWAK/WAC had ministerial rank. However, this experience was not seen as a gain, probably because people felt that women had been given positions more to ensure women's support for government or party policies than to promote equal rights in decision making. As a result, in the post-conflict period, this experience has not been used by women of either side to justify demands for women's greater participation in decision making and politics.

Women in the post-conflict period

Although economic liberalisation started in the mid-1980s, the major socio-economic change in Cambodia occurred in May 1989, with the shift from a planned to a market economy. Private property was re-established and the country was opened up to foreign trade and investment while the armed conflict (and peace negotiations) were still in progress. The impact of the changes was accelerated and multiplied in 1991 by the arrival of 22,000 civilian and military UNTAC staff, and thousands of foreign aid workers and business people. The rapid change of economic system led to a deterioration in health and women's education indicators, the closing of childcare centres and state factories, the disappearance of rice rations and subsidies on basic commodities, and a rise in the cost of living.

Following the first post-conflict elections in 1993, the percentage of women in parliament and in national government decreased. Some of these losses were eventually regained in the early 2000s once peace was achieved. The perceived increase in violence against women in the post-conflict period[3] was usually blamed on the loss of traditional family values, and hence loss of respect for women, brought about by the Khmer Rouge regime, rather than on the new socio-economic context.

Because in general women, like men, saw nothing positive in the regime of the armed conflict period, there was no perception of the post-conflict period as a loss. On the contrary, women tended to emphasise what they saw as its positive points, namely freedom and new economic opportunities, in particular freedom of movement which allowed them to do business or to seek paid work.

Women's organisations

During the war, women's organisations on both sides implemented welfare programmes for women, especially for war widows. They also received financial and technical assistance from international agencies: the RWAK/WAC to implement education and economic programmes for women all over the country, and the KWA to provide social services and education programmes to women in the refugee camps.

Gender issues had a high profile in the 1993 electoral campaign and the new constitution provided for equal rights. This, and the well-established role of official women's organisations on both sides in the 1980s, may have been factors in the decision of the new government to establish a State Secretariat and then a Ministry of Women's Affairs. The new institution absorbed staff from the WAC and donor-funded projects, and also hired staff from the other two political parties in the government coalition, including former KWA personnel.

The new institution therefore started with a nationwide organisational structure reaching every village and a pool of women with organisational skills and experience in managing development projects and disseminating information. Initially, relations between the two former warring parties were not easy. Former WAC staff managed the ministry's main resource – the donor-funded projects – while decision making was in the hands of another party, as the first state secretary, later the minister, was from the minority party in the government coalition. Tensions eased with time, especially during the ministry's second term, when more resources became available and a new minister was appointed who assigned responsibilities to staff more on the basis of qualifications than political affiliation.

Women's organisations of the armed conflict period also played a role in developing NGOs during the post-conflict period. Some former KWA staff founded NGOs working on women's issues. Former KWA and WAC staff worked with international and local NGOs on women's issues. The Phnom Penh branch of the WAC, which had been one of the strongest provincial branches, became a local NGO specialising in women's issues. It was the first local NGO to work on sensitive issues such as family planning, HIV and AIDS prevention and sexual exploitation, and it became one of the leading women's advocacy NGOs.

Returning refugees

As with other local NGOs created during the transition period, many local NGOs working on women's issues were established or encouraged by Cambodians who had recently returned from exile in North America, Australia or Europe, or from the refugee camps in Thailand.

Prior to the 1990s Cambodia had no tradition of NGOs or membership-based associations. The political regimes in power between 1975 and 1991 did not allow the existence of civil society organisations, and international isolation prevented Cambodians from communicating with civil society organisations in other countries. After years of authoritarian rule, many Cambodians who had never left the country were fearful of taking a leadership role, as the new freedom was still fragile. Meanwhile, Cambodians who had lived overseas had been exposed to democracy, human rights and civil society organisations, as well as to the role and status of women in western societies. Cambodians who lived in the refugee camps in Thailand were exposed to the work of international NGOs in the camps, had contacts with many western aid workers and received training in democracy and human rights in preparation for repatriation and the national elections.

These returnee women NGO leaders hired and trained Cambodians who had never left the country. Women from inside the country quickly followed their example and created local NGOs too, helped by the large amounts of international aid available. Mu Sochua, the first woman minister of women's affairs, and the first who succeeded in giving a high profile to gender issues in the government agenda, lived and studied in Europe and the US for several years, worked in the Cambodian refugee camps in Thailand, and returned to Cambodia in the late 1980s. She founded the first Cambodian NGO in 1991 and became a leader of the Cambodian women's movement. She helped found several local NGOs and was appointed adviser on women's issues to one of the prime ministers in 1995.

The role of organisations and institutions

Local NGOs
Local NGOs established during the transition period played a major role in putting women's issues and gender equality on the political agenda and encouraging women to vote and run as candidates in the 1993 elections. NGOs worked together to raise public awareness, seeking recognition of the role of women and arguing for equal rights in the lead-up to the Fourth World Conference on Women in Beijing. The 80-member Cambodian NGO delegation to

Beijing led a panel on women and peace and the Women Weaving the World initiative. The appointment of women's issues advisers to the two prime ministers and the creation of the NGO Committee on CEDAW were outcomes of all these activities.

From 1994 much of the advocacy and public awareness work of the local NGOs focused on violence against women, in particular sexual exploitation and trafficking, and domestic violence and sexual abuse. This included lobbying for legislation and law enforcement. In the 1998 national elections, and even more so in the local elections in 2002 and the national elections in 2003, local NGOs – in particular Women for Prosperity (WFP) – succeeded in increasing the number of women candidates. WFP is supporting and training regional networks of women commune councillors.

Government institutions
During its first five-year term the Secretariat of State (later the Ministry) of Women's Affairs, led by a man from the minority party in the government coalition, had little impact. Its staff were experienced in managing social and economic programmes but not in policy development, advocacy or gender analysis. The institution was unable to develop a strategic plan, attract significant resources or build its staff's capacity for new areas of work. Mostly it implemented economic, education and health projects proposed by donors, many of them inherited from the WAC.

During the second five-year term, however, the ministry achieved a great deal thanks to its head, Mu Sochua. A prominent leader of the Cambodian NGO women's movement and highly regarded in the international community, she was able to attract major international financial and technical assistance and to give a high profile to women's and gender issues. The ministry formulated a strategic plan and placed considerable emphasis on building the capacity of its staff. Its major achievements were the mainstreaming of gender in most national policies and in some sectoral policies, in particular education; the drafting of legislation on domestic violence and sexual exploitation (although this has yet to be adopted); the establishment of a high level inter-ministerial National Council for Women in charge of monitoring national policies and laws in the framework of CEDAW; and the establishment of gender focal points in line ministries and local councils.

International organisations
Whereas throughout the 1980s the country was assisted by three UN agencies and 10 international NGOs, the 1990s witnessed the

arrival of more than 100 international NGOs, 10 UN and other multilateral agencies and at least 15 bilateral agencies. These agencies have provided political, financial and technical support in various ways: direct project implementation; funding of government institutions; funding of local NGOs; creation of local NGOs; and transformation of international NGOs into local NGOs. The international community's political commitment to the development of civil society has been important.

From the beginning, local NGOs were totally dependent on international aid both for core and programme costs, and this remains the case today. This is because the private sector is too small to fund civil society projects, there is no tradition of civil society organisations or membership-based associations, and practically no government funding is available for NGOs. Most of the budget of government institutions covers core costs; the majority of services and programmes are funded by international aid. This dependence is likely to continue and poses problems of sustainability and long term planning.

Many educated people were killed under the Khmer Rouge, and international isolation in the 1980s slowed down reconstruction of the education system and made it difficult for the few educated survivors to update their knowledge and skills. As a result, Cambodia still suffers from a dire lack of qualified professionals. The quality of public and private education remains poor, and the range of subjects offered in higher education is limited, so this situation is likely to continue. Educated women are even rarer than educated men. An additional problem is that, because government salaries are extremely low, many qualified staff have been leaving the civil service to work with international agencies, or local and international NGOs, which offer higher salaries. Consequently, most local NGOs and the State Secretariat/Ministry of Women's Affairs have relied heavily on foreign advisers for training and technical assistance. However, the assistance provided has sometimes been inadequate, owing to limited knowledge or understanding of the country's recent history, politics, society, culture and language.

Donors have had a significant influence on the programmes of both local NGOs and government institutions. During the UNTAC period of operation, international agencies played an important role in orienting activities to ensure women's issues were on the agenda during the electoral campaign, and they helped to create some local NGOs. Initially, most local organisations focused only on economic, social and education programmes for women, reflecting what they saw as immediate needs as well as donors' 'women in development' approach of the time. Reproductive health and HIV and AIDS programmes were first introduced by donors. The increased emphasis on sexual exploitation and trafficking, and other issues of violence against women in the mid and late 1990s, was a response to real and growing problems. But it was also due to the large amounts of funding made available for these issues, while funding for socio-economic programmes decreased.

Gender mainstreaming was also introduced by donors, especially by multilateral and bilateral organisations working with government institutions, and by international NGOs. With the shift from needs-based to rights-based approaches came a focus on women's rights, political participation and legal literacy. The emphasis of the Ministry of Women's Affairs 2005-2009 plan on mainstreaming gender in poverty reduction, good governance, human rights, and administrative and judicial reform reflects the priorities of multilateral and bilateral donors at global level.

This donor influence had a positive impact, in that it addressed problems which were previously ignored and brought new ideas. But it also resulted at times in local demands being set aside or in poor implementation of programmes owing to lack of ownership, understanding or acceptance, or because they did not adequately address the reality of the situation.

Some lessons learned

- Local NGOs and the government institution have been working both on women's immediate practical needs and on long term gender strategic goals.

The majority of local NGOs and the Ministry of Women's Affairs initially focused on socio-economic programmes because of the many unmet needs, a lack of awareness and understanding of the importance of long term strategies, and a lack of capacity to carry out other types of programmes. The main worry of most Cambodian women has continued to be daily survival: food security, access to water, access to education and health services, and economic resources for themselves and their families. Many women have been affected by sexual exploitation, domestic violence, sexual abuse or HIV and AIDS. Line ministries have been unable to respond to all these pressing problems, so both local NGOs and the ministry have continued to provide direct assistance to women in these areas.

Outside the NGOs and the Ministry of Women's Affairs, few

women and even fewer men are aware of the importance of women's right to participate in politics and government, of changing gender roles and gender relations, or of the need to mainstream gender in government policies, statistics, budgets, laws and programmes. While local NGOs and the ministry have experience of implementing social, educational and economic programmes, they lack the skills and expertise to engage in advocacy and policy development for gender equity. As a result, they have begun to tackle gender analysis, research, law, and national planning and budgeting only in recent years with international technical assitance.

- Cooperation between local NGOs and the ministry has had a positive impact on advocacy and public awareness.

Ever since they were established, local NGOs and the State Secretariat/Ministry of Women's Affairs have worked together on public awareness and advocacy with government. During the first five-year term of the secretariat/ministry, local NGOs usually took the initiative of launching activities, inviting the government institution to join as president. At that time the ministry lacked capacity and resources while NGOs were receiving large amounts of funding and had active leaders with many ideas. During the second five-year term, the minister often took the lead in launching joint ministry/NGO activities. The new ministry also established mechanisms to coordinate work with the NGOs and sent representatives to the meetings of NGO networks. The ministry has subcontracted some activities to NGOs, for example a reproductive health programme, gender training for commune councils, and internships and training for line ministry gender focal points.

- Inter-agency networks were formed at an early stage and have played an important role in coordination, information exchange, public awareness and advocacy.

An inter-agency 'women in development' group was established in 1989 as a coordination and information exchange mechanism by foreign workers of UN agencies and international NGOs which had been in the country since the early 1980s. During the transition period, new local NGOs, newly-arrived multilateral, bilateral and international NGOs, and government institutions joined the group and soon the majority of the members were Cambodian women.

Starting with the 1993 National Women's Summit, the group has been organising joint public awareness activities on international women's day and for international conferences. It has lobbied for specific pieces of legislation and written country reports and joint statements for the meetings of the donors' consultative group. In 1997 it took the name of GADNET. Since 2000 it has been coordinated by GAD/C, the local NGO which came out of the gender and development (GAD) project.

It seems that in the last few years, the group has abandoned its coordinating role. Yet this is important to avoid duplication, fill gaps and optimise resources – even more so when funding opportunities are diminishing and other inter-agency bodies working on women's issues have been created: the NGO Committee on CEDAW in 1995, the NGO Forum Gender Working Group in 1997, and the Cambodian Committee for Women in 2000.

- Governmental and non-governmental institutions specialising in capacity building in gender need further strengthening, but have already had an impact.

Part of the mandate of the Ministry of Women's Affairs is to train and assist other government institutions to mainstream gender in their policies, laws, programmes, statistics and monitoring systems. The initial results achieved by the ministry during its second five-year mandate, despite its shortage of qualified personnel, shows that this is an efficient strategy.

On the NGO side, in 1995 the 'women in development' sectoral group identified the need for an institution that would build local capacity and act as a resource and coordinating body on gender. Following a needs assessment, the GAD Project was established in 1997 under the NGO umbrella organisation. It became an autonomous local NGO, GAD/C, in 2000. Initially, its main activity was to provide gender training to the staff of international NGOs, UN agencies and local NGOs at the request of donor agencies. In recent years, in addition to conducting gender training for a wider range of audiences, it has expanded its gender resource centre, produced handbooks on gender, published a regular bulletin, conducted research on women in various sectors, coordinated GADNET, organised two GAD national conferences and established a Cambodian Men's Network (see below). GAD/C needs to focus on strengthening local NGOs and NGO networks, and on reaching out to a wider group of women, in rural areas in particular.

The current strategic plans of the ministry and GAD/C include similar objectives and activities, so coordination will be important to avoid overlap and duplication. The two institutions are necessary and complementary, and both need to be strengthened.

- The fact that the country had not yet developed certain national laws and policies made it easier to include gender.

Although the constitutions of 1981 and 1989 included equal rights for women and men, the writing of a new constitution in 1993 provided an opportunity to include more specific provisions on gender. With the arrival of international financial institutions in the post-conflict period, national five-year plans were developed. National statistics systems, national census and demographic and health surveys were updated or established in the 1990s. The legislation drafting process initiated in 1979 had not been completed when the peace agreements were signed and the new civil and criminal codes were still at draft stage at the end of 2004. A decentralisation process started in 2002.

It has probably been easier to include gender issues into law and policy in Cambodia than in countries which already have a complete legal framework and long-established policies, planning and budgeting processes, and national statistics systems. During its second five-year mandate, the Ministry of Women's Affairs took advantage of this opportunity.

- Men's engagement with gender issues is a recent but promising development.

The Cambodian Men's Network for the Elimination of Violence against Women, formed in 2000 by GAD/C, has been conducting annual 'white ribbon' campaigns and participated in the second national GAD conference in 2002. For the moment, the network's membership is limited to local NGO staff and some youth activists. To really have an impact, it needs to reach other sectors of the male population. It could also expand its mandate to other aspects of gender equity, for example the promotion of women's access to education.

Conclusion
The post-conflict period provided the context in which a Cambodian women's movement could emerge. Political, financial and technical support from international agencies was an important factor in the creation and the development of local NGOs, as well as in strengthening the ministry for women. However, neither would have developed without the leadership and dedication of

Cambodian women, who made the most of the new context and the assistance offered. The existence of women's organisations on both sides during the armed conflict also contributed to the establishment of local NGOs and of a government institution for the advancement of women.

There has been considerable activity on women's rights. A framework of institutions, mechanisms, laws and policies has been established. Training, advocacy and public awareness activities have taken place. Information programmes and specialised social and legal services have been created to address sexual exploitation, domestic violence, sexual abuse and HIV and AIDS. Programmes for women's economic empowerment have been expanded, reproductive health services have been established and a gender mainstreaming strategy has been developed in education. All this activity has had some results: progress has been made in raising awareness among the public and in government about gender equality in general and violence against women in particular; women's participation in politics and government has increased; and law enforcement in cases of violence against women has improved somewhat.

But so far, despite the activities and their results, the actual impact on the lives of most women has been limited. The number of women victims of violence reached by specialised services, and the number of women reached by economic programmes, is well below the number of women who need them. The incidence of violence against women and of women's poverty has not diminished. Limited progress has been made in increasing access to and quality of education and health services. Besides lacking coverage, programmes and services are often hindered by structural problems.

Lack of education impedes women's access to economic resources. It undermines their ability to avoid sexual or labour exploitation, and to defend themselves against abuse and seek legal redress. It also affects their participation in politics and decision making. The shortage of qualified women and men is also the main weakness of the Ministry of Women's Affairs and of local NGOs working for the advancement of women.

In addition to poverty, gender roles are at the root of women's lower education rates, and gender relations are a key factor in the areas of domestic violence, sexual abuse, sexual exploitation and HIV and AIDS. Changing gender roles and gender relations is a long term endeavour which requires diverse approaches, such as working with children from an early age, as well as with men and with women themselves. The Cambodian women's movement has not yet been able to reach a large number of women, particularly in rural areas, so awareness of gender issues among women remains low.

Women's immediate needs for education, health and economic resources cannot be ignored (see the statistics in appendix 8). Information, legal and social services, and improved law enforcement will be needed as long as violence against women exists. The strategies to address these issues – and the roles of NGOs, the Ministry of Women's Affairs and line ministries in addressing them – have to be defined. Meanwhile, the longer term work of changing gender roles and gender relations, and increasing women's participation in politics and decision making, must not be forgotten.

Notes

1   Figures for 1975, Documentation Centre of Cambodia.

2   1998 Census.

3   Although the information available is limited, it is generally believed that domestic violence and sexual abuse during the armed conflict were particularly common in war zones and in the refugee camps, but were rarely reported. After the war, awareness-raising campaigns and the creation of social and legal services resulted in increased reporting of violence. Sexual exploitation existed during the armed conflict, but on a small scale. It expanded when the country shifted to the market economy owing to an increase in demand from urban men who had more money and rural men who came to look for employment in the city. On the supply side, trafficking (around 50 per cent of the women are sold or tricked), poverty, domestic violence, sexual abuse and family conflicts have led women into the sex trade.

Chapter 10
Women beyond independence: the challenges ahead

> Gender inequality is the surest way to transmit poverty to future generations of men and women. Therefore, reducing gender inequality and enhancing women's productivity will be integral elements of the country's development and poverty reduction strategies.
>
> *East Timor National Development Plan, 2002*[1]

This book has shown how leading women activists in East Timor have worked to enhance women's rights and opportunities, introducing a gender analysis to the roles that women and men play in their newly independent country. It has compared their experiences with those of women in three other countries emerging from conflict: Mozambique, Namibia and Cambodia.

This chapter looks at what has been achieved so far in East Timor, the dilemmas women's organisations face now, and the debate about human rights-based and efficiency approaches to gender. It evaluates the international intervention and the progress of East Timor's national machinery for mainstreaming gender. It draws on the case studies of other countries for key lessons for women activists in East Timor in building a more unified movement, modernisation, coalition building, and nurturing and accepting leadership. It also looks at how the mechanisms for implementing the women's rights convention can be used to improve the accountability of government and discusses whether the backlash some East Timorese men have threatened can be averted.

Concrete advances – but enduring poverty

Clearly women's organisations and activists in East Timor have made some important and far-reaching advances during the transition and in the first two years of independence. In the run-up to the first elections women's organisations achieved a common platform for action and increased their participation in political processes. They gained much improved political representation, including, by 2002, the appointment of two female ministers and three vice-ministers. Legislative and constitutional measures which enshrine rights for women were passed, and legislation on domestic violence was submitted to parliament. The government also recognised the need for some degree of affirmative action to improve the representation of women at managerial level in public decision-making bodies.

It is nonetheless important to keep this in perspective. For the vast majority of East Timorese women, who are farmers living in remote, rural areas, life has yet to change. Poverty remains pervasive.[2] The United Nations Development Programme Human Development Index in 2002 placed East Timor in the 'low human development' category, ranked 158 among 177 countries.[3] The female literacy rate remains very low. Women are an insignificant proportion of the labour force and most are concentrated in lower-skilled jobs.[4]

New structures for a new era

Women activists have had to modify their strategies to accommodate the new reality of independence amid widespread poverty. One dilemma the East Timorese women's movement faces now is the challenge of developing appropriate structures to hold the government to account for the implementation of gender equity policies, particularly as they affect the poorest. As with any set of organisations sharing common interests, they need to find a way to co-exist which enhances those interests.

Many East Timorese women activists believe there is a need to reconcile and harness the joint energies of the Organização Popular da Mulher Timorense (OPMT – Popular Organisation of East Timorese Women) and the Organização da Mulher Timorense (OMT – Organisation of Timorese Women), two long-standing women's networks, each with considerable reach throughout East Timor at grassroots level. Clearly the tensions between the two divert energy which could be directed at securing women's interests. Has the time come for these long-established movements to give way to newer, more relevant arrangements? This will have to be balanced against the value or relevance of their experience, solidarity and coverage. Can they be updated? Would Rede Feto (the East Timorese women's network) provide a sufficient platform for cooperation? Rede Feto has had considerable input from East Timorese women activists as well as foreign donors, and has grown stronger since 2002. It might serve as a bridge between all women's organisations, if they allow it to.

Paradoxically, it may take external pressure (the loss of a significant number of parliamentary seats for women in future elections, for example) to force the different parts of the women's movement to resolve these internal fractures. There may be lessons from similar situations elsewhere. In Mozambique, for example, the Organização da Mulher Moçambicana (Organisation of Mozambican Women) went through several mutations, including turning into a non-party non-governmental organisation (NGO) before eventually re-attaching itself to Frelimo. In post-conflict Mozambique, as in East Timor, the number of women's organisations and civil society organisations concerning themselves with various women's issues has certainly created a much more complex and diverse landscape.

One issue which has united women across all sorts of boundaries is that of violence, and domestic violence in particular. There is clearly a need for concerted action, given that the legal reforms will take time to have any effect. Efforts at cultural change will be very important. Another issue of increasing concern is trafficking. There have been reports of the trafficking of women from Thailand, Indonesia, Vietnam and the People's Republic of China for purposes of forced prostitution. According to a US State Department briefing of 2004, the East Timorese government is aware of the problem and anxious to act, but has found it difficult to distinguish trafficked persons from illegal migrants.[5]

The challenges facing the East Timorese women's movement are not so different from those facing East Timorese civil society in general. Political movements in East Timor need to move beyond the protest model developed during the liberation struggle to diversify their range of approaches. Major changes in tactics are needed. Liberation struggles do not prepare civil society movements for mature and constructive dialogue and engagement with government. On the other hand, new governments can often feel intimidated by a healthy civil society engagement, particularly when former resistance colleagues find themselves on opposite sides of the table.

The role of civil society in East Timor has developed strongly in the four years since the departure of the Indonesian army. NGOs have proliferated, coordinated to some degree by the NGO Forum, set up in 2000 and generously resourced by international donors.[6] Similarly, although labour unions were banned under the Indonesians, after their departure East Timorese workers began to establish their own unions with encouragement from Australian union organisations.[7]

The press was also controlled until the end of Indonesian rule, but today a free press operates, mostly centred on Dili, and a number of NGOs and women activists use their own newsletters and radio to stimulate debate. Women have also used regular slots on radio and TV to good effect. An enthusiastic civil society group in 2003 organised the production of a film, *Sirana* – the story of a young actress asked to perform the role of Rosa Bonaparte in a musical.[8] The film raises a number of issues, including domestic violence, and has been very successful in provoking debate.

Political representation

Perhaps once some of the structural issues of the women's movement have been addressed, it will be in a better position to encourage women members of parliament to push for issues of common concern. Women members of parliament have found it difficult to resist pressure from their own political parties to toe the party line in debates and when voting on legislation.

The Women's Caucus (see chapter 5) has been encouraging political parties to nurture women candidates and working with women members of parliament, particularly on domestic violence legislation. In general, organisations seeking to foster cooperation among women parliamentarians of different parties have found the going tough. Further thoughtful and creative thinking, and delicate action, are needed to build capacity and consensus in this area.

In both Namibia and Mozambique, women had more success in local elections than at national level. In East Timor, at least so far, the opposite seems to be true. The Women's Caucus has tried to encourage greater female representation at local level in East Timor, on village councils in particular.[9] Research by the National Democratic Institute shows that most East Timorese invest huge faith in their local leaders (*chefe de suco* and *chefe de aldeia*); they want them to be directly elected, and to have greater powers and support locally.[10] Most East Timorese living in rural areas have little information about national politics, and local politics have a much greater influence on their daily lives.

Women stood in the *chefe de suco* elections in Oecusse and Bobonaro (both traditionally matrilineal communities) in 2004. A quota was set at three out of seven places on local councils to be allocated to women. However the Office for the Promotion of Equality (OPE) and the Women's Caucus were unable to mount a sufficiently strong campaign to influence the outcomes, and only one woman was elected as a *chefe de suco*. The OPE and the Women's Caucus felt the failure was mainly due to the organisation of the campaign: there were simply not enough people active at the crucial time to influence the outcome. They planned a bigger effort for the next round of *chefe de suco* elections in 2005.

International intervention and foreign funding

International intervention brought advantages and disadvantages. In general terms, East Timorese activists found the huge influx of foreign personnel a great imposition at times, and reacted strongly against being treated as amateurs in relation to the development of their own country. They were not afraid to object, and the United Nations (UN) was forced on a number of occasions to modify its plans, and to accommodate more power-sharing in the interim administration.[11]

Women activists were determined that with or without the international community they were going to challenge their political leaders and push for greater participation and representation. Some felt that the international involvement had been supportive without being unduly interventionist. Others felt that resources had not been used to the greatest effect. Undoubtedly, support for gender and development activities in the East Timorese transition was an attractive option for international donors because of the obvious energy, commitment and enthusiasm of the many activists on hand to implement programmes and activities. There was a strong likelihood that such projects would be successful.

Nevertheless, there were some difficulties along the way. Rede Feto suffered a hiatus in funding for about 18 months after the United Nations Development Fund for Women (Unifem) unexpectedly pulled out for a time. Staff were forced to work unpaid for several months, and the network lost impetus. Organisations such as the OPMT have complained bitterly about their inability to raise funds from international sources because of their party political affiliations. Other women's organisations – such as Fokupers (the East Timorese Women's Communications Forum) – seem to have found it relatively easy to attract foreign donors.

The question arises, how sustainable are women's organisations likely to be in the long term? Overwhelmingly, women's organisations and networks in countries in transition and post-conflict periods are dependent on foreign donors. Capacity building among key personnel in women's organisations and networks will be crucial to safeguard their long term sustainability. President Xanana Gusmão has actively encouraged civil society organisations to raise their own funds. Communities have been encouraged to work together to raise money for common projects such as the establishment of schools.

Women in civil society can also be trained in the lobbying skills needed to access government funds through the OPE. This often requires the nurturing of key supporters and advocates in government, parliament and key ministries.

The backlash

Some East Timorese women activists wonder whether they have alienated their men from the concept of gender equality by making them feel as if they are enemies rather than partners in this particular struggle. The introduction of quotas in civil service and police recruitment, for example, is felt by some men as a very direct threat to their former privileges. Women activists have seen the need to explain more clearly that men can also gain from gender equality.

The right to vote, written laws, and access to better education are essential, but will not lead to equality by themselves. If gender equality is to be achieved, men must take personal responsibility for promoting change in their own lives. Because most leaders and decision makers are male, they have a great responsibility as role models: their words and actions contribute to the perpetuation or mutation of cultural rules. Unless they signal that equality is a key issue for women and men, little will change. The challenge for East Timorese women activists therefore is to find ways of convincing their male leaders to set the necessary example, not only in rhetoric, but in their personal behaviour.

For East Timorese men opposed to cultural change in gender relations, blaming the UN for importing feminist or 'western' ideas has been both logical and easy. Some men have threatened to campaign for a return to women's subordination when the UN leaves. The backlash has led women activists to reconsider the rights-based approach that has framed their strategies over the past decade.

Rights-based approaches are sometimes criticised for emphasising legal reform. It is clear from experience in many countries in transition that laws have little practical effect unless they are implemented, and that cultural change is also needed. Yet the passing of legislation can make states responsible for delivering improvements to women's lives, and that means that governments can be held to account. By framing violence against women as a rights issue, women activists were able to obtain protection under the law. Activists nonetheless recognise the need for longer term work on cultural change.

Rights-based approaches have other drawbacks. Manuela Pereira, the director of Fokupers, explains:

Fokupers first approached its work by talking about women's rights. They did this for five years. Then we did an evaluation with our constituents and what came out was that talking about women's rights was not very effective. Women would often respond: 'We can't listen to all this talk about rights because my husband does not know about rights.' So now we are changing our approach. We are talking instead about improving women's economic prospects and reaching out to the communities – that is the process that we use. We talk about people's rights through their work.[12]

Some East Timorese women's organisations are concentrating on economic projects, enabling women to generate income which can help their families. With high unemployment, practical necessities often take over from what some regard as theory. Much of this work is in the tradition of the efficiency or 'women and development' approaches of the 1980s and early 1990s, before the rights-based 'gender and development' approaches became popular. In practice, however, the rights-based approach to achieving gender justice in East Timor has not been abandoned. The two approaches are working alongside one another, addressing gender 'needs' and gender 'interests' simultaneously.

Government machinery[13]

The OPE has made much progress on gender mainstreaming in East Timor, with training extended to most government departments. With a decentralised structure in mind the head of the OPE, Maria Domingas Fernandes, has encouraged these departments to designate gender focal points: key staff (men as well as women) have been given the responsibility for mainstreaming gender throughout their ministry. The OPE still has to evolve mechanisms to hold government accountable for the advancement of women. This will require sex-disaggregated data and budgets, performance indicators, reporting to legislative bodies and reporting under international agreements, in particular the Convention on the Elimination of All Forms of Discrimination Against Women (CEDAW).

In many countries, there has been distrust between the women's movement and the government machinery set up to mainstream gender. This is not generally the case in East Timor, possibly because Maria Domingas Fernandes herself has a strong record of civil society organising. East Timorese women activists believe that the OPE has done well so far and the Second East Timorese

Women's Congress, held in August 2004, demanded the upgrading of the OPE to a ministry for women.[14]

It is important that the relationship between civil society and government on gender issues is healthy and constructive. Civil society representatives interviewed for this book affirmed the need to ensure that the OPE maintains an independent voice, respects the diversity of civil society women's organisations and refrains from favouring one over another. The OPE could benefit from working more closely with women's organisations, without presuming that they can, or should, implement its programmes. It is also incumbent on civil society organisations to support the OPE and hold it to account, while respecting the parameters that bind a government office.

For this to be a long term reality, the OPE will need continued support and resources from government. At present its office running costs and five of the seven salaries are paid for by the government, but the remaining salaries and its activities depend on funding from foreign governments, of which Ireland has so far been the most generous. The government's commitment to provide resources for the OPE will be something to monitor over the coming years.

In the light of the demands for it to become a full ministry, the OPE has been looking for models in neighbouring countries, in particular Cambodia and the Philippines. The two countries have different approaches: Cambodia has a minister for women, while the Philippines does not. The Cambodian minister is part of the Cabinet, which would imply that gender is part of decision making at the highest level. However, Timorese visitors to the Cambodian women's ministry felt that the structure may have become overly bureaucratic.

The OPE will also be responsible for implementing CEDAW and submitting reports to the monitoring committee. In years to come civil society organisations will monitor the information provided to the CEDAW committee, and have the option to submit their own information in a shadow report. The CEDAW monitoring process should ensure that all rights, whether civil and political, or economic, social and cultural, are taken into consideration in evaluating the government's performance on implementation.

Working with men

To change social attitudes it is necessary to challenge dominant models of masculinity, and that means working with men. The men's group Mane Kontra Violencia is an encouraging development. It has had some modest success in challenging cultural norms. Marito Araujo, a founder of the group, believes that men of all classes are beginning to change their attitudes towards women.[15] The prospect of going to jail for wife-beating, for example, has been something of a wake-up call. Mane Kontra Violencia has been challenging definitions of culture at village level in discussions with elders, using simple but effective arguments. Exploring the anger that leads to violence can also lead to a critical examination of traditional customs such as bride price, which can cause tensions in marriage. Questioning the norms and searching for creative alternatives could reduce such tensions in the future.

Key questions

The issues confronting East Timorese women activists are similar to those encountered by women's movements in other countries emerging from conflict. The experiences in Mozambique, Namibia and Cambodia can offer lessons for East Timor on some key questions:

1 What challenges are likely to stand in the way of progress towards gender equality?
2 Will foreign funding prevent women's organisations from setting their own agenda?
3 What do women's movements need to do to modernise, how can they best build a unified movement and how do they handle leadership?
4 How are the gains of the first elections to be safeguarded against a backlash?

What challenges are likely to stand in the way of progress towards gender equality?

While societies remain poor, progress in improving gender relations for empowerment of women will be limited. When women have to concentrate on the survival of their children and families, addressing gender 'needs' will often prevail over the furtherance of gender 'interests'. Thus poverty reduction strategies that take gender into account can help to pave the way for long term advances for women by improving their health, education, participation, representation and so on. Issues such as land tenure rights, access to markets, and transport are fundamental to transforming the lives of poor, rural, uneducated women. Such issues therefore need to be on the agenda of activists on women's issues, as well as those of women and men representatives in local and national government. Economic, social and cultural rights must be addressed alongside civil and political rights. A holistic approach is needed.

HIV and AIDS
With assistance from international financial institutions and governments, East Timor is developing poverty reduction strategies with gender components. Yet the fruits of such strategies could be wiped out by factors beyond the control of governments and institutions: natural disasters, famine and disease.

East Timor does not yet have a serious HIV and AIDS problem,[16] but international experts have warned that conditions exist in the country for a major epidemic. The government has recognised the need for prevention and awareness campaigns, but these need resources and impetus if spread of the disease is to be averted. The devastating consequences for women of widespread HIV and AIDS can be seen in Africa, where women have borne the brunt of the pandemic, both in terms of vulnerability to the infection and caring for others already afflicted. Women's groups in East Timor are aware of this danger and are becoming more involved in government HIV and AIDS prevention and awareness-raising schemes.

Neoliberalism
The effects of neoliberal economic policies and the risk of running into debt are also potential threats to East Timor, despite the government's current resolve not to borrow money. So far, East Timor has survived on grant aid from 10 donor countries, channelled through the Trust Fund for East Timor, jointly administered by the Asian Development Bank and the World Bank.

International involvement in the transitions of Mozambique, Namibia and Cambodia brought certain benefits such as peace keeping and emergency relief, an introduction to international legal norms, and international aid. But it also imposed neoliberal economic policies. World Bank structural adjustment programmes in Mozambique reversed previous development gains and many East Timorese see those lessons as a dire warning.

In Mozambique in particular, women and girls were hard hit by the structural adjustment programmes of the 1980s and early 1990s. They were the first to lose their jobs, and as health and education standards dropped, girls were the first to suffer malnutrition and to be pulled out of school. Women struggled to maintain their families in the informal economy as their menfolk were thrown out of work.[17]

East Timor has few economic assets. Even though the Timor Gap oil and gas fields may eventually provide much-needed revenue, the proceeds have yet to come on-stream, and the Australian government has driven a hard bargain over division of the eventual benefits.[18] Meanwhile, international aid has been tailing off. Although international donors have pledged a further US$360m, this may not be enough to finance the government's economic and social policies.

The World Bank and International Monetary Fund (IMF) arrived in East Timor before the Indonesians left in 1999. Both institutions played a major part in shaping East Timor's development strategies, including its first national development plan. Some civil society activists fear this will be followed by a Poverty Reduction Strategy Paper (PRSP), the successor to structural adjustment programmes.[19] Countries eligible for debt relief under the Heavily Indebted Poor Countries (HIPC II) initiative must produce a PRSP as a condition for receiving debt relief and future concessional loans. The World Bank promotes PRSPs as a new generation of policies, country-driven and country-owned, based on learning from the failures of the past. But the economic growth agenda behind them remains the same. Once the PRSP is formulated, it is presented to the joint board of the IMF and World Bank to judge whether they 'constitute a suitable basis for their own lending programmes'.[20]

One example of the World Bank's influence on East Timorese economic policy is in relation to coffee production. East Timor's most important export, after oil, is its fine arabica coffee. In 2001, the price of coffee on the world market fell, and the East Timorese coffee farmers asked the government to subsidise the price. The World Bank strongly advised against this.

Many Timorese civil society organisations are worried that if their government is forced to negotiate concessional loans from the international financial institutions, there could be dire consequences in terms of economic liberalisation, food insecurity, land ownership and privatisation of utilities such as water, power, finance and agricultural support. Although the World Bank professes to take account of gender issues in the participatory processes used in the formulation of PRSPs, the practice has been found to fall short of the rhetoric.[21] East Timorese women's organisations will need to monitor this.

Will foreign funding prevent women's organisations from setting their own agenda?

To what extent do foreign donors influence the agendas of the organisations and departments they choose to support? The views of those interviewed for this book were mixed. While some felt that the international NGOs had refrained from imposing policy directions, others felt that the very presence of foreign donor funding inevitably exerts considerable influence on the women's and civil society movements. The question arises whether this could ever be positive. From the experience in Cambodia, it appears that positive outcomes could emerge despite high levels of dependency on foreign funding, but that civil society organisations need to think clearly about the sources of their funds and the purposes to which they put them. They should also be aware of the consequences of doing without donor funds.

In East Timor from the early 1990s, funding and other support to local women's organisations and networks became an increasingly prominent component of international assistance, particularly after 1999. In Namibia, in contrast, funders were anxious to channel their resources into government institutions. Both Cambodia and East Timor benefited from the trend towards funding civil society organisations and NGOs, with strong cooperation between the UN, international NGO donors, women activists and returnees. The cooperation seems to have been particularly fruitful in Cambodia although it is not clear what would have existed without foreign funding, and what will exist in the future should the funding tail off.

It is clear that East Timorese women played a proactive role in organising for gender equity, and that they would have done so even without the assistance of the UN and international organisations. Nevertheless, the end of funding may signal the demise of certain initiatives unless creative ways can be found to sustain them. At the beginning of 2005, women activists in East Timor believed that funding was accessible and that they were able to negotiate terms acceptable to them. The key question remains the ability of women's organisations to work more effectively together to implement projects.

What do women's movements need to do to modernise, how can they best build a unified movement and how do they handle leadership?

Tensions are bound to arise when women from opposing political camps suddenly find themselves working alongside each other after an armed conflict. These tensions were eased in Cambodia by the availability of sufficient funding accompanied by even-handed management from the minister for women. East Timorese women's organisations have on occasions resented their rivals' access to funding. The competition for funds could intensify if, as seems likely in the long term, the sources start to dry up.

The reconciliation effort in East Timor may have helped ease political tensions, unlike the case in Namibia. The Comissão de Acolhimento, Verdade e Reconciliação (CAVR – Commission for Reception, Truth and Reconciliation) addressed the experiences and needs of women victims to some extent (although many would argue, not far enough). Women activists also encouraged the government to recognise female combatants and offer them compensation. The CAVR paid particular attention to documenting women's stories, and held a specific session for women victims to give testimony about the abuse they had endured during the civil war and Indonesian occupation.

The tensions between home-based activists and returnees also affected Cambodia and Namibia. Returning activists can often appear elitist and out of touch to those who stayed behind, whatever the skills they have to contribute. The lesson here seems to be that women's movements need to work hard to build inclusive new movements from the grassroots upwards, with fluid structures that encourage diversity and acceptance.

The question of who leads is often contentious. Women interviewed for this book often described other women leaders as 'arrogant', particularly if they belonged to rival organisations or political camps. Yet there is a sense in which leaders have to be given a chance to prove their abilities and allowed to lead. Provided democratic means exist for the periodic change of leaders, organisations have the means to govern themselves in a transparent manner.

How are the gains of the first elections to be safeguarded against a backlash?

Even in Mozambique, where women make up 30 per cent of the parliament, progress towards gender equality is slow, while in Namibia women's representation fell in the national elections in November 2004. The Namibian case showed that once women have achieved a milestone, they need to consolidate it. In Namibia, women were not well positioned on party lists, and lost heavily as a result. Women parliamentarians need strong and continuing support if they are to be effective agents of change and gender justice. International experts such as Lesley Abdela[22] emphasise the need to work with parliaments as a group and to win the support of male politicians for female ones in order to make structures of governance more equitable.

As in Mozambique, East Timorese women have identified the cultural attitudes that lie at the roots of the violence against women. They have fought for domestic violence legislation and mounted a national campaign to ensure that it is implemented. Education has an important part to play, as Milena Pires has stated:

> As a product of their own societies, women often help to maintain the status quo and perpetuate gender stereotypes. Education cannot be overemphasised, as it provides alternatives and helps to change attitudes with time. It must start in schools to promote generational change as well as target young women, professional and older women. And since decision making and power often remains in the hands of men, education of boys and men is also vital.[23]

Strategies to improve gender relations need to include work with men as well as with women. That is why the work of Mane Kontra Violencia in East Timor is so important: for men to challenge male behaviour and social norms can be a particularly powerful agent of change. As in East Timor, some Cambodian men set up a group to look at masculinities and men's role in cultural change. This helps to challenge and change role models for young people, male and female. The experience shows that such challenges must start in the family home, but crucially, must be backed up by policy at state level.

In Mozambique, women are more inclined to include men in their organisations – something which also seems to be under consideration in East Timor. It is also important for the groups to work together to reinforce each other's messages. In June 2004 men from Mane Kontra Violencia marched with East Timorese women in protest at the rape of a woman by a group of police officers in Dili. This sent a powerful signal to other men.

There is a need to broaden support for gender equity throughout civil society, even among the groups that seem most resistant.

Conclusion

UN involvement, and the strengthening of international legal norms on women's rights, together with constitution-framing processes which took account of these, have undoubtedly contributed considerably to women's increasing sense of progress. Yet it would be unhelpful to exaggerate their impact. As Brigitte Sonnois points out in chapter 9, in Cambodia the volume of activity has been immense but the results have been modest, and the impact on most women's lives has been limited. The same applies in all the countries discussed in this book.

In all these countries, there is a need to improve living conditions, not only for women, but for their societies as a whole. Women activists should not be discouraged at this reality. They have the determination and inner resources, and they will go on doing what is necessary to work for a better future for their daughters and sons, communities and nations. It is important to recognise that everyone who participates in civil society movements is working incrementally for a long term objective. These movements need to take a historical view of their part in this ultimate goal, regardless of short term indicators and the monitoring frameworks of international donors. East Timorese women and men have made a convincing start, and without a doubt deserve the continuing support of the international community to accompany them on their way.

In the words of Maria Lourdes Martins Cruz:

Women now have a voice that they did not have before and this is new for East Timorese men. Now we can have a new life. Women started to develop themselves in groups and during Indonesian times education and training were made available. Lots of Timorese women care deeply for their country. What we need now is to create greater equality.... We need to educate our boys and girls with a strong vision for the future, and we need to educate our men to be able to accommodate change, and to internalise the changes necessary. The Indonesians had a negative effect on the mentality of our menfolk. They did not organise themselves in the same way that we women did. They grew up in a hard time. But women cannot wait for men to change – we have to get on with our own change....

A luta continua – the struggle continues.[24]

Notes

1   UNDP (2002), *East Timor National Development Plan 2002*, United Nations Development Programme, p6.

2   The Asian Development Bank and the government of East Timor signed a poverty reduction partnership agreement in October 2003. Work on East Timor's second Human Development Report in 2005 will include looking at how progress towards the Millennium Development Goals, including enhanced strategies for gender mainstreaming, can be measured.

3   Taken from 'Human development index trends', *Human development report 2004*, United Nations Development Programme, 2004 (http://hdr.undp.org/statistics/data/pdf/

hdr04_table_2.pdf, accessed July 2005).

4　Asian Development Bank (2004) *Country strategy and programme update 2005-2006: Timor Leste.*

5　US State Department (2004) *Trafficking in persons report*, US State Department, Washington, 11 June 2004.

6　By mid-2001, 130 national and 73 international NGOs had registered at this forum. See Bano, A (2001) 'The role of civil society organisations' in Anderson, R, and Deutsche, C (eds) *Sustainable development and the environment in East Timor: Proceedings of the conference on sustainable development in East Timor, 25-31 January 2001*, Timor Aid, Dili.

7　For example, the Australian People for Health Education and Development Abroad, the humanitarian wing of the Australian trade union movement – see Mather, C (2000) *The labour situation and workers' support groups in Timor Lorosae (East Timor) – Report of a research visit, 15-25 May 2000*, unpublished report, UK.

8　This was the first film made by East Timorese about their own history, a fact of which the organisers of the project were justifiably proud.

9　Teresa Cardoso in an interview with Catherine Scott, June 2004.

10　National Democratic Institute (2003) *Government within reach: A report on the views of East Timorese on local government*, Dili.

11　Yayasan HAK (2000) *From scorched earth operation to humanitarian operation* – a *note on the conduct of international NGOs and UN institutions in post-referendum Timor Lorosae*, compiled by the Working Group for Study and Examination, Yayasan HAK, Dili.

12　Interview with Catherine Scott, June 2004.

13　The Beijing Platform for Action sets out the role of national machineries as 'the central policy coordinating unit inside the government. Its main function is to support government wide mainstreaming of a gender-equality perspective in all policy areas.' (Paragraph 201.)

14　Declaration and plan of action, Second National East Timorese Women's Congress, 27-31 July 2004.

15　Interview with Catherine Scott, June 2004.

16　USAID Bureau for Global Health (2004), *Country profile on East Timor*, USAID, Washington DC, November 2004. This document quotes the 2002 figure of 0.64 per cent prevalence.

17　A critique of the gender implications of structural adjustment programmes was developed from the mid-1980s by feminist economists such as Isobel Bakker and Diane Elson: see Elson, D (1995) *Male bias in the development process*, Manchester University Press. They exposed the social consequences for women and children of policies which concentrated almost exclusively on economic growth.

18　For a full discussion of the dispute between Australia and East Timor over the Timor Gap, see Catry, J-P (2004) 'Australia's offshore oil grab in the Timor Gap' in *Le Monde Diplomatique*, December 2004.

19　The World Bank displays the East Timor National Development Plan in the Poverty

Reduction Strategy Paper section of its website, although it does not list the country as having completed a PRSP.

20 IMF/Institute of Economic Development (2002) *Evaluation of Poverty Reduction Strategy Papers and the Poverty Reduction and Growth Facility*, International Monetary Fund, Washington DC.

21 For an in-depth evaluation of the implementation of gender analysis in the World Bank PRSP process with reference to Nicaragua and Honduras, see Bradshaw, S, and Linneker, B (2002) *Challenging women's poverty: Perspectives on gender and poverty reduction strategies from Nicaragua and Honduras*, Catholic Institute for International Relations, London.

22 Director of Project Parity and Shevolution, based in the UK.

23 Pires, M (2004) 'Timor-Leste: Promoting women's post-conflict participation' in *Cross Currents*, Unifem, March 2004.

24 Interview with Catherine Scott, June 2004.

Appendices

Feminism/feminist
Advocacy of the rights of women – 'minimally, the term implies
the identification of women as systematically oppressed; the
belief that gender relations are neither inscribed in natural
differences between the sexes, nor immutable, and a political
commitment to their transformation' (Andermahr, S, Lovell, T,
and Wolkowitz, C, 1997, *A concise glossary of feminist theory*, OUP,
New York).

Gender and development (GAD)
An approach to development that looks at women's and men's
socially constructed roles and their impact on one another. It
analyses gender relations in terms of power. GAD approaches
focus on changing the attitudes of men as well as women. It has
largely superseded the earlier women in development (WID) and
women and development (WAD) approaches.

Gender mainstreaming
The United Nations Economic and Social Council (ECOSOC)
defines gender mainstreaming as:

> ... the process of assessing the implications for women and
> men of any planned action, including legislation, policies or
> programmes, in any area and at all levels. It is a strategy for
> making the concerns and experiences of women as well as
> of men an integral part of the design, implementation,
> monitoring and evaluation of policies and programmes in
> all political, economic and societal spheres, so that women
> and men benefit equally, and inequality is not perpetuated.
> The ultimate goal of mainstreaming is to achieve gender
> equality. [See www.sdnp.undp.org/gender/capacity/
> gm_intro.html, accessed July 2005]

Gender 'needs' and gender 'interests'
These concepts, orginally defined by Maxine Molyneux
('Mobilisation without emancipation?' in *Feminist Studies*, Spring
1985) distinguish between women's immediate practical concerns
– welfare, food, shelter, etc – and more strategic, longer term

goals such as a greater role in community decision making, the ability to meet in groups and organise with other women, and so on.

Patriarchy
The 'rule of the father': the dominance of men and subordination of women in society at large.

Rights-based approach
An approach to development which sets rights and justice as the starting point from which interventions should be formulated and draws on international human rights standards to monitor their effectiveness.

Sex and gender
'Sex' refers to the biological difference between male and female human beings or other animals. 'Gender' refers to the socially constructed roles of males and females. All societies have different rules of behaviour for women and men, although these may differ enormously from one society to another.

Women and development (WAD)
This successor to women in development (WID) theory recognised women as actors in their own development, but justified interventions in terms of 'efficiency', arguing that policies and progress for women could improve economic productivity. It failed to consider women's rights and social position.

Women in Development (WID)
This was the first attempt at recognising that women needed to be taken account of in development. It focused on women as a separate group, but most of the approaches related to welfare interventions.

Women's issues
Concerns relating to family, society or world events which particularly affect and challenge women and which become a focus for group action.

Appendix 2: Women's human rights

The UN Charter holds fundamental human rights to be core principles and objectives of the United Nations, and affirms the equal rights of men and women.

The Universal Declaration of Human Rights (1948) holds that all people are entitled to all the rights and freedoms enshrined in it, regardless of 'race, colour, sex, language, religion, political or other opinion, national or social origin, property, birth or other status'.

The International Covenant on Civil and Political Rights (1966) provides that states shall 'ensure the equal right of men and women to the enjoyment of all civil and political rights set forth in the present Covenant'.

Women's rights were addressed specifically in the Convention on the Elimination of All Forms of Discrimination Against Women (CEDAW) of 1979. It commits its signatories to condemn violence against women, to create legal and social protections against violence, and to refrain from invoking custom, tradition or religion to avoid these obligations.

From the 1990s onwards, a series of treaties, covenants and action plans has sought to build on CEDAW:

1993   The World Conference on Human Rights in Vienna declares that 'violations of the human rights of women in situations of armed conflict are violations of the fundamental principles of international human rights and humanitarian law [and] require a particularly effective response'.

   The UN General Assembly adopts the Declaration on the Elimination of Violence Against Women.

1993-4 The statutes of the International Criminal Tribunal for the Former Yugoslavia and the International Criminal Tribunal on Rwanda explicitly include rape as a war crime.

   The UN Commission on Human Rights appoints a UN Special Rapporteur on violence against women.

1995   The Fourth World Conference on Women in Beijing produces the Global Platform for Action which elaborates on states' obligations under CEDAW and reinforces state responsibility to protect women and girls.

1998   The Rome Statute of the International Criminal Court defines rape, sexual slavery, enforced prostitution, forced pregnancy, enforced sterilisation, and other grave forms of systematic sexual violence as crimes against humanity. The statute entered into force on 1 July 2002.

        Optional protocol for CEDAW introduced, allowing an individual complaint process.

2000   The Beijing Plus Five Review, New York, reiterates concerns about human rights violations against women. UN Security Council passes Resolution 1325 on women in conflict and peacebuilding.

2000-1 G8 statements allude to gender issues, as do guidelines on conflict, peace and development cooperation from the Organisation for Economic Cooperation and Development (OECD) Development Assistance Committee.

Appendix 3: Resolution of the Conselho Nacional da Resistência Timorense (CNRT – National Council of Timorese Resistance), August 2000

We, the undersigned, delegates of CNRT National Congress, concerned with:

1 the continuing discrimination and inequality of opportunities for women in East Timorese society;

2 the violence against women within and outside of the house;

3 the polygamy and lack of participation of women in decision making;

4 the absence of laws that protect Timorese women;

We call for this historic CNRT National Congress to adopt policies that can really contribute towards an inclusive, equitable and law abiding society, and for all the elected CNRT members to gather their efforts to call upon:

1 UNTAET [the United Nations Transitional Administration in East Timor] and the future East Timor Government to make available sufficient resources for the development and empowerment of East Timorese women;

2 the National Council of UNTAET to establish laws and legal mechanisms that can protect women victims of domestic and sexual violence;

3 UNTAET and the future government of East Timor to create mechanisms at the government level that can meet and guarantee gender equity;

4 UNTAET to carry out an education campaign on women's and children's rights to end the practice of discrimination against women, including traditional practices.

Appendix 4: Women's Charter of Rights in East Timor

This charter was drawn up by women's organisations, who presented it to the Constituent Assembly elected in 2001.

Article 1: Equality
1 The Constitution must prohibit all forms of discrimination.
2 The State may implement positive measures to promote equality between men and women.
3 Men and women are guaranteed equality before the law.

Article 2: Right to security of the person
1 The Constitution must protect women's right to live free from any form of violence.

Article 3: Political rights
The Constitution must guarantee equal rights of women in political activities and public life as follows:
1 The right to vote and be elected.
2 The right to participate in government policy decision making.
3 The right to participate in organisations concerned with communal and national politics.

Article 4: Right to health
1 The Constitution must protect all people's right to basic health care of the same quality.
2 The State must provide reproductive health care for women.

Article 5: Right to education
1 The Constitution must guarantee equal rights to formal and non-formal education for men and women.
2 Women must have equal opportunity to study, and have equal access to scholarship opportunities and literacy programmes.

Article 6: Social rights
1 The Constitution must guarantee the rights to livelihood, shelter, sanitation, electricity, water, transportation and communication, health and education.
2 Women must participate in development programmes at every level.

3 The right to social security in case of sickness, unemployment and incapacity to work.

Article 7: Labour rights
1 The Constitution must guarantee equal pay for equal work.
2 Women must have a right to maternity leave without loss of salary, job or position.
3 Women's health needs must be protected in the workplace.
4 Women have the right to safe working conditions.
5 Dismissal must be prohibited in cases of pregnancy or maternity leave.

Article 8: Tradition and women's rights
1 Equal rights to inheritance.
2 The Constitution must regulate the dowry system to prevent violence against women.
3 Women must be guaranteed participation in traditional decision-making processes.

Article 9: The right to freedom from exploitation
1 The Constitution should prohibit prostitution and slavery.

Article 10: Children's rights
The Constitution must protect children's basic rights:
1 Rights to food, shelter and social services.
2 The right to be cared for by parents and family.
3 The right not to carry out work beyond the child's age capacity.

Appendix 5: Extracts from the Constitution of the Republic of East Timor

Preamble, Section 6: Objectives of the State
The fundamental objectives of the state shall be:
   j) To create, promote and guarantee the effective equality of opportunities between women and men.

General Principles, Section 16: Universality and Equality
   1 All citizens are equal before the law, shall exercise the same rights and shall be subject to the same duties.
   2 No-one shall be discriminated against on grounds of colour, race, marital status, gender, ethnic origin, language, social or economic status, political or ideological convictions, religion, education and physical or mental condition.

General Principles, Section 17: Equality between women and men
Women and men shall have the same rights and duties in all areas of family, political, economic, social and cultural life.

Appendix 6: Women's Platform for Action, Second East Timorese Women's Congress, August 2004

- Reduce the level of female illiteracy.
- Improve women's access to continuing education, vocational training, and science and technology.
- Increase women's and men's understanding of gender at all levels of society in order to implement the Convention on the Elimination of All Forms of Discrimination Against Women (CEDAW).
- Facilitate women's equal access to employment and productive resources.
- Promote women's participation in sustainable development processes.
- Strengthen women's economic capacity.
- Strengthen preventative programmes that promote women's maternal health.
- Promote women's knowledge, access and use of traditional medicine and traditional ecological knowledge.
- Undertake gender-sensitive initiatives to address sexually transmitted diseases, HIV and AIDs, and sexual and reproductive health issues.
- Increase women's access during their life cycle to information and affordable, quality health services.
- Take measures to ensure women's equal access and participation in power and decision-making structures.
- Resolve the maritime boundary dispute between Timor Leste and Australia.
- Recognise the service of women in the struggle for independence.
- Promote and protect the rights of minority groups in society.
- Strengthen and protect women's access to formal justice.
- Eliminate gender-based violence.
- Take action to guarantee justice for women victims of the war for national liberation 1974-1999.
- Change public opinion about the aspects of culture that have negative impacts on women, young women and girls.
- Create laws on cultural practices that uphold international human rights standards and ensure the practical realisation of these principles.
- Combat negative portrayals of women in media communications – electronic, print, visual, and audio – that negatively affect women and their participation in society.

Appendix 7: Women's organisations in East Timor

Alola Foundation
Founded: 2001 by Kirsty Sword Gusmão
Current leader: Kirsty Sword Gusmão
Purpose: The foundation works to boost the status and well-being of East Timorese women and children through programmes in the areas of maternal and child health, education, economic empowerment and advocacy. The foundation is named after Juliana dos Santos, known as Alola, a young woman abducted by a violent militia leader in 1999 and taken to West Timor, where she remains his prisoner to this day.

ET-Wave
East Timorese Movement Against Violence Towards Women and Children; formerly Gertak (Gerakan Wanita Anti-Kekerasan)
Founded: 1998 by Olandina Caeiro
Current leader: Olandina Caeiro
Purpose: ET-Wave focuses on violence against women and children. Its main aims are to collect testimonies from women and children who have been victims of violence and to use these testimonies to bring the perpetrators to justice. It also provides assistance, such as food and access to health and psycho-social services, to the victims of abuse. It helps victims to give evidence before the UN Commission on Human Rights and has helped to set up several women's magazines.

Fokupers
Forum Komunikasi Untuk Perempuan Lorosae – East Timorese Women's Communications Forum
Founded: 1997 by Maria Domingas Alves
Current leader: Manuela Pereira
Purpose: Women's development and advocacy with special focus on violence against women. Fokupers gives counselling and other forms of assistance to women victims of human rights violations, including former political prisoners, war widows, wives of political prisoners and victims of domestic violence. Its mandate also includes promoting women's human rights. Fokupers works with the women's movement of Indonesia.

Grupo Feto Foinsae Timor Lorosae
GFFTL – East Timor Students Women's Group
Founded: 1998 by students of the University of East Timor,
including Teresa de Cavalho, Angelina Atanasia Pires, Elisa da
Silva.
Current leader: Rosa Xavier
Purpose: Helped to organise free speech dialogues throughout
East Timor in 1998 and worked for reconciliation. In November
1998, the group co-organised a conference on the situation of
Timorese women, the first conference of its kind in 23 years of
occupation. Since 2002 GFFTL has conducted a citizenship
education and literacy programme for women, targeting remote
areas. It has begun to expand this to include basic education in
democracy, in the hope of empowering women at the grassroots
and encouraging them to take a more active role in their
communities.

Organização da Mulher Timorense
OMT – Organisation of Timorese Women
Founded: 1998
Current leader: Florentina Smith
Purpose: The OMT was set up as a counterpart to the Conselho
Nacional da Resistência Timorense (CNRT – National Council of
Timorese Resistance), as a women's umbrella organisation that
embraced women from all political and non-political affiliations.
After the CNRT dissolved, OMT members decided to maintain the
OMT as an independent non-partisan women's organisation.
OMT activities are similar to those of the OPMT: income-
generating projects for widows and orphans, self-sufficiency and
literacy programmes.

Organização Popular da Mulher Timorense
OPMT – Popular Organisation of East Timorese Women
Founded: 28 August 1975 by Rosa Bonaparte, Maia Reis, Aicha
Bassarawan, Dulce da Cruz, Isabel Lobato, Maria do Ceu and
others.
Current leader: Regina Soares
Purpose: The OPMT is the women's wing of the political party
Frente Revolucionária de Timor Leste Independente (Fretilin –
Revolutionary Front for an Independent East Timor). Rosa
Bonaparte described it as 'a mass organisation of Fretilin – which
will work to enable women to participate in the revolution'. The
OPMT also aimed to fight discrimination against women and to

promote the emancipation of women in all aspects of life. During the war it became an essential part of the armed and clandestine struggle. It continued for 25 years underground and came out into the open at the Fretilin congress in 2000.

After independence the OPMT set up income-generating projects, for example weaving cooperatives and sewing classes, especially for widows, orphans and other socially disadvantaged women. This programme is perceived as crucial to the OPMT's objectives because it helps women to achieve a degree of economic self-sufficiency.

Rede Feto Timor Lorosae
The East Timorese Women's Network
Founded: 2000
Current executive director: Ubalda Elves
Purpose: Serves as an umbrella to forward the agendas of periodic Women's Congresses, the most recent of which (at the time of writing) was held in July 2004. Currently has 18 member organisations.

Women's Caucus
The East Timor Women's Political Caucus
Founded: May 2001
Current executive director: Teresa Cardoso
Purpose: To encourage women's direct participation in the political process through political parties and government, and indirect participation through other channels within civil society. The Caucus organises monthly lunches for all women parliamentarians and key women activists to discuss current issues affecting women and their roles in the development of the country and how policy decisions affect women. In the run-up to the Constituent Assembly elections in 2001 the Women's Caucus helped register women as independent candidates. Post-election, the Caucus helped form gender working groups to develop a charter on women's rights, continued to advocate for its adoption in the draft constitution, and publishes a popular newsletter to encourage women's participation in public life. The Caucus also promotes women candidates for the village-level elections scheduled for 2005 and 2006.

In addition to these women's organisations, several East Timorese NGOs have also developed their own women's – and feminist – divisions and projects.

Appendix 8: Comparative statistics: East Timor, Mozambique, Namibia and Cambodia

Source: UNDP Human Development Report 2005, unless otherwise indicated

Basic data

	East Timor	Mozambique	Namibia	Cambodia
Life expectancy at birth (2003)	54.5 years	41.1 years	47.6 years	52.4 years
Adult literacy (2003)	58.6%	46.5%	85%	73.6%
Adult literacy (female)	36%*	31.4%[†]	83.5%	64.1%
Adult literacy (male)	51%*	62.3%[†]	86.8%	84.7%
GDP per capita (US$ PPP) (2003)	$1,033 (estimate)	$1,117	$6,180	$2,078
Population (2003)	0.8 million	19.1 million	2 million	13.5 million

PPP = purchasing power parity

* United Nations Office in Timor-Leste (www.unmiset.org), data not dated (overall adult literacy figure for East Timor is for 2003, taken from UNDP Human Development Report 2005)

[†] 2002

Gender, economic activity and income

	East Timor	Mozambique	Namibia	Cambodia
Female economic activity rate* (2003)	73.1%	82.6%	53.7%	80.1%
Female economic activity rate as % of male rate (2003)	86%	92%	68%	97%
Estimated earned income for women (US$ PPP) (2003)	N/A	$910	$4,201	$1,807
Estimated earned income for men (US$ PPP) (2003)	N/A	$1,341	$8,234	$2,368
Ratio of female to male earned income	N/A	0.68	0.51	0.76

* Economic activity rate = percentage of population aged 15 or over who are economically active
PPP = purchasing power parity

Health and education

	East Timor	Mozambique	Namibia	Cambodia
Maternal mortality rate* (2000)	660	1,000	300	450
Births attended by trained medical staff (1995-2003)	24%	48%	78%	32%
Contraceptive prevalence (1995-2003)	10%†	6%	29%	24%
HIV prevalence (2003)	0.64%**	12.2%	21.3%	2.6%
Female adult literacy (2003)	N/A	31.4%	83.5%	64.1%
Female youth literacy (ages 15-24) (2003)	N/A	49.2%	93.5%	78.9%
Primary enrolment ratio for girls (02/03)	63%‡	53%	81%	91%
Secondary enrolment ratio for girls (02/03)	N/A	10%	50%	19%

* Per 100,000 live births – adjusted to account for well documented problems of underreporting and misclassification of maternal deaths

† Source: UNICEF Multi Indicator Cluster Survey 2002

** Source: USAID Bureau for Global Health, *Country profile on East Timor*, 2004

‡ Figure for female primary school net attendance 1996-2003. Source: *The state of the world's children 2005*, UNICEF

Women in parliament (as of 28 February 2005)

Country	No of lower house seats	No of seats occupied by women	Percentage of seats occupied by women	Position in the world
Mozambique	250	87	34.8%	9th
East Timor	87	22	25.3%	21st
Namibia	72	18	25%	22nd
Cambodia	123	12	9.8%	84th

Source: Inter-Parliamentary Union

Bibliography

(for East Timor chapters)

Abrantes, L, and Domingo Fernandes, M (2003) *Hakerek ho ran (Written in blood)*, Office for the Promotion of Equality, Dili.

Aditjondro, G (1997) *Violence by the state against women in East Timor: A report to the UN Special Rapporteur on Violence Against Women, including its causes and consequences*, Australia East Timor Human Rights Centre, Fitzroy.

Aditjondro, G (2001) 'Women as victims vs women as fighters: Redressing asymmetry in East Timorese discourse' in *Asian Exchange*, vol 16 no 1.

Almeida, I (1998) 'Convention offers little to Timorese women's movement' in *Timor Link*, August 1998.

Amnesty International (1995) *Women in Indonesia and East Timor: Standing against repression*, AI Index ASA21/51/95, Amnesty International, London.

Amnesty International (2004) *Indonesia and Timor Leste: Justice for Timor Leste – the way forward*, AI Index ASA21/006/2004, Amnesty International, London.

Anderson, R, and Deutsche, C (eds) *Sustainable development and the environment in East Timor: Proceedings of the conference on sustainable development in East Timor, 25-31 January 2001*, Timor Aid, Dili.

Asian Development Bank (2004) *Country strategy and programme update 2005-2006: Timor Leste.*

Bell, E, et al (2002) *National machineries for women in development: Experiences, lessons and strategies,* Institute of Development Studies, UK.

Boyce, D (1995) *East Timor: Where the sun rises over the crocodile's tail*, Dili (self-published); and in *Asia Pacific Journal of Anthropology*, vol 2 no 2, September 2001, pp89-113.

Bradshaw, S, and Linneker, B (2002) *Challenging women's poverty: Perspectives on gender and poverty reduction strategies from Nicaragua and Honduras*, Catholic Institute for International Relations, London.

Brownmiller, S (1975) *Against our will: Men, women and rape*, Simon and Schuster, New York.

Byrne, B, et al (1996) *National machineries for women in development: Experiences, lessons and strategies for institutionalising gender in development policy and planning*, Institute of Development Studies, UK.

Carey, P, and Carter Bentley, G (eds) (1995) *East Timor at the crossroads: The forging of a nation*, University of Hawaii, Honolulu.

Carey, P (2001) 'Challenging tradition, changing society: The role of women in East Timor's transition to independence' in *Lusotopie*, 2001, pp255-267.

Carvalho, M (2001) *Os dois lados da moeda*, Instituto Brasileiro de Análises Sociais e Econômicas (Brazilian Institute of Social and Economic Analysis) (www.ibase.br), translation by Catherine Scott.

CAVR (2003) *Report on National Public Hearing on Women and Conflict*, Commission for Reception, Truth and Reconciliation, 5 May 2003 (see www.easttimor-reconciliation.org).

CIIR (1989) *I am Timorese – testimonies from East Timor*, Catholic Institute for International Relations, London, on behalf of the Christian Consultation on East Timor.

CIIR (1996) *East Timor: The continuing betrayal*, Catholic Institute for International Relations, London.

CIIR (1999) *Humanising peace: The impact of peace agreements on human rights*, Catholic Institute for International Relations, London.

CIIR (2001a) *East Timor: Transition to statehood*, Catholic Institute for International Relations, London.

CIIR (2001b) *Report of the CIIR observer mission to the East Timor Constituent Assembly election, 30 August 2001*, unpublished report, Catholic Institute for International Relations, London.

CIIR (1985-2003) *Timor Link*, Catholic Institute for International Relations, London.

Clery, C (1994) 'Expatriate tells of continuing horrors facing East Timor' (interview with Elizabeth Exposto), *Irish Times*, 12 December 1994.

Cockburn, C (2000) 'The women's movement – boundary crossing on terrains of conflict' in Cohen, R, and Rai, S (eds) *Global social movements*, Athlone Press, London.

Coles, M (1993) 'The forgotten war of East Timor' (interview with Maria Braz), *The Guardian*, 10 November 1993.

Coomaraswamy, R (1998) *Report of the Special Rapporteur on Violence Against Women*, United Nations Commission on Human Rights, 54th session, Item 9a, E/CN.4/1998/54.

Coomaraswamy, R (1999) 'Integration of the human rights of women and the gender perspective: Violence against women', addendum to *Mission to Indonesia and East Timor on the issue of violence against women*, United Nations Economic and Social Council, Item 12a, E/CN.4/1999/68/Add.3.

Cristalis, I (2002) *Bitter dawn: East Timor – a people's story*, Zed Books, London.

De Fatima, M (2002) 'Mobilising women for the sustainable rebuilding of East Timor', paper contributed to the Sustaining our Communities conference organised by Adelaide City Council in March 2002.

Defert, G (1992) *Timor Est: Le génocide oublié. Droits d'un peuple et raisons d'etat*, L'Harmattan, Paris.

El-Bushra, J (2003) *Women building peace: Sharing know-how*, International Alert, UK.

Fokupers (1999) *Gender-based human rights abuses during the pre and post-ballot violence in East Timor: Preliminary report, Jan-Oct 1999*, unpublished report, Forum Komunikasi Untuk Perempuan Lorosae, Dili.

Fox, J, and Soares, D (eds) *Out of the ashes*, Crawford House Publishing, Adelaide.

Furusawa, K, and Inglis, J (1998) 'Violence against women in East Timor under the Indonesian occupation' in Lourdes Sajor, I (ed) *Common grounds: Violence against women in war and armed conflict situations*, Asian Centre for Women's Human Rights, Quezon City.

Gunn, G (1999) *Timor Lorosae: 500 years*, Livros do Oriente, Macao.

Hicks, D (1976) *Tetum ghosts and kin: Fieldwork in an Indonesian community*, Mayfield Publications, Palo Alto.

Hicks, D (1984) *A maternal religion: The role of women in Tetum myth and ritual*, Special Report No 22, Monograph Series on Southeast Asia, DeKalb Center for Southeast Asian Studies, Northern Illinois University.

Hill, H (1978) *Fretilin: The origins, ideologies and strategies of a nationalist movement in East Timor*, MA thesis, Monash University, Australia.

ICTJ (2003) *Intended to fail: The trials before the ad hoc human rights court in Jakarta*, International Centre for Transitional Justice, New York.

International Alert (2000) *From kitchen table to the negotiating table*, International Alert, London.

International Alert (2001) *Gender and peace support operations: Opportunities and challenges to improve practice*, International Alert, London.

IRC (2001) *If not now, when? Post-conflict situation in East Timor*, International Rescue Committee, Dili.

IRC (2002) *Gender based violence: Challenges and ways forward – A report of focus groups in four districts*, International Rescue Committee, Dili.

Jolliffe, J (1978) *East Timor nationalism and colonialism*, University of Queensland Press, St Lucia, Queensland.

Jolliffe, J (2001) 'Timor's haunted women' in *The Age* (Melbourne), 3 November 2001.

JSMP (2004a) *An analysis of a sexual assault decision from the Dili District Court, Dili, East Timor, July 2004*, Judicial Systems Monitoring Programme, Dili.

JSMP (2004b) *Women in the formal justice sector*, Judicial Systems Monitoring Programme, Dili.

JSMP (2004c) *Access to justice for women victims*, Judicial Systems Monitoring Programme, Dili.

JSMP (2005) *Statistics on cases of violence against women in Timor Leste*, Judicial Systems Monitoring Programme, Dili.

Kohen, A (1999) *From the place of the dead*, St Martin's Press, New York.

Linton, S (2001) 'Rising from the ashes: The creation of a viable criminal justice system in East Timor' in *Melbourne University Law Review*, vol 25.

Martinkus, J (2002) 'Beyond justice' in *The Bulletin*, 11 June 2002.

Mather, C (2000) *The labour situation and workers' support groups in Timor Lorosae (East Timor) – Report of a research visit, 15-25 May 2000*, unpublished report, UK.

Meintjes, S, Pillay, A, and Turshen, M (eds) (2001) *The aftermath: Women in post-conflict transformation*, Zed Books, London.

National Democratic Institute (2003) *Government within reach: A report on the views of East Timorese on local government*, National Democratic Institute, Dili.

O'Kane, M (2001) 'The men's war is over: now the women begin their fight' in *The Guardian*, 22 January 2001.

O'Keefe, C, and Whittington, S (2002) *Women in East Timor: A report on women's health, education, economic empowerment and decision-making*, Office for the Promotion of Equality/Ireland Aid, Dili.

Ospina, S, and Hohe, T (2001) *Traditional power structure and the community empowerment and local governance project*, Final Report, World Bank, Dili.

Panter, M, and Rogers, B (2001) *Report on a visit to East Timor 28 April-5 May 2001*, Christian Solidarity Worldwide, Hong Kong/Australia.

Pereira, M (2001) 'Domestic violence: A part of women's daily lives in East Timor' in *La'o Hamutuk Bulletin*, vol 2 no 5, August 2001.

Pinto, C, and Jardine, M (1997) *East Timor's unfinished struggle*, South End Press, Boston, MA.

Pires, M (1999) 'Towards a gendered approach to post-conflict reconstruction and development', unpublished paper for a conference on a strategic development plan for East Timor, Melbourne, 4-9 April 1999.

Pires, M (2004) 'Timor-Leste: Promoting women's post-conflict participation' in *Cross Currents*, Unifem, March 2004.

Rehn, E, and Sirleaf, E (2002) *Women, war, peace*, Unifem, New York.

Retboll, T (ed) (1998) *East Timor: Occupation and resistance*, International Work Group for Indigenous Affairs, Denmark.

Reuters (1995) 'East Timorese women yearn for freedom from rape', Reuters Information Service, 3 September 1995.

Rimmer, S (2003a) *The rights of East Timorese women and the Catholic Church*, unpublished paper, Australian National University.

Rimmer, S (2003b) *Untold numbers: East Timorese women and transitional justice*, unpublished paper, Australian National University.

Rimmer, S (2003c) *Building a feminist model of transitional justice: Women in East Timor*, unpublished paper, Australian National University.

Rodriguez, J (1994) *Our Lady of Guadalupe: Faith and empowerment among Mexican-American Women*, University of Texas Press.

Rowlands, J (1997) *Questioning empowerment: Working with women in Honduras*, Oxfam, Oxford.

Scott, C (1997) *Women, faith and empowerment*, MA dissertation, University of East Anglia, Norwich.

Scott, C (2001a) *East Timor: Transition to statehood,* Catholic Institute for International Relations, London.

Scott, C (2001b) 'Women of East Timor' in *The Tablet*, 15 September 2001.

Scott, C (2003) *Are women included or excluded in post-conflict reconstruction? A case study from East Timor*, published 30 June 2003 on the website of PeaceWomen: Women's International League for Peace and Freedom (see www.peacewomen.org/resources/Timor-Leste/CIIRWomensPart03.html).

Scott, C and Pires, M (1998) 'The feminine face of the resistance' in Retboll, T (ed) (1998).

Sissons, M (1997) *From one day to another*, East Timor Human Rights Centre, Melbourne.

Smythe, Fr P (1995) *The crucifixion of East Timor*, MA dissertation, Leeds University.

Storey, S (1995) *Coercive birth control and settler infusion: The Indonesian prophylactic against East Timorese self-determination*, University of Melbourne.

Swaine, A (2003) *Traditional justice and gender-based violence*, International Rescue Committee, Dili.

Sword-Gusmão, K (2001) *Still fighting to be free: East Timorese women, survivors of violence*, paper contributed to Seeking Solutions' inaugural domestic violence and sexual assault conference, September 2001, Gold Coast (see www.aifs.gov.au/acssa/onlinedocs/diverse.html).

Tanter, R, Selden, M, and Shalom, S (eds) *Bitter flowers, sweet flowers: East Timor, Indonesia and the world community*, Rowman & Littlefield, Maryland.

TKTB (2000) *Violence against IDP/refugee women: Report of TKTB findings in IDP/refugee camps in West Timor*, Tim Kemanusiaan Timor Barat, Kupang, West Timor.

Traube, E (2001) 'Housing the nation', unpublished paper presented at the Pacific Islands, Atlantic Worlds symposium, Asian/Pacific American Studies Programme, New York University, 26 October 2001.

Turner, M (1992) *Telling East Timor: Personal testimonies, 1942-92*, New South Wales University Press, Sydney.

Turshen, M, and Twagiramariya, C (eds) (1998) *What women do in war time: Gender and conflict in Africa*, Zed Books, London.

UNDAW (2003) *Peace agreements as a means for promoting gender equality and ensuring participation of women: A framework of model provisions*, United Nations Division for the Advancement of Women, Canada.

UNDP (2002) *East Timor National Development Plan 2002*, United Nations Development Programme.

USAID (2000) *Aftermath: Women and women's organisations in post-conflict Cambodia*, USAID evaluation highlights no 67, Center for Development Information and Evaluation, US Agency for International Development, Washington.

USAID Bureau for Global Health (2004), *Country profile on East Timor*, US Agency for International Development, Washington.

Wallace, A (1869) *The Malay archipelago*, Macmillan & Co, London, reissued by Oxford University Press, 1989.

Wandita, G (2001) 'Left behind by death' in *Inside Indonesia*, April-June 2001, Issue 66.

Ward, J (2002) *If not now, when? Addressing gender-based violence in refugee, internally displaced, and post-conflict settings: A global overview*, Reproductive Health for Refugees Consortium.

Whittington, S (2000) 'The UN Transitional Administration in East Timor: Gender Affairs' in *Development Bulletin* vol 53.

Winters, R (ed) (1999) *Buibere: Voice of East Timorese women*, vol 1, East Timor International Support Centre, Australia.

World Council of Churches and Christian Conference of Asia (1999) *Women to women: A solidarity visit to Indonesia and East Timor 23 June – 1 July 1999* (see www.wcc-coe.org/wcc/what/international/indon.html).

Xia, C (1995) 'Bella's Story: East Timorese woman speaks out for justice' in *The Activist*, No 17, April 1995, Toronto, Canada.

Yayasan HAK (2000) *From scorched earth operation to humanitarian operation – a note on the conduct of international NGOs and UN institutions in post-referendum Timor Lorosae*, compiled by the Working Group for Study and Examination, Yayasan HAK, Dili.

Authors and contributors

Irena Cristalis is a freelance journalist and photographer who has been working in Asia since the mid-1980s. She is now based in New Delhi. She has documented and reported on East Timor since the mid-1990s for international media like the BBC, *The Economist* and Radio Netherlands and is the author of *Bitter dawn: East Timor – A people's story* published by Zed Books in 2002.

Catherine Scott has worked with CIIR's Asia programme in a variety of roles, but particularly on advocacy, over the past 17 years. She has written extensively on East Timor and edited the CIIR newsletter *Timor Link* between 1992 and 2002. She has been visiting East Timor regularly since 1993.

Isabel Casimiro and Ximena Andrade are based at the Centre of African Studies at the University of Eduardo Mondlane in Maputo, Mozambique They have both been active in Mozambican women's movements since the 1980s, and have contributed to the ongoing Women and Law in Southern African project. Isabel Casimiro has also served as a member of the Mozambican legislature.

Ruth Jacobson is a visiting research fellow at the Department of Peace Studies, University of Bradford. She has worked on issues of gender, armed conflict, political settlement and longer term peace building over two decades.

Brigitte Sonnois lived in Cambodia from 1988 to 2002, where she worked on 'women in development' and child protection programmes for Unicef as well as some international NGOs. (The opinions in chapter 9 are those of the author and do not necessarily reflect those of the institutions she worked with.)

Caroline Roseveare has worked in international development and human rights for over 20 years. She was based in southern Africa for 10 years, including a period in Windhoek as Oxfam's country representative for Namibia. She has completed a doctoral thesis on women's civil and political organisation in Namibia's democratic transition.